THE 36 DEADLY BUBISHI POINTS

AUTHOR'S AND PUBLISHER'S NOTE

The techniques in this book can cause severe bodily injury and even death. The ability to do bodily damage and to kill—and to train others in techniques that may do so—imposes grave responsibilities. The potentially lethal techniques in this book should never be used except for defensive purposes in the most extreme life-and-death situations. Knowledge of these techniques requires high levels of maturity and responsibility, and no one who lacks such maturity should be using this book at all.

The techniques in this book should be practiced only in consultation with a trained martial arts teacher who can provide advice about their safe and responsible use. The physical activities described in this book are strenuous and should not be attempted by anyone who is not in good physical health. The author and publisher disclaim responsibility for any harmful effects, on yourself or others, whether intended or unintended.

THE 36 DEADLY BUBISHI POINTS

The Science and Techniques of Pressure Point Fighting

RAND CARDWELL

TUTTLE Publishing

Tokyo | Rutland, Vermont | Singapore

"Books to Span the East and West"

Tuttle Publishing was founded in 1832 in the small New England town of Rutland, Vermont [USA]. Our core values remain as strong today as they were then—to publish best-in-class books which bring people together one page at a time. In 1948, we established a publishing office in Japan—and Tuttle is now a leader in publishing English-language books about the arts, languages and cultures of Asia. The world has become a much smaller place today and Asia's economic and cultural influence has grown. Yet the need for meaningful dialogue and information about this diverse region has never been greater. Over the past seven decades, Tuttle has published thousands of books on subjects ranging from martial arts and paper crafts to language learning and literature—and our talented authors, illustrators, designers and photographers have won many prestigious awards. We welcome you to explore the wealth of information available on Asia at www.tuttlepublishing.com.

Published by Tuttle Publishing, an imprint of Periplus Editions (HK) Ltd.

www.tuttlepublishing.com

Copyright © 2019 by Rand Cardwell

Library of Congress cataloging in process

ISBN: 978-0-8048-5024-7

First edition
26 25 24 23 22
10 9 8 7 6 5 4   2203TP

Printed in Singapore

TUTTLE PUBLISHING® is a registered trademark of Tuttle Publishing, a division of Periplus Editions (HK) Ltd.

DISTRIBUTED BY

North America, Latin America & Europe
Tuttle Publishing
364 Innovation Drive
North Clarendon, VT 05759-9436 U.S.A.
Tel: (802) 773-8930
Fax: (802) 773-6993
info@tuttlepublishing.com
www.tuttlepublishing.com

Japan
Tuttle Publishing
Yaekari Building, 3rd Floor
5-4-12 Osaki, Shinagawa-ku
Tokyo 141 0032
Tel: (81) 3 5437-0171
Fax: (81) 3 5437-0755
sales@tuttle.co.jp
www.tuttle.co.jp

Asia Pacific
Berkeley Books Pte. Ltd.
3 Kallang Sector #04-01
Singapore 349278
Tel: (65) 6741-2178
Fax: (65) 6741-2179
inquiries@periplus.com.sg
www.tuttlepublishing.com

TABLE OF CONTENTS

Acknowledgments..7

Foreword..9

Introduction..11

PART I:
The Extraordinary Vessels

Chapter 1: THE HUMAN BATTERY....................................25

Chapter 2: THE CONCEPTION VESSEL.............................31

Chapter 3: THE GOVERNING VESSEL...............................44

Chapter 4: THE THRUSTING VESSEL................................59

Chapter 5: THE GIRDLE VESSEL..67

Chapter 6: THE HEEL VESSELS..73
            THE YIN HEEL VESSEL..74
            THE YANG HEEL VESSEL..78

Chapter 7: THE LINKING VESSELS....................................87
            THE YIN LINKING VESSEL......................................89
            THE YANG LINKING VESSEL...................................93

PART II:
Laws, Theories, Concepts and Interactions

Chapter 8: THE LAW OF YIN/YANG..................................103

Chapter 9: FIVE ELEMENT THEORY.................................109

Chapter 10: ELEMENTAL BODY TYPES..............................117

Chapter 11: EXTRAORDINARY VESSEL INTERRELATIONSHIPS...................123

Chapter 12: BODY ALARM REACTION................................129

Chapter 13: **PRIMARY ENERGETIC TARGETS** 141

Chapter 14: **SEALING THE QI** 159

Chapter 15: **DEFENSE** 165

PART III:
Vital Points of the Original Bubishi

Chapter 16: **THE 36 VITAL POINTS** 173

Conclusion 207

Appendix 211

Bibliography 215

Point Index 217

General Index 220

ACKNOWLEDGMENTS

There were numerous people that assisted in making this book a reality. Undertaking a project of this level requires not only personal commitment, but much assistance from others to bring it into completion. I would like to express my gratitude to everyone that helped along the way but specifically to the following: to Patrick McCarthy for the inspiration of his work on the historical Okinawan *Bubishi* and for writing the foreword for this book; we have communicated numerous times through the last couple of decades and I have always enjoyed his kindness and true gentlemanly manner; without his efforts, this book would have never materialized; to Josh Jones, Chris Seals and Randy Pressley for playing the part of the opponent in the photographs; the numerous photography sessions and various unforeseen issues such things as positioning and lighting (and a few thumps) were all completed in a fun manner; to the photographer, Amanda Jones, who had to bear with me as we captured the correct angles, and for her help editing the photographs; and to Robert Goforth, my editor, for his guidance on making this book truly something special.

FOREWORD

The *Bubishi* is probably the single most important historical document for anyone pursuing more than just a cursory study of karate. How fortunate I was to have stumbled upon a book of such magnitude, never anticipating what an important impact it would have on my life.

I published my translation of the *Bubishi* in 1987 but had no idea how well received it would be by the global martial arts community. What was once hidden from all but the most serious students has now been made available to all. It has opened many eyes to the true depth and sophistication of the unarmed Okinawan fighting arts.

Taking on a classical study of work of this magnitude, without a formal academic background in Traditional Chinese Medicine (TCM), made understanding the theoretical and functional applications of bioelectrical energy, the Five Element Theory, Yin/Yang Theory, the Meridians and the Diurnal Cycle (as they pertained to addressing the habitual acts of physical violence) damn near impossible. Had it not been for the unselfish assistance of many wonderful people along the way my translation would have simply never been made possible. Even now, years later, it is only because of the studies of researchers like Rand Cardwell that I am able to completely understand the most ambiguous sections of the Bubishi—the Dim Mak pressure points.

Mr. Cardwell has done an admirable job of analyzing some of the most difficult sections of the *Bubishi* that pertain to the 36 Vital Points. His work provides the Western reader with a much clearer picture of the implications of attacks to those points. The last few decades have identified to Western students of the martial arts that the fighting traditions of the East are deeply rooted in the knowledge of Traditional Chinese Medicine. Endeavoring to understand those abstract concepts, the majority of Western martial artists fail to grasp the implications of Chinese methodology. Subsequently, they generally have a lesser knowledge in comparison to the old masters that developed many of the systems practiced today. Information that was once considered secret is now available in the West.

I have long been a supporter of Mr. Cardwell's research and I highly recommend his work to any and all students of the fighting arts looking to better understand secrets that I myself was unable to unravel or adequately explain. I am delighted that other researchers have accepted the challenge of studying my work and taking it to greater heights. I applaud the brilliant efforts of Rand Cardwell and wish him great success with this publication.

Patrick McCarthy
Hanshi 9th Dan
Australian Black Belt Hall of Fame Inductee, 2000
Canadian Black Belt Hall of Fame Inductee, 2012

INTRODUCTION

The information what is presented in this book is the result of over two decades of extensive research into the martial applications of Traditional Chinese Medicine. There are numerous resources available to gain an understanding of Traditional Chinese Medicine, but hardly any reference material for its martial application. A practice that is common among pressure point researchers is "reverse engineering" of the healing aspects of Chinese medicine. This enables the researcher to gain understanding of the martial implications of attacks that are aimed at the energetic system of the body. Much of the information that is presented in this book was gained through the "reverse engineering" method. Additionally, a great deal of insight was added by practicing Chinese Medicine acupuncturists that reviewed my research and offered their expert advice.

I was very fortunate to have been involved in the martial arts during the development of Western pressure point fighting in the last decade of the 20th century. Rarely does one expect to find themselves in an era that that is pivotal in the development of the martial arts. The introduction of pressure point fighting applications, and its associated science, is such a juncture in the Western world. Numerous instructors have attempted to understand this science from a Western perspective. Much of which has been to no avail. The science of Traditional Chinese Medicine views the body in a totally different manner than it is viewed in the west. Attempts to understand what occurs to the body during a pressure point technique from a Western medicine perspective are elusive. Some pressure point pioneers took the path of attempting to understand Traditional Chinese Medicine from an Eastern perspective and apply that hard gained knowledge to the martial arts. That path has led to many "discoveries" concerning martial applications of Chinese medicine. Being involved with these early Western efforts determined the path of study that I took to arrive at the conclusions that are presented in this book. It is unfortunate that some martial artists have capitalized on the application of Traditional Chinese Medicine to the martial arts. Their quests for profit and fame, using various nonsense like No-Touch knockouts, have hurt the legitimate, historically accurate, and combat effective techniques within this spectrum of knowledge.

The ability to utilize the information from Traditional Chinese Medicine grew with the collective understanding of the science. The intense examination of its various laws, theories and concepts has opened numerous doors for the martial artist. During that development, which has been occurring over the last thirty years, attacks to the twelve Main Meridians have been the majority of focus. Those meridians have been attacked with the laws of Yin/Yang, Five Element Theory, Quadrant Theory and a host of other concepts from the Eastern perspective—all with great success. One area that has received very little attention is the Extraordinary Vessels, which are considered by the Chinese as the primary energy system of the body.

The Extraordinary Vessels are the focus of this book. Their function and interaction with the twelve Main Meridians will be covered in great detail. The understanding of which of the twelve Main Meridians is the primary energetic target of the body will be answered. I decided to take you through a step-by-step process to show you the answer, which is validated by numerous Traditional Chinese Medicine textbooks, rather than just state the answer. Some of this martial research is being presented to the reader for the first time. Information concerning Body Alarm Reaction, which is the automatic physical response to stress, will be examined from both an Eastern and Western perspective. The application of that Western-based theory has extreme merit to the martial artist. This book will explain in detail why the Extraordinary Vessels are the most important of the energy systems of the body. It will describe methods to attack this energetic system to effectively drop or even kill an opponent.

For over two hundred years, and possibly much longer, on the island of Okinawa, the ancient document called the *Bubishi* has been passed down from generation to generation. Information from that document such as the 36 Vital Points, *Shichen* points and bi-hourly attacks will be examined. This book will not discuss the history of the original *Bubishi*. Nor will it provide any insight into the healing and philosophical aspects that it contains. Patrick McCarthy, whose translation of the *Bubishi* is discussed below, has already amply covered that in his excellent work. This book will answer some of the questions posed by the information that was presented in the original *Bubishi* concerning martial science. That document, which is cryptic in many ways, basically states that there are thirty-six points on the body that are vital from a combative perspective. No explanation was given to why the points were selected or how they are to be attacked. This book will provide the answer to those questions and many more by examining the original *Bubishi* by using the laws, theories and concepts of Traditional Chinese Medicine.

Extraordinary Vessels

In the Far East the eight Extraordinary Vessels are referred to as *Qi Jing Ba Mai*.[1] The word *Qi* refers to something that is wonderful, rare, strange, unusual, exceptional or extraordinary. These translations follow the development of Eastern thought as the healing and diagnostic qualities of the energetic system were discovered over the last three thousand years. Unfortunately, as Western minds started examining the more complicated aspects of Traditional Chinese Medicine, as well as the combative applications that evolved from it, the translation of "extraordinary" falls short of an easily understandable term to grasp the system. A different character represents Qi[2]—the life force or energy of the universe.

After several years of studying the Extraordinary Vessels, and their association with the combative fighting systems and Chinese *Qigong*,[3] a more Western term comes to mind in describing the interaction of these vessels with the twelve Main Meridians. That term is "Root Vessels" and it will be used on occasion throughout this book. Why does the term "Root Vessels" provide an easier mental picture of the function of this energetic system? If we use the analogy of a tree, rather than that of water as the Chinese did, in describing the *Qi Jing Ba Mai* then they become the "Root Vessels" and the twelve Main Meridians become the "Branch Meridians." The twelve "Branch Meridians," or Main Meridians, serve to move energy/*qi* to and from the organs of the body as understood in Traditional Chinese Medicine. They are the branches of the tree, and like the branches of a tree they will die if there is not a healthy root system to support the growth and maintenance of the organism.

The Extraordinary Vessels comprise the energetic system of the body that stores and releases energy to the twelve Main Meridians.[4] They are the source of energy in the human body and the term of "root" more fully describes their

[1] Iona Marsaa Teeguarden, M.A., *A Complete Guide to Acupressure* (Tokyo: Japan Publications, 1996) p. 55.

[2] *Qi* is a Chinese term that is used to describe the life energy that flows in the body. It is associated with the ancient Taoist traditions and is a cornerstone of Traditional Chinese Medicine.

[3] *Qigong* are various Chinese exercise methods that are designed to increase the energy, or *qi*, levels of a person. There are numerous systems that teach these exercises. They are often referred to as *Chi Kung*.

[4] Kiiko Matsumoto & Stephen Birch, *Extraordinary Vessels* (Brookline, MA: Paradigm Publications, 1986) p. 16.

interaction with the entire energy system. The Extraordinary Vessels, when working properly, move energy in a continuous manner to adjust and moderate the flow of energy throughout the twelve Main Meridians. Understanding how the Extraordinary Vessels do this is essential to gaining an advanced knowledge of the combative aspects of the martial arts, as well as Traditional Chinese Medicine in general.

This book will describe how the Extraordinary Vessels operate as well as their related functions. It will provide a detailed examination of the interactions of the system with the twelve Main Meridians. It will discuss why attacks to the Extraordinary Vessels are more lethal than attacks to the Main Meridians. It is only natural that the martial artist, who seeks to understand Traditional Chinese Medicine, as applied to the fighting arts, eventually gravitates towards the Extraordinary Vessels. Up to this point there has been precious little documentation on this advanced element of the Eastern practices for anyone to study. There are numerous references to the Extraordinary Vessels that are available, but all of those are written from a healing perspective. By reverse engineering the information provided by those sources, and the interjection of Western theories concerning Body Alarm Reaction, a greater understanding of the combative aspects of the martial arts will be presented to the reader.

Historical Perspective

The study of Extraordinary Vessels is comprised of four major components: the pathways or trajectories, the description of their functions, the healing aspects of their treatment, and the implications of martial attacks focused upon their interruption. Two early documents are of interest concerning the first known introduction of the concept in Traditional Chinese Medicine. The *Su Wen*[5] and *Ling Shu*[6] were written between 300 BC and 100 BC, according to Chinese scholars. These documents present the first mention of the Extraordinary Vessels and are basically focused on their pathways. The next major examination occurs in the *Nei Jing*,[7] which is an important early acupuncture text that expands on the knowledge of the two previously mentioned works. The pathways, which were forwarded by the *Su Wen* and *Ling Shu*, are de-

---

[5] *Su Wen* (Beijing: People's Hygiene Publishing Company, 1978).
[6] Maoshing Ni, Ph.D., *Ling Shu* or *The Yellow Emperor's Classic of Medicine* (Boston: Shambhala Publications, 1995).
[7] *Nei Jing* or *Classic of Difficulties*, c. 100 BC–AD 100.

scribed with more precision and simplification. The *Huangdi Nei Jing* starts defining the energetic theory surrounding the Extraordinary Vessels. The author of the *Huangdi Nei Jing* is unknown, and may have consisted of several acupuncturists, but the work became the base of knowledge in the clinical applications of Traditional Chinese Medicine.

The *Zhen Jiu Da Quan*,[8] written in 1439, marks the first complete treatment descriptions of the Extraordinary Vessels. It also defines the eight Master points[9] or treatment points associated with the Extraordinary Vessels. Close to 200 years later the *Zhen Jiu Da Cheng*[10] was introduced and further expanded on the treatment of the healing aspects that were presented in the *Da Quan*. Additionally, the *Da Cheng* described detailed information pertaining to the use of the biorhythmic treatments.[11]

The development of Extraordinary Vessel knowledge can be traced to these various sources. They concern themselves with the descriptions of the pathways, function and treatment of the Extraordinary Vessels. It was not until much later that the martial aspects of interruption of the Extraordinary Vessels would surface.[12]

---

[8] Xu Feng, *Zhen Jiu Da Quan* or *Complete Textbook of Acupuncture and Moxibustion* (Taiwan: Han Wu publishing Co., 1974) – originally published c. 1439.

[9] Master/Opening Points, or *Jiaohu* Points, are specifically used in acupuncture treatment to adjust energy levels in the Extraordinary Vessels. They are SP-4, PC-6, SI-3, BL-62, GB-41, TW-5, LU-7, and KI-6. According to Xu Feng, the author of *Zhen Jiu Da Quan*, these points were divided into four paired sets. SP-4 is associated with the Thrusting Vessel. PC-6 is associated with the Yin Linking Vessel and is paired with SP-4. ST-3 is associated with the Governing Vessel and is paired with BL-62, which is associated with the Yang Heel Vessel. GB-41 is associated with the Girdle Vessel and is paired with TW-5, which is associated with the Yang Linking Vessel. LU-7 is associated with the Conception Vessel and is paired with KI-6, which is associated with the Yin Heel Vessel. Needling these points singularly or as a pair helps to control and cure many disorders, which are associated with more systematic problems of Extraordinary Vessel energy imbalances.

[10] Yang Shang San, *Zhen Jiu Da Cheng* or *Compendium of Acupuncture and Moxibustion* (Taiwan: Hong Ye Shu Ju Publishing Company, 1976) — originally published c. 1601.

[11] Biorhythmic treatments are associated with the Diurnal Cycle. That cycle represents the peak energy levels of the twelve Main Meridians as they occur during a twenty-four hour period. The *Bubishi* makes reference to attacking specific Main Meridians at the point when they are at their highest level of energy according to the Diurnal Cycle. This corresponds with the research of the author concerning attacking energetic points, or meridians, while they are in an excessive state.

[12] Erle Montaigue, *Advanced Dim-Mak* (Boulder, CO: Paladin Press, 1994), pp. 1-4, - There is evidence which suggests that Vital Point Striking was utilized as early as the fourteenth century by Chang Sangfeng.

The *Bubishi*

Patrick McCarthy,[13] a martial arts historian and authority, published a translation of an ancient document concerning the martial applications of Eastern fighting disciplines in 1987. This document had been passed down for centuries by some of the top karate practitioners in Okinawa and China. The *Bubishi*[14] is considered a classic work on philosophy, strategy, Traditional Chinese Medicine, and martial technique. (I highly recommend McCarthy's book. Details on the *Bubishi* can be found in the Bibliography.) Chojun Miyagi, the founder of *Goju-ryu*, referred to the *Bubishi* as "the bible of karate." The *Bubishi* has had a dramatic impact on the development of the fighting disciplines of the Far East. Many of the legendary masters have studied it and applied its teachings to their individual methods. With the publication of McCarthy's translation the Western world was exposed to the depth of knowledge that it contained.[15] Unfortunately, the fact that it was transcribed by hand through the years allowed for some literary erosion. Likewise, some of the information is presented without explanation with only crude diagrams or drawings.

From examination of the material presented in the historic document, it becomes quickly apparent that martial techniques were aimed at acupuncture points.[16] This leads to the fact that the author(s) had an understanding of Traditional Chinese Medicine. Coupled with the development of the healing aspects of Traditional Chinese Medicine, there was development of fighting techniques that derived themselves from the same knowledge base. Given the verbal transmission traditions of the early martial arts, the history of that development does not mirror the better represented healing traditions as in the *Su Wen, Ling Shu, Nei Jing, Zhen Jiu Da Quan*, and the *Zhen Jiu Da Cheng*. McCarthy presents some excellent historical accounts of early Chinese martial artist that developed systems that utilized striking vital points. He also discusses

---

[13] Patrick McCarthy has written a number of excellent books on Okinawan based fighting disciplines and martial history, in addition to his translation of the *Bubishi*. He has recently established Koryu Uchinadi, which is an art that is based on the ancient combative methods of Fujian China and Okinawa.

[14] Patrick McCarthy, *The Bible of Karate: Bubishi* (Boston: Tuttle Publishing, 1995).

[15] It should be noted that George Alexander and Ken Penland published a translation of the *Bubishi* in 1993. In the opinion of the author, the McCarthy translation is the better of the two. It includes information from other classic martial texts and excellent commentary by McCarthy. The Alexander version is more purely a translation, in that it includes a minimal amount of commentary and lacks the extensive research that is exhibited with the McCarthy translation. It appears that both McCarthy and Alexander received copies of the *Bubishi* from different sources, which coincides with the fact that it was passed down in many different branches of Okinawan karate. See the Appendix on page 211 for additional information.

[16] McCarthy, *The Bible of Karate: Bubishi*, pp. 107–147.

the development of some of the kata,[17] or *taolu*,[18] that were originally designed with the purpose of attacking vital points.

Vital Points are one of the major focuses of the *Bubishi*. The information presented on these points provides solid proof that Traditional Chinese Medicine was used as a knowledge base to understand the interactions of the energetic system of the human body. It is pure conjecture to state that the author(s) of the *Bubishi* had advanced knowledge of acupuncture and the associated theories of Traditional Chinese Medicine, but that knowledge base is obviously the foundation of the document. Information concerning the biorhythmic cycle of striking specific points at their most active times is included. This further substantiates that the author(s) had knowledge of acupuncture or Traditional Chinese Medicine. The 36 Vital Points[19] of combat are listed in the document. These points are what the author(s) of this document considered as the most important acupuncture points from a martial perspective. McCarthy's *Bubishi* translation provides information concerning biorhythmic attacks to the body. Those biorhythmic attacks were separated into two distinct methods. One method is referred to as *Dim Hsueh*, or Blood Gate Attacks.[20] This method is for attacking a point that provides easy access to a vein or artery. Several such locations feature this accessibility on the human body. The second method is called *Dim Ching*,[21] or Nerve Plexus Attacks. This method revolves around attacks to the acupuncture points of Traditional Chinese Medicine. Both *Dim Hsueh* and *Dim Ching* are collectively referred to as the method of *Dim Mak*,[22] which is known as the "Death Touch." The vital points, which will be examined in detail in this book, are listed by point name and are included in Table I-1.

---

[17] Kata is an Okinawan term that is used to describe specific physical sets of movements that are associated with the martial arts. They are designed to allow the practitioner the ability to memorize and engrain martial techniques to vital points of the body. *Kata* are often given abstract names, but some are named after a specific number. For instance, *Seisan* (Thirteen), *Seipai* (Eighteen), *Niseishi* (Twenty-four), *Nepai* (Twenty-eight), *Sanseiru* (Thirty-six), *Useishi* (Fifty-four), *Peichurrin* (One Hundred and Eight). It is the opinion of the author that those *kata* represent attacks to the specific number of vital points represented by the name. Unfortunately, the interpretation of those movements by the majority of Western martial arts schools does not include the knowledge of vital point attack.

[18] *Taolu* refers to the Chinese term for *Kata*.

[19] McCarthy, *The Bible of Karate: Bubishi*, p. 114; George W. Alexander and Ken Penland, *Bubishi: Martial Art Spirit* (Lake Worth, FL: Yamazato Publications, 1993), p. 85.

[20] Ibid., pp. 24–28.

[21] Ibid., pp. 18-28, 66–79.

[22] Ibid., p. 24.

	McCarthy Translation						
#	**Point**	**#**	**Point**	**#**	**Point**	**#**	**Point**
1	GV-22	10	ST-9	19	BL-51	28	HT-5
2	GV-24	11	CV-22	20	GV-1	29	LU-8
3	GB-3	12	ST-12	21	CV-4	30	LI-4
4	Eyes	13	GV-16	22	CV-1	31	TW-2
5	Ears	14	GV-14	23	GB-24	32	GB-31
6	TW-17	15	CV-18	24	LV-13	33	BL-40
7	GV-26	16	CV-15	25	LV-11	34	KI-6
8	CV-24	17	HT-1	26	LU-3	35	BL-62
9	SI-16	18	BL-43	27	LI-10	36	LV-3

Table I-1: *The Thirty-six Vital Points: McCarthy Translation.*[23]

During the early part of the twentieth century, after the Boxer Rebellion and the fall of the Qing dynasty in China, the combative art of vital point fighting went into decline, as did the majority of unarmed fighting methods. The heavy introduction of firearms ushered in a new era and the emphasis on unarmed fighting techniques suffered. The sweeping social changes in China, which was the result of the introduction of communism, further reduced the practice of the "old ways" and the knowledge of vital point striking basically started to evaporate. The accumulated knowledge of thousands of years of combative science declined to the point that few practitioners today understand vital point striking. The martial arts in China shifted from the effective combative disciplines to a more recreational and artistic expression of their former selves.[24] That trend has repeated itself throughout the Asian world and was dominant during the time that the martial arts were introduced to the west. Unfortunately, the recreational and artistic aspects have further entrenched themselves in the west by the overly commercial emphasis of character development, tournaments and the huge student enrollment focus of many Western instructors. They are producing a generation of people that believe that they practice the martial arts, but in reality are not. These modern "martial artists" are practicing a child's version of the true combative arts which is far removed from the ancient teachings of China and Okinawa. What is even more unsettling is that many of these "martial artists" do not understand the difference.

---

[23] McCarthy, *The Bible of Karate: Bubishi*, p. 114.
[24] Ibid., p. 112.

Terminology

This book assumes that the reader has a basic understanding of such terms as *qi*, meridians, acupuncture points, Yin/Yang and Five Element Theory. If you a little unclear on any of these concepts please skip ahead to Part II and familiarize yourself with the Law of Yin/Yang and Five Element Theory. One of the major problems I encountered while researching this book was the dealing with the various Chinese and Japanese terms used by other authors to describe concepts and in the naming of meridians and points. Those terms have been "Americanized," but I am providing a brief explanation of the oriental terms in the course of this book. Chinese words, when used, will be italics. I have used the Pinyin Romanization System for all Chinese words. For example, *ch'i*, will be spelled as *qi*. Confusion that is caused by use of Chinese terms is apparent in the information that was presented in the Alexander/Penland translation of the *Bubishi*, a translation slightly different than McCarthy's that is more thoroughly discussed in the Appendix. The Chinese term for the various points will be included in the point descriptions that you will find in this book.

Many Westerners that start to study Traditional Chinese Medicine, as applied to the martial arts, become overwhelmed by many of the words and terms used to describe that science. I hope to eliminate some of that confusion in this book by attempting to use terms that the average Westerner can understand.

Abbreviations are used in this text for the acupuncture points. Those used are standard in the majority of Traditional Chinese Medicine textbooks. For example; when a reference is made to Stomach Meridian Point Nine it will be noted as ST-9. Please refer to Table I-2 for an explanation of the Meridian abbreviations.

Meridian or Vessel	Abbreviation
Stomach	ST
Spleen	SP
Heart	HT
Small Intestine	SI
Bladder	BL
Kidney	KI
Pericardium	PC
Triple Warmer	TW
Gall Bladder	GB
Liver	LV

Meridian or Vessel	Abbreviation
Lung	LU
Large Intestine	LI
Conception	CV
Governing	GV

Table I-2: *Abbreviations of the Meridians and Vessels.*

Point Descriptions

There are numerous descriptions of acupuncture points that are covered in this book. The format that is used in Part I, the section that goes into detail on all the points of the Extraordinary Vessels, will first list the associated meridian, which will utilize the abbreviations in Table I-2. The actual point number (**CV-1** for example) will followed by the **Chinese point name** and then the **English translation**. **Special attributes** of the point will be listed next (Intersection point, Alarm Point, etc.). If the point is bilateral, which means that it is found on both the right and left sides of the body, this will be stated. Some Extraordinary Vessel points are not bilateral. Next will be a short description of the physical **location** of the point from a TCM perspective, followed by general **Western anatomy** features that are present at the location. Last will be a **comments** section that will provide methods that can be utilized to attack the point will be given and the energetic effects of the strike may be mentioned. You will find that there are a small amount of points that are found in more that one of the Extraordinary Vessels. These are Intersection Points between two Extraordinary Vessels and are listed under both the vessels. This might be a little redundant to the reader, but I believe it is important to have the information readily available in the event that someone is studying one specific vessels. It is only six points, but I want to make you aware. For a more detailed examination of point locations I suggests several of the Chinese Medicine textbooks that are mentioned in the Bibliography.

In Part III there is a complete list of the 36 Vital Points found in the *Bubishi* with detailed comments on their combative utilization. Seventeen out of the 36 Vital Points are Extraordinary Vessels Points which were covered under basic point descriptions in Part I. Part III goes into much more detail about the points. I want to make the reader aware of this distinction. Part I contains general point descriptions of all the points of all the Extraordinary Vessels. Part III contains more detailed point descriptions of thirty-six points that are found in the *Bubishi*, seventeen of which are Extraordinary Vessels points. I hope that eliminates any confusion.

Defensive Aspect

Though the *Bubishi*, and true combative arts in generally, focuses on the offensive application, it is important to address defensive applications to such attacks. Incorporating defense against someone that is attacking your vital points should be an important aspect of your personal training. It will develop a well-rounded ability to not only utilize vital point striking, but also how to defend against such attacks. Adding this to your training regimen will help you development into a more capable martial artist. As you read this book, you will find photographs of offensive use of vital point utilization and striking. Following those photographs will be another set that shows defensive counters to the offensive technique. These are not set in stone. Through thoughtful examination, study of the vital points and how to attack them (proper angle and direction), and your own understanding of your specific martial system, you should be able to devise numerous other counters to vital point attacks. These are added as one example, but are open to individual interpretation.

The Western Bubishi

In 2004, I self-published *The Western Bubishi*, which more than a decade later became the basis for this book. If you happen to have a copy of it, you will notice that this book contains much greater detail than my first effort. The chapter on the Thirty-Six Vital Points of the *Bubishi* contains a more in depth examination of each of those points. I felt compelled to include a chapter concerning defensive aspects of unarmed combat that I hope will provide some insight into an almost exclusive offensive mindset of true unarmed combatives. Additionally, you will find photographs of attacks to various vital points, which were included in *The Western Bubishi*, but also photographs of several defensive variations to those attacks, which were not. This book is built on that first amateur effort, but still holds to the original research that went into it, though greatly expanded.

PART I
Extraordinary Vessels: Functions, Trajectories and Point Descriptions

Chapter 1

THE **HUMAN BATTERY**

"This is why we can say the du mai, ren mai and chong mai have different names but are all the same."[1]

Wang Bing

The Extraordinary Vessels are the basic "battery pack" of the human body. Energy, or *qi* as the Chinese refer to it, is stored in the Extraordinary Vessels, or transported to the twelve Main Meridians,[2] by this system according to Traditional Chinese Medicine.[3] Many martial artists have placed a great deal of importance on the twelve Main Meridians. These meridians are designed to adjust the energy levels of their specific organs. They are secondary to the Extraordinary Vessels. Using the tree analogy ask yourself the following question. Can a branch survive, grow and maintain itself without a root? The answer is obvious. It can not do any of those functions without the nourishment provided by the tree's root system. Likewise, the human body cannot survive, grow or maintain itself without a solid root system. Can a tree survive if you cut off a limb? Can a human being survive if you remove a limb? Of course, but remove the ability of the root system to supply the limbs with nourishment and both the tree and the human will die. The concepts presented in this book will hopefully allow the student to gain a more solid understanding of the interaction between the Extraordinary Vessels and the twelve Main Meridians.

Of the eight meridians that consist of the Extraordinary Vessel subsystem,

---

[1] Wang Bing, *Su Wen*, This classic Chinese text is dated between 300 BC and 100 BC. The Chinese term for the Governing Vessel is *Du Mai*, the Conception Vessel is *Ren Mai*, and the Thrusting Vessel is *Chong Mai*.

[2] The Twelve Main Meridians are responsible for the energy flow to the associated organs and bowels according to Traditional Chinese Medicine. A detailed examination of the Main Meridians will not be covered in this book, which is focused on the Extraordinary Vessels and the thirty-six vital points listed in the original *Bubishi*. Specific points of the Main Meridians that intersect the Extraordinary Vessels will be examined.

[3] Claude Larre & Elisabeth Rochat de la Valle, *The Eight Extraordinary Meridians* (Cambridge, England: Monkey, 1997), p.1.

Matsumoto & Birch, *Extraordinary Vessels*, pp. 16–17.

Teeguarden, *A Complete Guide to Acupressure*, pp. 53–57.

Giovanni Maciocia, *The Foundations of Chinese Medicine* (New York: Churchill Livingstone, 1989), p. 355.

three of those meridians make up what can be considered as the "Human Battery." They are the Conception Vessel, Governing Vessel, and the Thrusting Vessel.[4] Many Traditional Chinese Medicine textbooks examine these three vessels independently, but numerous sources make mention of the interrelation. The *Nei Jing* discusses the concept of the energetic center of the body in the following manner in Chapter 8:

> *The root of the twelve meridians,*
> *fundamental to the five yin and six yang organs;*
> *The source of the triple warmer, the gate of breathing;*
> *The source of vital qi.*[5]

This can be rather cryptic to the Western reader, but consider the *Nei Jing* placed a great deal of importance on the "Human Battery." It states that it is the root of the twelve meridians. This indicates that the twelve Main Meridians are secondary in function to that of the Extraordinary Vessels, which make up the energy center of the body. That it is fundamental to the organs of the body, the gate of breathing, the source of the Triple Warmer, and the source of vital *Qi*. The importance should be obvious to the martial artist.

The three meridians that make up the "Human Battery" originate directly from the Kidneys and flow down to the center core of the body to the point known as Conception Vessel 1 (CV-1), at that location they take different pathways. The Conception Vessel flows up the abdomen following the centerline of the body. The Governing Vessel flows up the back following the centerline of the body. The Thrusting Vessel flows up the inside of the abdomen along the Kidney Meridian (one of the twelve Main Meridians). This "Human Battery" is the source for all the other Extraordinary Vessels and twelve Main Meridians. It is the energetic center of the body and is vital to the life of the organism.

This energetic center of the body is the location of many transformations of *qi*, or energy, according to Traditional Chinese Medicine.[6] The energies that are produced in that center are those used for nutrition, protection from elements and disease, and to feed the twelve Main Meridians. The Extraordinary Vessels directly controls those twelve Main Meridians, which consist of the Stomach, Spleen, Heart, Small Intestine, Bladder, Kidney, Pericardium, Triple

---

[4] The Thrusting Vessel is sometimes referred to the Penetrating Vessel in Traditional Chinese Medicine textbooks.

[5] *Nei Jing*, Chapter 8.

[6] Matsumoto & Birch, *Extraordinary Vessels*, pp. 8–18.

Warmer, Gall Bladder and Liver Meridians. All life force flows from the Extraordinary Vessels. From a health perspective they are essential to the proper function of the organism. From a martial perspective the Extraordinary Vessels represent a series of targets that quickly disables the body from readjusting *qi* levels that have been disrupted or allow for instant attacks to the primary energy source of the body. Attacks to the Extraordinary Vessels cause greater damage to the body than those aimed at the twelve Main Meridians. Later in this book, data will be presented that supports the concepts of "sealing the energy" or "sealing the *qi*."[7] This information will show the location of finishing blows that theoretically disables the Extraordinary Vessels from adjusting the energy levels of specific organs that have been attacked. This can have a lethal effect on your opponent by "sealing," or otherwise stopping, the ability of the Extraordinary Vessels to correct the energy level of an attacked organ. This can result in death in certain circumstances according to Traditional Chinese Medicine.

As a martial artist you are aware of numerous attacks to the centerline of the body. These attacks are engrained by the hours of practice that you have committed to refining your individual art. Strikes to an opponent will be more effective if your focus and angle of attack are towards the center core of the body and down at 45 degrees. This will be true with any strike that you aim at the centerline of the body. Why is that? It is because you are striking into the energetic core of the body. You can try this out when you train to illustrate the point.

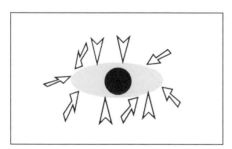

Figure 1-1: Strikes to the body reflect the random directions of impact common in the majority of martial arts systems.

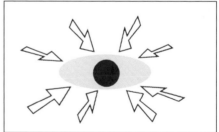

Figure 1-2: Strikes to the body reflecting attacks to the energetic core, which are more damaging to the energetic system of the body.

Assume a solid forward stance and have a training partner throw a medium to hard reverse punch on a completely flat, horizontal plane into your stomach on the centerline.[8] Notice the impact and the effect of the strike. Now have your

---

[7] Rick Moneymaker, *Torite-Jutsu Reference Manual* (Chattanooga, TN: Northshore Communications, 1997), p. 81.

[8] If you are trained in one of the Okinawan Martial Arts you will probably be familiar with *Sanchin* kata.

training partner throw another reverse punch aimed at the same location, but this time they will throw it so that it rises up at a 45-degree angle. Again, notice the impact and effect of the strike. Last, have your training partner throw another reverse punch aimed at the same location, but this time they throw it at a downward angle of 45 degrees. Notice the impact and the effect of the strike. If you think the effects of the three strikes might be cumulative, then do only one of the strikes per day. You will just need to mentally register the effect of the strike and your training partner will have to remember how much force they used when throwing the reverse punch. Depending on the striking ability of your partner you will discover that the first two strikes have little to no effect on you. The last strike, the one aimed in and down at a 45-degree angle, will produce the most discomfort and will more than likely upset your stance by causing you to lean forward at the waist. This exercise should illustrate the effect of a properly thrown strike to the centerline. I have done this demonstration before and on numerous occasions the volunteer, after easily withstanding the level and upward punches, was knocked to the ground (to their great surprise) by the downward trajectory punch. So, be careful with the amount of power of this test.

When you examine the effect of causing you to bend forward, think of the martial implications of striking an opponent and get-

Centerline punch on flat trajectory.

Centerline punch on upper trajectory.

Centerline punch on downward trajectory.

Some styles utilize a method of testing the posture and strength of a students called *Shime*, which is often done while the student performs *Sanchin* kata. Consider this test of strike angle as *Shime* and assume the tense and strong manner of *Sanchin* kata during the execution as described.

ting that effect. Their stance will be disrupted and their ability to attack will be greatly hindered. They will fold at the waist and their hips will move backward. This will present their head to you for follow-up strikes. This minor adjustment in understanding how to attack the centerline of the body, and the "Human Battery," will increase your effectiveness as a martial artist.

Another curious observation concerning the Governing and Conception Vessels is that according to the point numbering system used in Traditional Chinese Medicine, both vessels appear to flow towards the head. The point numbers start with the low numbers in the pelvic region and become larger as the vessels ascends to the head. After intense study of the Extraordinary Vessel subsystem, it appears that the numbering system for these two vessels are for reference purposes only and are not indicative of the direction of flow of energy. Direction of energy flow is indicated in the twelve Main Meridians in this manner, but it does not suit the function of the Extraordinary Vessels.[9]

The Extraordinary Vessels can "flow" in either direction and are not limited to energy movement in any particular direction. As energetic fluctuations occur in the twelve Main Meridians, the Extraordinary Vessels either move energy to, or away, from the Main Meridians depending on the imbalance.[10] They accomplish this process with the Yin and Yang Linking Vessels. These functions will be covered later in this book.

The easiest manner to understand the function of the Extraordinary Vessels is to consider it the "Human Battery." Through normal processes like breathing and eating the body takes in energy to use for proper function. *Qigong* exercises can increase the natural level of energy the body according to Traditional Chinese Medicine. All the various energies that enter the body (breathing, eating and *Qigong*) go through a number of transformations in the Energy Core of the "Human Battery."[11] The Thrusting, Conception, and Governing Vessels make up the energetic subsystem that is responsible for storing that energy.[12] There can never be too much energy in the "Human Battery," but there can be too little. When there is an abundance of energy in the "Human Battery" the body is healthy and the person radiates energy in everyday functions. When there is a deficient amount of energy in the "Human Battery" the body will be sick and the person will be fatigued. In Traditional Chinese Medicine when the

---

[9] Larre & Vallee, *The Eight Extraordinary Meridians*, pp. 46–47.

[10] Teeguarden, *A Complete Guide to Acupressure*, pp. 53–54.

[11] This is a simplified description of the energetic transformation according to Traditional Chinese Medicine. For a more detailed analysis of the process I suggest several of the TCM related textbooks that are listed in the Bibliography.

[12] Teeguarden, *A Complete Guide to Acupressure*, p. 57.

"Human Battery" runs low all manner of sickness and disease will likely manifest. When the "Human Battery" runs out of energy the person dies. Hopefully, this simplified explanation of the function of this three-vessel subsystem (Thrusting, Conception, and Governing Vessels) provides a clearer understanding of the importance of the Extraordinary Vessels.

Chapter 2

THE CONCEPTION VESSEL

*"Among the eight extraordinary channels, the conception,
governing and thrusting are of the greatest importance."*
Nei Jing: Chapter 60

The Conception Vessel is the Yin aspect of the "Human Battery." It runs along the centerline of the abdomen from the CV-1 point, which was discussed in the previous chapter, and connects with the Governing Vessel at the upper lip. The Governing Vessel is the Yang half of the "Human Battery" subsystem. Some Traditional Chinese Medicine sources state that it ends at the point known as CV-24, but a more intense examination of texts show a continuation of the meridian that encircles the mouth and extends to ST-1 under each eye.[1] The majority of the textbooks that I have researched include this interpretation and it is included in this book.

The Conception Vessel is responsible for regulating the energy levels, and correcting energetic imbalances, of all yin associated meridians.[2] The exact method that it uses to accomplish this function will be covered in later chapters. The three Yin associated meridians of the feet all connect with the Conception Vessel. This allows for direct adjustments to these bilateral Main Meridians.[3] The Conception Vessel is often referred to as the *Ren Mai* or the Directing Vessel.

There are a number of acupuncture points that the Conception Vessel passes through as it ascends from CV-1. Some of them have a varying degree of interest to the martial artist, but a detailed examination of each point will be given in this text. Major points of interest to martial artists will be outlined in the descriptions.

---

[1] Jwing-Ming Yang, *Muscle/Tendon Changing & Marrow/Brain Washing Chi Kung* (Jamaica Plains, MA: YMAA Publication Center, 1989), p. 184.

[2] Andrew Ellis, Nigel Wiseman, and Ken Boss, *Fundamentals of Chinese Acupuncture* (Brookline, MA: Paradigm Publications, 1991), p. 345.

[3] Jwing-Ming Yang, *The Root of Chinese Chi Kung* (Jamaica Plains, MA: YMAA Publication Center, 1989), p. 232.

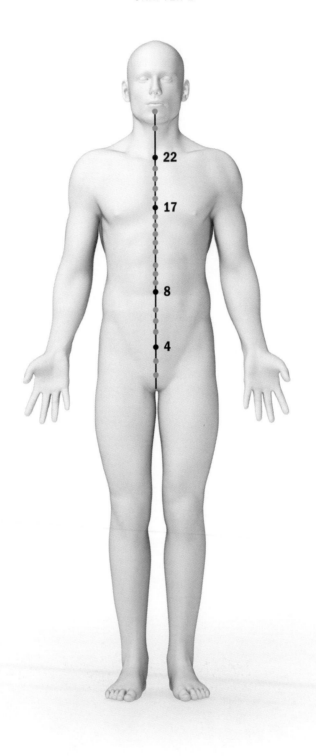

Attacks to the Conception Vessel are commonly taught as "attacking the centerline" in the majority of martial arts schools. We are all familiar with techniques that are aimed at the centerline on the front of the body, which is even without any knowledge of Traditional Chinese Medicine. Understanding the function of the Conception Vessel should allow you to gain proficiency in attacking it from an energetic perspective.

Conception Vessel Point Descriptions

CV-1   **Chinese Point name:** *Hui Yin;*[4] **English translation:** "Meeting of Yin;" **Special Attributes:** Intersection Point of the Conception, Governing, and Thrusting Vessels. It is one of the 36 Vital Points listed in the *Bubishi*; **Location:** Midway between the anus and the bottom of the genitals; **Western Anatomy:** Branches of the perineal artery and vein, as well as a branch of the perineal nerve are present; **Comments:** Given the naturally protected location of this point it is difficult to strike in a combative situation, but if your opponent is kicking for your head or if they are prone on the ground and you have control of one of their legs it can be accessible. A strike, if one is possible, to this point is devastating to an opponent.

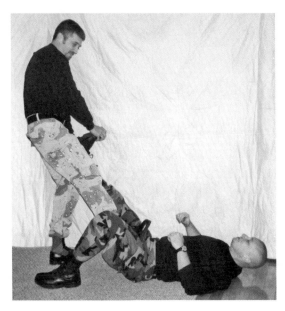

CV-1 being stomp kicked on a dropped opponent after an attempted kick and takedown.

---

[4]   Andrew Ellis, Nigel Wiseman, and Ken Boss, *Grasping the Wind: An Exploration Into The Meaning of Chinese Acupuncture Point Names* (Brookline, MA: Paradigm Publications, 1989), p. 303.

CV-2   Chinese Point name: *Qu Gu;*[5] English translation: "Curved Bone;" Special Attributes: Intersection point with the Liver Meridian; Location: just above the top of the pubic bone on the centerline of the front of the body; Western Anatomy: Branches of the inferior epigastric artery and obturator artery, and a branch of the iliohypogastric nerve are present; Comments: Strikes to this point should be at a downward 45-degree angle, if possible, and can break the pubic bone causing great pain in the opponent. Downward aimed punches and hard driving straight kicks to this region can be effective in a combative situation.

CV-3   Chinese Point name: *Zhong Ji;*[6] English translation: "Central Pole;" Special Attributes: Alarm Point for the Bladder Meridian and the Intersection Point for the Spleen, Kidney, and Liver Meridians; Location: about one inch above CV-2 or about four inches below the navel; Western Anatomy: Branches of the superficial epigastric and inferior epigastric arteries and veins, and a branch of the iliohypogastric nerve are present; Comments: From a martial perspective, strikes to an intersection point tend to cause more damage to the overall energetic system. It should be noted that forceful strikes will cause disruption to specific points of attack and others in close proximity.

CV-4   Chinese Point name: *Guan Yuan;*[7] English translation: "Origin Pass;" Special Attributes: Alarm point of the Small Intestine Meridian and the intersection point of the Spleen, Kidney, and Liver Meridians, It is one of the 36 Vital Points listed in the *Bubishi*; Location: About three inches below the navel; Western Anatomy: the anterior cutaneous nerve of the subcostal nerve is present; Comments: It should be attacked in the same manner as CV-2 and 3. Additional details available in Chapter 16.

CV-5   Chinese Point name: *Shi Men;*[8] English translation: "Stone Gate;" Special Attributes: Alarm Point for the Triple Warmer Meridian; Location: About one inch above CV-4 or about two inches below the navel; Western Anatomy: Branches of the superficial epigastric and inferior epigastric arteries and veins, and the anterior cutaneous branch of the eleventh intercostal nerve are present. Comments: This point should be attacked in the same manner as CV-2 through 4 for similar results.

---

[5] Ibid., p. 304.
[6] Ibid., p. 305.
[7] Ibid., p. 306.
[8] Ibid., p. 308.

CV-6   Chinese Point name: *Qi Hai;*[9] English translation: "Sea of Qi;" Location: About .5 of an inch above CV-5 or about 1.5 inches below the navel. Western Anatomy: Branches of the superficial epigastric and inferior epigastric arteries and veins, and the anterior cutaneous branch of the eleventh intercostal nerve are present; **Comments:** Strike in same manner as CV-2 through CV-5 for similar results.

CV-7   Chinese Point name: *Yin Jiao;*[10] English translation: "Yin Intersection;" Location: About one inch below the navel on the centerline of the body; Western Anatomy: Branches of the superficial epigastric and inferior epigastric arteries and veins are found at this location. Also, the anterior cutaneous branch of the tenth intercostal nerve is present; **Comments:** Attack this point with a downward 45-degree strike to collapse the hips of the opponent backwards and disrupt the energetic center of the body.

CV-8   Chinese Point name: *Shen Que;*[11] English translation: "Spirit Tower Gate;" Location: In the center of the navel; Western Anatomy: A branch of the inferior epigastric artery and vein are found along with the anterior cutaneous branch of the tenth intercostal nerve; **Comments:** Attack this point in the same manner as CV-7 for similar results.

CV-9   Chinese Point name: *Shui Fen;*[12] English translation: "Water Divide;" Location: About one inch above the navel on the centerline of the body. Western Anatomy: A branch of the inferior epigastric artery and vein are found along with the anterior cutaneous branch of the tenth intercostal nerve; **Comments:** Strike in the same manner as CV-7 and 8 for similar results.

CV-10   Chinese Point name: *Xia Wan;*[13] English translation: "Lower Venter;" **Special Attributes:** Intersection Point of Spleen Meridian and the Conception Vessel; Location: About two inches above CV-9 or two inches above the navel on the centerline of the body; Western Anatomy: A branch of the inferior epigastric artery and vein are found along with the anterior cutaneous branch of the tenth intercostal nerve; **Comments:** Attack this point in the same manner as CV-8 and 9 for similar results.

---

[9] Ibid., p. 309.
[10] Ibid., p. 310.
[11] Ibid., p. 311.
[12] Ibid., p. 312.
[13] Ibid.

An attack on the string of centerline Conception Vessel points with a downward strike. Strikes in this manner will disrupt the energetic core of the body. The initial strike is near CV-10. A follow through of the initial strike attacks the lower CV points. The strike will cause the opponent to fold at the waist and bend forward. This exposes the neck and head for additional strikes.

Defensive Counters

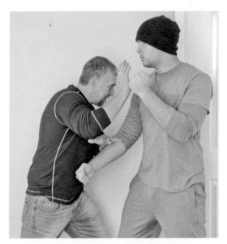

As the attacker (right) launches a centerline punch towards your midsection, deflect it downward with your lead arm and prepare for counter.

Move aggressively toward your attacker and perform an Open Palm strike to their chin.

CV-11   Chinese Point name: *Jian Li*;[14] **English translation:** "Interior Strengthening;" **Location:** About three inches above the navel on the centerline of the body; **Western Anatomy:** Branches of the superior and inferior epigastric arteries, and the anterior cutaneous branch of the eighth intercostal nerve are present. **Comments:** Strike downward at a 45-degree angle for disruption of the energy center.

---

[14] Ibid., p. 313.

CV-12   Chinese Point name: *Zhong Wan;*[15] English translation: "Central Venter;" Special Attributes: Intersection Point of the Small Intestine, Triple Warmer, and Stomach Meridians with the Conception Vessel. It is also the Alarm Point for the Stomach Meridian; Location: About four inches above the navel on the centerline of the body; Western Anatomy: Branches of the superior epigastric artery and vein, and the anterior cutaneous branch of the seventh intercostal nerve are present; Comments: This is an important energy disruption point due to it being a major intersection point and an Alarm Point. Strikes should be downward at a 45-degree angle for the best results.

CV-13   Chinese Point name: *Shang Wan;*[16] English translation: "Upper Venter;" Special Attributes: Intersection Point for the Stomach and Small Intestine Meridians with the Conception Vessel; Location: About five inches above the navel on the centerline of the body; Western Anatomy: Branches of the superior epigastric artery and vein, and the anterior cutaneous branch of the seventh intercostal nerve are present; Comments: Strikes should be in the same manner as attacking CV-12.

CV-14   Chinese Point name: *Ju Que;*[17] English translation: "Great Tower Gate;" Special Attributes: Alarm Point for the Heart; Location: About six inches above the navel on the centerline of the body; Western Anatomy: Branches of the superior epigastric artery and vein, and the anterior cutaneous branch of the seventh intercostal nerve are present; Comments: This point being the Heart Alarm Point offers excellent attack value. Alarm points are generally considered as diagnostic indicators of energetic imbalances of the associated organ. Simple finger pressure on the alarm point of specific organs will produce some pain if there is a disease present. From a combative perspective the alarm points generally are located over the organ in question. It is not true in this case, as the heart is located approximately four inches higher than the Traditional Chinese Alarm point that it is associated. Regardless, strikes to this point should be downward at a 45-degree angle for best results, but an upward strike can effectively knock the air out of the lungs.

CV-15   Chinese Point name: *Jui Wei;*[18] English translation: "Turtledove Tail;"

---

[15] Ibid., p. 314.
[16] Ibid., p. 315.
[17] Ibid., p. 316.
[18] Ibid., p. 317.

Special Attributes: It is the Connecting Point for the Conception Vessel. It is also one of the 36 Vital Points listed in the *Bubishi*; **Location:** About seven inches above the navel on the bottom of the xiphoid process; **Western Anatomy:** Branches of the superior epigastric artery and vein, and the anterior cutaneous branch of the seventh intercostal nerve are present; **Comments:** Strike in same manner as CV-14 for similar results. Strikes may break the xiphoid process.

CV-16 Chinese Point name: *Zhong Ting*;[19] **English translation:** "Central Palace;" **Location:** On the centerline of the body about nine inches above the navel. **Western Anatomy:** Branches of the internal mammary artery and vein, and the anterior cutaneous branch of the sixth intercostal nerve are present; **Comments:** Strikes should be aimed downward at a 45-degree angle to get the best results. Hard strikes can break the breastbone.

CV-17 Chinese Point name: *Shan Zhong*;[20] **English translation:** "Chest Center;" **Special Attributes:** Intersection Point of the Spleen, Small Intestine, Triple Warmer and the Conception Vessel. Additionally, it is the alarm point for the Pericardium Meridian; **Location:** On the centerline of the body on the same level as the nipples; **Western Anatomy:** Branches of the internal mammary artery and vein are found with the anterior cutaneous branch of the fourth intercostal nerve; **Comments:** This is a major point of interest to combative martial artists. A blow to CV-17 can affect the electrical pattern of the heart resulting in arrhythmia. Western science refers to this as *Commotio cordis* and it is documented with strikes to the chest as in a baseball striking the chest of a child. While interviewing a former infantry point man who served in Vietnam confirmation was added to the lethality of a strike to CV-17. According to this individual, a life-long karate practitioner, while he was walking point one night he actually bumped into an enemy soldier who was traveling down the same trail from the opposite direction. The American struck the Viet Cong with a strong punch to CV-17 killing him instantly. His small frame combined with the larger stature of the American allowed for a perfect 45-degree strike (strikes to CV-17 should be downward at a 45-degree angle). These strikes will generally be open palm or hammer fist type strikes given the height of an average sized opponent and the location of the point. Additional energetic disruption can be added by rotating your striking hand outward on contact.

---

[19] Ibid., p. 318.
[20] Ibid., p. 319.

A strike to CV-17 after a blocking technique. A forceful strike to this point will activate several of the centerline CV points in the general area. Note that CV-17 sits over the heart.

Defensive Counters

As the attacker (right) attempts to strike CV-17, twist your center line to the side, drop your lead arm over the attacking arm.

Reinforce your hand and deliver a nailing elbow strike to the attacker's chest.

CV-18 Chinese Point name: *Yu Tang*;[21] **English translation:** "Jade Hall;" **Special Attributes:** It is one of the 36 Vital Points listed in the *Bubishi*; **Location:** On the centerline of the body about 1.5 inches above CV-17; **Western Anatomy:** Branches of the internal mammary artery and vein are found along with the anterior cutaneous branch of the third intercostal nerve; **Comments:** Strikes should be the same as those to CV-17. Given the close physical location

---

[21] Ibid., p. 320.

between CV-17 and CV-18, these two points should both be considered as striking directly over the heart.

CV-19 **Chinese Point name:** *Zi Gong;*[22] **English translation:** "Purple Palace; **Location:** About 1.5 inches above CV-18 on the centerline of the body; **Western Anatomy:** Branches of the internal mammary artery and vein are found with the anterior branch of the second intercostal nerve; **Comments:** Strikes should be the same as those to CV-17 and 18.

CV-20 **Chinese Point name:** *Hua Gai;*[23] **English translation:** "Florid Canopy;" **Location:** About 1.5 inches above CV-19 on the centerline of the body; **Western Anatomy:** Branches of the internal mammary artery and vein are found with the anterior cutaneous branch of the first intercostal nerve; **Comments:** Strikes should be the same as those to CV-17, 18, and 19.

CV-21 **Chinese Point name:** *Xuan Ji;*[24] **English translation:** "Jade Pivot;" **Location:** On the centerline of the body midway between CV-20 and CV-22; **Western Anatomy:** Branches of the internal mammary artery and vein are found along with the medial supraclavicular nerve and the anterior cutaneous branch of the first intercostal nerve; **Comments:** Strikes should be in the same manner as those to CV-17, 18, 19, and 20.

CV-22 **Chinese Point name:** *Tian Tu;*[25] **English translation:** "Celestial Chimney;" **Special Attributes:** this is an Intersection Point of the Yin Linking Vessel and the Conception Vessel. It is listed as a Vital Point in the *Bubishi*; **Location:** On the centerline of the body at the center of the suprasternal notch. That structure is the commonly referred to the "horseshoe notch" at the base of the throat; **Western Anatomy:** the jugular arch and a branch of the inferior thyroid artery are superficially represented. The trachea, or windpipe, is found deeper and the posterior aspect of the sternum, the innominate vein and aortic arch are also present; **Comments:** This point is of particular importance the martial artist as it is the intersection point of the Yin Linking Vessel and the Conception Vessel. The interrelationship between these two vessels will be covered in detail later in the book. Additionally, the structure of the suprasternal notch is an

---

[22] Ibid., p. 321.
[23] Ibid., p. 322.
[24] Ibid., p. 323.
[25] Ibid., p. 324.

excellent "touch point" for situations when sight is reduced and you find yourself at extremely close range with your opponent.

CV-23   Chinese Point name: *Lian Quan;*[26] English translation: "Ridge Spring;" Special Attributes: Some Traditional Chinese Medicine textbooks state that this location is an intersection point for the Yin Linking Vessel and the Conception Vessel; Location: On the centerline of the throat just above the Adam's apple; Western Anatomy: the anterior jugular vein, a branch of cutaneous cervical nerve, the hypoglossal nerve, and branch of the glossopharyngeal nerve are present; Comments: Strikes to this point should directly inward, or slightly upward, to bust the structure of the Adam's apple and disrupt the energy flow to the head. Generally, any strike to the throat area will activate a number of sensitive acupuncture points and attacks the structural weakness of this part of the human body.

CV-24   Chinese Point name: *Cheng Jiang;*[27] English translation: "Sauce Receptacle;" Special Attributes: It is the intersection point of the Stomach and Large Intestine Meridians. Some sources state that the Governing and Conception Vessels intersect at this location. It is one of the 36 Vital Points listed in the *Bubishi;* Location: On the centerline of the head at the slight depression on the upper aspect of the chin; Western Anatomy: Branches of the inferior labial artery and vein are found with a branch of the facial nerve. Comments: The translation of the Chinese term for the point, "Sauce Receptacle," is illustrative in that if one were to drip sauce from their mouth while eating it would accumulate at this point of their chin. This point is another interesting point for the martial artist. Strikes to this point are generally most effective when aimed downward at a 45-degree angle. A hammerfist strike to this point, with enough force, will not only cause an instant knockout, but can dislocate the jaw.

ST-1   Chinese Point name: *Cheng Qi;*[28] English translation: "Tear Container;" Special Attributes: It is an intersection point of the Stomach Meridian, the Yang Heel Vessel, and the Conception Vessel (according to some sources). It is also bilateral; Location: Directly in line with the pupil of the eye and on the ridge of the infraorbital ridge. This point is bilateral; Western Anatomy: Branches of the infraorbital and ophthalmic arteries and veins, branches of the

---

[26] Ibid., p. 325.
[27] Ibid., p. 326.
[28] Ibid., p. 56.

intraorbital, oculomotor and facial nerves are present. **Comments:** Strikes should be upward at a 45-degree angle and aimed toward to the center of the head. Forceful strikes can break the cheekbone and damage the eye.

Another strike to CV-22. Again, these are serious strikes and should never be used unless your life is threatened.

Defensive Counters

Drop your lead arm across the top of the arm attacking your throat. Push the attackers arm down.

Step towards the attacker (on right) and pin his lead arm against his body. Prepare to deliver an open palm strike to his face.

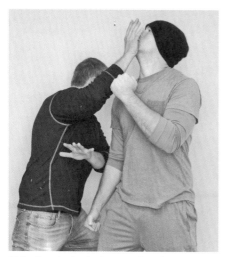

Strike the attacker in the centerline of their face.

This strike needs to be strong and violent with a long follow-through.

Chapter 3

THE GOVERNING VESSEL

"The Governing Vessel is the sea of the yang channels."
Su When

The Governing Vessel is the Yang aspect of the "Human Battery." It starts at the intersection of CV-1 and runs posteriorly to Governing Vessel 1 (GV-1) at the tip of the coccyx bone at the end of the spine. From GV-1 the Governing Vessel ascends the centerline of the body running over the spine to GV-15, which is the point that the head and the spine connect. From GV-15 the Governing Vessel follows the centerline of the head up and over onto the face. It then descends down the centerline of the face until it connects with Conception Vessel at GV-28.

Given the yang characteristics of the Governing Vessel it is harder and more resilient to strikes than the softer Conception Vessel. Consider how the body is designed according to Traditional Chinese Medicine and Western Science. The Yang surfaces of the body are the natural shock absorbers of the body. Let us say that someone is going to strike you with a whip. Will you just stand there and take the strike across the front of your body? I doubt it. Your natural defenses will cause you to turn your back to the strike. The strike would fall on the Yang surfaces of the body. Thus allowing you to protect the more vulnerable yin surfaces. This description illustrates the difference between a Yang surface and a Yin surface. The Yang surfaces of the body can take more physical abuse than the Yin surfaces. This should be a major clue to the martial artist. The fact that the body is designed to protect the Yin over the Yang illustrates that attacks to *Yin* are more traumatic to the body.[1]

It has the primary function of transferring energy to/from the Yang Linking Vessel, which will then transfer the energy to/from the Main Meridians. The energy that is transferred from the Governing Vessel is often referred to as "Yang energy" in Chinese texts.[2] A common term used by Traditional Chinese Med-

---

[1] Moneymaker, *Torite-Jutsu Reference Manual*, pp. 11–17.
[2] Larre & Rochat, *The Eight Extraordinary Meridians*, p. 26.

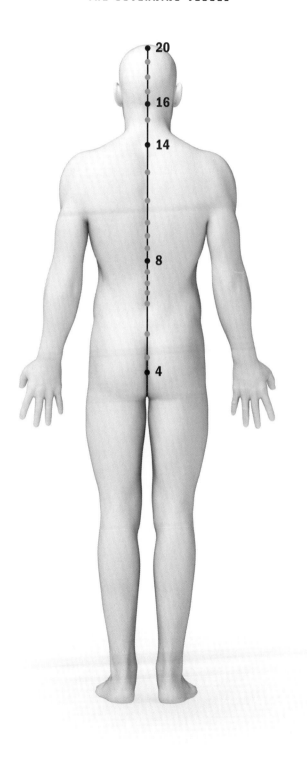

icine textbooks for the Governing Vessel is the "sea of yang meridians."[3] These terms can seem cryptic to the Western student. It is easier to consider the Governing Vessel simply as the Yang aspect of the "Human Battery." That it is connected to the Yang Linking Vessel, which enables smooth transfer of energy between the Extraordinary Vessel Subsystem and the twelve Main Meridians.

From a Western anatomy perspective, the trajectory of the Governing Vessel takes it along the hard skeletal structure of the spine and skull. Those skeletal structures are in great contrast to the softer tissue that runs along the centerline of the front of the body. Asians observed this distinction as well, and associated the hardness of the back of the torso with Yang and the softness of the front of the torso with Yin. They simply applied the physical structure of the body to the Taoist logic that is the root of traditional Chinese philosophy. There is no Yang energy or Yin energy as some pressure point instructors have stated at seminars. There is just energy, which the Chinese refer to as *Qi*. Yin and Yang are just comparative terms that are applied to every aspect of the human body in that model. Additionally, they are utilized by the Chinese to compare everything in nature. *Qi* can be observed in the same manner. It can have Yin qualities or it can exhibit Yang qualities, both of which are associated with the diurnal cycle. Regardless, it remains just *qi* and is not to be considered as yin *qi* or yang *qi*. The Law of Yin/Yang will be covered in detail later in this book.

The Governing Vessel is of great importance to the overall Extraordinary Vessel subsystem. Besides being the Yang aspect of the "Human Battery" of the torso, it has the function of moving energy to the Yang associated Main Meridians to correct energetic imbalances. It only does this directly through the intersection point with the Bladder Meridian. It is also accomplished indirectly through the connection with the Yang Linking Vessels, which are bilateral and interact with all Yang associated Main Meridians.

Governing Vessel Point Descriptions

GV-1 **Chinese Point name:** *Chang Qiang*;[4] **English translation:** "Long Strong;" **Special Attributes:** the intersection point for the Kidney Meridian, Gall Bladder Meridian, and Governing Vessel. It is also listed as one of the 36 Vital Points of the *Bubishi*; **Location:** Just below the coccyx bone on the end of

---

[3] Ellis, Wiseman and Boss, *Fundamentals of Chinese Acupuncture*, p. 369.

[4] Ellis, Wiseman, and Boss, *Grasping the Wind*, p. 327.

the spine; **Western Anatomy:** branches of the inferior hemorrhoid artery and vein are present. Also, the posterior ramus of the coccygeal nerve, and the hemorrhoid nerve are found; **Comments:** Remember that strikes to intersection points have greater energetic effect on the body. Strikes to this point should be upward at a 45-degree angle. This places the force of the blow as being aimed at the energy center of the body. From a martial perspective, this point is generally difficult to hit, but situations when you move to the back of your opponent open the possibility of knee strikes aimed in the coccyx bone. These types of strikes are extremely effective in dropping an opponent. Hard knee strikes to this region not only shock the energy core of the body, but also shock the entire nervous system with the connection of the coccyx bone to the spine.

After evading an opponent's initial attack it is possible to gain superior position on the outside. It is possible to grasp the opponent's clothing and, after manhandling the opponent into a tactically weak position, deliver a forceful knee strike to GV-1 Note that while in this dominant position several such knee strikes can be thrown. There is no need to change positions or move to a different technique once you have established this type of advantage over your opponent.

Defensive Counters

The attacker (right) has gained positional advantage and is establishing control on your shoulder and arm.

Turn quickly to face the opponent as you start to raise the arm they are attacking.

Continue to raise your arm as you step closer to the attacker.

Deliver an elbow smash to the attacker's chest.

GV-2   **Chinese Point name:** *Yao Shu;*[5] **English translation:** "Lumbar Shu;" **Location:** About 1.5 inches above GV-1 and is on the midline of the sacral hiatus; **Western Anatomy:** Branches of the median sacral artery and vein are present, with a branch of the coccygeal nerve; **Comments:** It should be struck in the same manner as GV-1.

GV-3   **Chinese Point name:** *Yao Yang Guan;*[6] **English translation:** "Yang Pass;"

---

[5] Ibid., p. 329.
[6] Ibid., p. 330.

Location: Just below the fourth lumbar vertebra on the centerline of the body; **Western Anatomy:** The posterior branch of the lumbar artery and the medial branch of the posterior ramus of the lumbar nerve are both present; **Comments:** Martial attacks to this point, and the majority of the Governing Vessel points on the back, are limited to situations when you are at your opponents back. Strikes to these areas will have to be forceful given the protective nature of the Yang surface of the back. If an opponent is prone on their stomach, after they have been dropped by another technique, then utilize heel stomps to the Governing Vessel to disable them. The hard stomping action will not only shock the energy core of the body, but might also cause structural damage to the spine.

The opponent has collapsed to the ground and turned their back. Notice the fetal-like position of the opponent. This is indicative of a Yin response.

Taking advantage of the opponent's position, the author delivers a forceful kick to the GV points in the center of the back.

Defensive Counters

TOP: One of your hands should grasp the attacker's heel and the other should grasp points just below the knee. Note: you can utilize your forearm for this.

LEFT: After being thrown to the ground, quickly roll towards the attacker (right).

Pull towards yourself with the hand on their heel and push away with the hand/ forearm just below their knee. This will drop the opponent to the ground.

GV-4   Chinese Point name: *Ming Men;*[7] **English translation:** "Life Gate;" **Location:** Just below the second lumbar vertebra on the centerline of the back; **Western Anatomy:** The posterior branch of the lumbar artery and the medial branch of the posterior ramus of the lumbar nerve are both present; **Comments:** Strike it in the same manner as GV-3.

GV-5   Chinese Point name: *Xuan Shu;*[8] **English translation:** "Suspended Pivot;" **Location:** Just below the first lumbar vertebra on the centerline of the back; **Western Anatomy:** The posterior branch of the lumbar artery and the medial branch of the posterior ramus of the lumbar nerve are both present; **Comments:** Strike it in the same manner as GV-3.

GV-6   Chinese Point name: *Ji Zhong;*[9] **English translation:** "Spinal Center;" **Location:** Just below the eleventh vertebra on the centerline of the back; **Western Anatomy:** The posterior branch of the eleventh intercostal artery and the medial branch of the posterior ramus of the eleventh thoracic nerve are present; **Comments:** Strike in the same manner as GV-3.

GV-7   Chinese Point name: *Zhong Shu;*[10] **English translation:** "Central Pivot;" **Location:** Just below the tenth thoracic vertebra on the centerline of the back; **Western Anatomy:** The posterior branch of the tenth intercostal artery and the medial branch of the posterior ramus of the tenth thoracic nerve are present: **Comments:** Strike in same manner as GV-3.

---

[7] Ibid., p. 331.
[8] Ibid., p. 332.
[9] Ibid.
[10] Ibid., p. 333.

GV-8   Chinese Point name: *Jin Suo*;[11] English translation: "Sinew Connection;" Location: Just below the ninth thoracic vertebra on the centerline of the back; Western Anatomy: The posterior branch of the ninth intercostal artery and the medial branch of the posterior ramus of the ninth thoracic nerve are present; Comments: Strike in same manner as GV-3.

GV-9   Chinese Point name: *Zhi Yang*;[12] English translation: "Extremity of Yang;" Location: Just below the seventh thoracic vertebra at the same level of the bottom point of the scapula; Western Anatomy: The posterior branch of the seventh intercostal artery and the medial branch of the posterior ramus of the seventh thoracic nerve are present; Comments: Strikes should be similar to GV-3, but aimed at the energy core of the body if possible (45-degree angle down if opponent is standing).

GV-10   Chinese Point name: *Ling Tai*;[13] English translation: "Spirit Tower;" Location: Just below the sixth thoracic vertebra on the centerline of the back; Western Anatomy: The posterior branch of the sixth intercostal artery and the medial branch of the posterior ramus of the sixth thoracic nerve are present; Comments: Strike in the same manner as GV-9.

GV-11   Chinese Point name: *Shen Dao*;[14] English translation: "Spirit Path;" Location: Just below the fifth thoracic vertebra on the centerline of the back; Western Anatomy: The posterior branch of the fifth intercostal artery and the medial branch of the posterior ramus of the fifth thoracic nerve are present; Comments: Strike in the same manner as GV-9.

GV-12   Chinese Point name: *Shen Zhu*;[15] English translation: "Body Pillar;" Location: Just below the third thoracic vertebra on the centerline of the back; Western Anatomy: The posterior branch of the third intercostal artery and the medial branch of the posterior ramus of the third thoracic nerve are present; Comments: Strike in the same manner as GV-9.

---

[11] Ibid., p. 334.
[12] Ibid.
[13] Ibid., p. 335.
[14] Ibid., p. 336.
[15] Ibid.

GV-13   Chinese Point name: *Tao Dao*;[16] English translation: "Kiln Path;" Location: Just below the first thoracic vertebra on the centerline of the back; Western Anatomy: The posterior branch of the first intercostal artery and the medial branch of the posterior ramus of the first thoracic nerve are present; Comments: Strike in the same manner as GV-9.

GV-14   Chinese Point name: *Da Zhui*;[17] English translation: "Great Hammer;" Special Attributes: This point is the intersection point of the six Yang meridians and the Governing Vessel. It is also listed as one of the 36 Vital Points in the *Bubishi*; Location: Between the seventh cervical vertebra and the first thoracic vertebra. It is generally about level with the shoulder; Western Anatomy: A branch of the transverse cervical artery, the posterior ramus of the eighth cervical nerve, and the medial branch of the posterior ramus of the first thoracic nerve are present; Comments: Strike in the same manner as GV-9.

GV-15   Chinese Point name: *Ya Men*;[18] English translation: "Mute's Gate;" Special Attributes: It is the intersection point of the Yang Linking Vessel and the Governing Vessel; Location: About .5 of an inch within the hairline on the centerline of the neck. This points marks the point in which the Governing Vessel leaves the back and ascends onto the head; Western Anatomy: Branches of the occipital artery and vein and the third occipital nerve are present; Comments: This point is of major importance to the martial artist. Strikes to this point should aimed at about a 30-degree upward angle. Considering that this point is located where the skull and spine connect, it is a structural weak location. Strikes to this point can cause death.

GV-16   Chinese Point name: *Feng Fu*;[19] English translation: "Wind Mansion;" Special Attributes: It is the intersection point of the Yang Linking Vessel and the Governing Vessel. It is one of the 36 Vital Points listed in the *Bubishi*; Location: About .5 of an inch above GV-15; Strikes to one of these points usually disrupt both given their close proximity. Western Anatomy: A branch of the occipital artery and branches of the third occipital and great occipital nerves are present; Comments: This is great importance to martial artist. Strike in the same manner as GV-15 for similar effect.

---

[16] Ibid., p. 337.
[17] Ibid., p. 338.
[18] Ibid., p. 339.
[19] Ibid., p. 340.

GV-17   Chinese Point name: *Nao Hu;*[20] **English translation:** "Brain's Door;" **Special Attributes:** It is an intersection point of the Bladder Meridian and the Governing Vessel; **Location:** About 1.5 inches above GV-16 on the centerline of the head; **Western Anatomy:** Branches of the occipital arteries and veins, and a branch of the great occipital nerve are present; **Comments:** Strike in similar manner as GV-15. This point is not as sensitive as GV-15 and 16, but can produce knockouts.

Gaining a position of dominance during a confrontation opens the back of the opponent's head to attack.

A hammerfist strike is aimed at GV-15 and 16. This technique can be lethal and should be only used in life or death situations.

---

[20] Ibid., p. 341.

Defensive Counters

As an attacker (right) initiates the strike, step towards them as you smother their attacking arm.

Twist your body so your centerline is not facing the attacker as you slide your elbow into their centerline.

Deliver a forceful nailing elbow strike to your opponent's chest.

GV-18   Chinese Point name: *Qiang Jian*;[21] **English translation:** "Unyielding Space;" **Location:** About 1.5 inches above GV-17 on the centerline of the head; **Western Anatomy:** Branches of the occipital arteries and veins, and a branch of the great occipital nerve are present; **Comments:** Strikes should be on 90-degree angle for best effect.

---

[21] Ibid., p. 342.

GV-19 Chinese Point name: *Hou Ding*;[22] English translation: "Behind the Vertex;" Location: About 1.5 inches above GV-18 on the centerline of the head. Western Anatomy: Branches of the occipital arteries and veins, and a branch of the great occipital nerve are present; Comments: Strikes should be aimed at about 30-degrees to the center of the head.

GV-20 Chinese Point name: *Bai Hui*;[23] English translation: "Hundred Convergences;" Special Attributes: This is an intersection point of the six Yang Meridians and the Governing Vessel; Location: About 1.5 inches above GV-19 on the centerline of the head; Western Anatomy: A large network of arteries and veins of the superficial temporal and occipital branches, from both sides of the head, are present. A branch of the great occipital nerve is also found; Comments: Chinese *Qigong* methods teach that this point is one of the major locations that *qi* enters the body. This makes it a target, if possible, for martial artist. Given the natural strength of the skull, strikes to this point will need to be forceful. Additionally, the point may only be accessible if the opponent is prone on the ground. Solid kicks to this point can not only disrupt the energetic system, but also traumatize the brain. Strikes should be straight down at a 90-degree angle.

GV-21 Chinese Point name: *Qian Ding*;[24] English translation: "Before the Vertex;" Location: About 1.5 inches to the front of GV-20; Western Anatomy: A network of the right and left superficial temporal arteries and veins, a branch of the frontal nerve, and a branch of the great occipital nerve are present; Comments: Strikes should be in the same manner as GV-20.

GV-22 Chinese Point name: *Xin Hui*;[25] English translation: "Fontanel Meeting;" Special Attributes: This point is listed in the 36 Vital Points of the *Bubishi*; Location: About 1.5 inches in front of GV-21 on the centerline of the head; Western Anatomy: A network of branches of the superficial temporal and frontal arteries and veins, and a branch of the frontal nerve are present; Comments: Strike in the same manner as GV-20.

---

[22] Ibid., p. 343.
[23] Ibid.
[24] Ibid., p. 345.
[25] Ibid.

GV-23 Chinese Point name: *Shang Xing;*[26] English translation: "Upper Star;" Location: About .5 of an inch in front of GV-22 and one inch within the hairline; Western Anatomy: Branches of the frontal and superficial temporal arteries and veins, and a branch of the frontal nerve are present; Comments: Strike in the same manner as GV-24.

GV-24 Chinese Point name: *Shen Ting;*[27] English translation: "Spirit Court;" Special Attributes: This is an intersection point of the Bladder Meridian, Stomach Meridian, and the Governing Vessel. It is also listed as one of the 36 Vital Points in the *Bubishi*; Location: About .5 of an inch in front of GV-23 and about .5 of an inch within the hairline; Western Anatomy: Branches of the frontal artery and vein and a branch of the frontal nerve are present; Comments: Strikes should be aimed downward at a 45-degree angle and very forceful.

GV-25 Chinese Point name: *Su Liao;*[28] English translation: "White Bone-Hole;" Location: On the tip of the nose; Western Anatomy: The lateral nasal branches of the facial artery and veins with the external nasal branch of the anterior ethmoid nerve are present; Comments: Strikes should be upward at a 45-degree angle to break the nose.

GV-26 Chinese Point name: *Shui Gou;*[29] English translation: "Water Trough;" Special Attributes: It is the intersection point of the Large Intestine Meridian and the Governing Vessel. It is also listed as one of the 36 Vital Points in the *Bubishi*; Location: Below in the nose and a little above the midpoint of the philtrum; Western Anatomy: The superior labial artery and vein, the buccal branch of the facial nerve, and a branch of the infraorbital nerve are present; Comments: This point can be struck or pinched. In a situation in which it is necessary to control an individual GV-26 can be pinched between the thumb and the forefinger with great effect. A strike should be aimed upward at a 45-degree angle. This strike, if thrown with force, will also hit GV-25.

GV-27 Chinese Point name: *Dui Duan;*[30] English translation: "Extremity of the Mouth;" Location: At the junction of the philtrum and the upper lip; West-

---

[26] Ibid., p. 346.
[27] Ibid., p. 347.
[28] Ibid., p. 348.
[29] Ibid., p. 349.
[30] Ibid., p. 350.

ern **Anatomy:** The superior labial artery and vein, the buccal branch of the facial nerve, and a branch of the infraorbital nerve are present; **Comments:** Strike in same manner as GV-26.

GV-28 **Chinese Point name:** *Yin Jiao;*[31] **English translation:** "Gum Intersection;" **Location:** Under the upper lip at the base of the gum line; **Western Anatomy:** The superior labial artery and vein and a branch of the superior alveolar nerve are present; It is the intersection point of the Stomach Meridian, Conception Vessel and the Governing Vessel. **Comments:** Strike in same manner as GV-26.

An upward strike to the centerline of the front of the head will disrupt several of the GV points.

Defensive Counters

As the attacker (right) attempts an uppercut to your centerline, deflect the strike to the outside with you inner forearm.

Strike the attacker's neck with your forearm as you violently close with him.

---

[31] Ibid., p. 351.

THE THRUSTING VESSEL

"Remember that acupuncture is for 'healing'
and it is much harder to heal than destroy."

Rusty McMains

T he Thrusting Vessel is the third and final energy channel of the "Human Battery" subsystem. It is extremely complex as it has many different functions along its internal pathways.[1] The Thrusting Vessel can be considered the origin of the other Extraordinary Vessels.[2] Likewise, the Extraordinary Vessels should be considered the origin of the twelve Main Meridians. The source of life essence, according to Traditional Chinese Medicine, is the kidneys and the Thrusting Vessel originates at that location. It connects to the other Extraordinary Vessels and spreads that energy throughout the rest of the energy system.[3]

The Thrusting Vessel connects to the Conception and Governing Vessels at CV-1. This connection enables the "Human Battery" to exchange energy with the twelve Main Meridians through their connection with the other Extraordinary Vessels.[4] The energy that is drawn from the twelve Main Meridians is returned to the Thrusting Vessel. Likewise, if the twelve Main Meridians need additional energy, to correct an imbalance, then it is taken from the Thrusting Vessel. The yin and yang aspects of the "Human Battery," which are the Conception and Governing Vessels, are the connection points for the Linking Vessels. The Linking Vessels are actually responsible for the transportation and exchange of energy with the twelve Main Meridians, but the Thrusting Vessel is responsible for the storage.[5]

Considering the internal pathways of the Thrusting Vessel is of little use from a martial perspective, in regards to striking it directly. The Thrusting

---

[1] Maciocia, *The Foundations of Chinese Medicine*, p. 360.
[2] Yang, *The Root of Chinese Chi Kung*, p. 234.
[3] Teeguarden, *A Complete Guide to Acupressure*, p. 56.
[4] Larre & Vallee, *The Eight Extraordinary Meridians*, p. 17.
[5] Ibid., pp. 212–213.

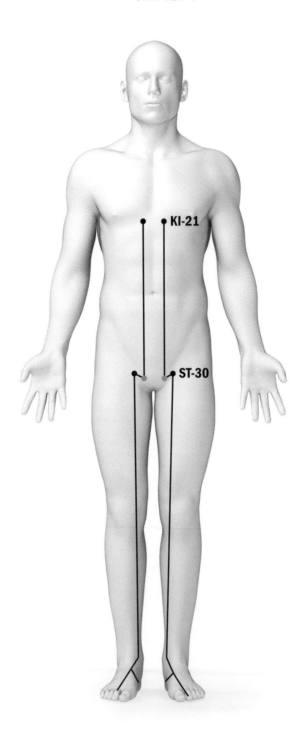

Vessel is sometimes referred to as the "Energy Core." The majority of the strikes to the torso are aimed towards the Energy Core. They are more effective than strikes thrown at random to the torso. The energetic shock to the "energy core" is the result of the kinetic energy transfer from a martial strike. The Thrusting Vessel is rarely struck directly, but the kinetic energy from a strike aimed at the torso can disrupt the normal energetic balance of the core.

The internal pathways of the Thrusting Vessel are as follows; the first path originates in the energy core of the lower abdomen and travels up the body internal to the Kidney Meridian until it disperses in the chest. The second path starts at that point and ascends to the through the throat and into the face. It terminates in the nasal cavity. The third pathway runs from the KI-11 downward to the sole of the foot. The fourth pathway descends from the ST-30 to the heel and terminates at the big toe. The last pathway separates from the energy core of the lower abdomen and ascends the internal aspects of the spine.

Some Traditional Chinese Medicine texts include KI-11 through KI-21 as shared points with the Thrusting Vessel. The majority of those texts maintain that the Thrusting Vessel runs deeper than the Kidney Meridian and does not include these points. There is a general consensus among those sources that the Thrusting Vessel connects to four acupuncture points. The Thrusting Vessel is sometimes referred to as *Chong Mai* or the Penetrating Vessel.

Martial techniques that attack CV-1 are devastating to an opponent from an energetic standpoint. Given the structural location of the point it is generally difficult to access during an aggressive encounter, but there are techniques that can blast it. Attacking CV-1, which is the intersection point of the Conception, Governing and Thrusting Vessels, has a major energetic influence on the state of the energy core of the body. Such an attack causes direct energetic disruptions to the core and can be life threatening according to the information contained in the *Bubishi*.

Thrusting Vessel Point Descriptions

CV-1 Chinese Point name: *Hui Yin;*[6] English translation: "Meeting of Yin;" **Special Attributes:** Intersection Point of the Conception, Governing, and Thrusting Vessels. It is one of the 36 Vital Points listed in the *Bubishi*; **Location:** Midway between the anus and the bottom of the genitals; **Western Anatomy:**

---

[6] Andrew Ellis, Nigel Wiseman, and Ken Boss, *Grasping the Wind: An Exploration Into The Meaning of Chinese Acupuncture Point Names* (Brookline, MA: Paradigm Publications, 1989), p. 303.

Branches of the perineal artery and vein, as well as a branch of the perineal nerve are present; **Comments:** Given the naturally protected location of this point it is difficult to strike in a combative situation, but if your opponent is kicking for your head or if they are prone on the ground and you have control of one of their legs it can be accessible. A strike, if one is possible, to this point is devastating to an opponent.

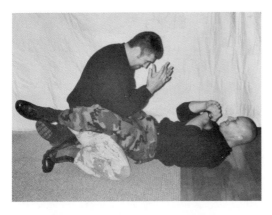

Here the opponent is in the classic guard position common to several forms of grappling.

Assume a squatted stance and bounces the opponent by their legs.

After gaining control of the legs, the author delivers a forceful kick to CV-1. Note that once this position is gained you should fire several such kicks.

Defensive Counters

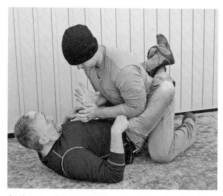

As the attacker (right) drives his elbows into the inner side of the thigh, take control of one of his wrists.

Forcefully pull the attacker forward and to the side to break his strong position. You will have to partially roll to one side to perform this technique correctly.

ST-30 Chinese Point name: *Qi Chong;*[7] English translation: "Surging Qi;" Special Attributes: It is an intersection point for the Stomach Meridian and the Thrusting Vessel. It is bilateral; Location: About five inches below the navel and two inches to either side of the Conception Vessel; Western Anatomy: Branches of the superficial epigastric artery and vein, the inferior epigastric artery and vein and the pathway of the ilioinguinal nerve are present; Comments: This point should be struck downward at the energetic core of the body.

KI-11 Chinese Point name: *Heng Gu;*[8] English translation: "Pubic Bone;" Special Attributes: It is an intersection point of the Kidney Meridian and the Thrusting Vessel. It is also bilateral; Location: About five inches below the navel and .5 of an inch lateral to each side of CV-2; This puts it in close proximity to ST-30 and CV-2. Western Anatomy: The inferior epigastric artery, external pudendal artery, and a branch of the iliohypogastric nerve are present; Comments: Strike in the same manner as ST-30.

KI-21 Chinese Point name: *You Men;*[9] English translation: "Dark Gate;" Special Attributes: This point is bilateral and is an intersection point of the Kidney Meridian and the Thrusting Vessel; Location: About six inches above the navel and about .5 of an inch lateral to each side of the CV-14; Western

---

[7] Ibid., p. 84.
[8] Ibid., p. 206.
[9] Ibid., p. 216.

Anatomy: Branches of the superior epigastric artery and vein and the seventh intercostal nerve are present; **Comments:** Strike this point downward towards the energetic core of the body.

Remember that strikes to the torso should be aimed at the energetic core of the body.

Defensive Counters

Use your lead arm to deflect the strike from the attacker (right) to the inside.

Drop your height as you prepare to counter.

Close with your attacker as you pin their arm to their torso.

Deliver an arching upward strike to their genitals with your forearm.

Repeat same strike if necessary.

Chapter 5
THE **GIRDLE VESSEL**

"A person's unbalance is the same as weight."
Tatsuo Shimabuku

The Girdle Vessel plays an important role in the Extraordinary Vessel subsystem. It is the only horizontal meridian of the body and is responsible for equalizing the energy in the torso and especially the lower abdomen. The Liver, Gall Bladder, Stomach, Spleen, Kidney, Bladder Meridians all transect this vessel. The Girdle Vessel controls the amount of energy that flows to these meridians. This function of the Girdle Vessel illustrates its place in equalizing the energy of the leg meridians. In cases of trauma to the torso or head, as in the result of a combative strike, the Girdle Vessel will "tighten" (which inhibits the energy flow to the legs) and quickly drop the energy flow to the leg meridians. This will cause the opponent to either bend at the knees or drop completely to the ground. The Girdle Vessel is often referred to as the Belt Vessel or the *Dai Mai*.

The points of the Girdle Vessel are shared with the Gall Bladder and Liver Meridians and indicate that this Extraordinary Vessel helps to maintain balance between this paired set of Wood Meridians.[1] It has no starting or ending point, as it connects to itself after encircling the body. The Girdle Vessel connects to the Gall Bladder and Liver Meridian points on both sides of the body. This forms a Girdle or Belt that is indicative of the name associated with this vessel.

Some Traditional Chinese Medicine textbooks partner the Girdle Vessel with Thrusting Vessel, but detailed research indicates that it is secondary to the functions of "Human Battery" that consists of the Conception, Governing, and Thrusting Vessels. Additionally, research by Mantak Chia[2] and Dr. Wilhelm Reich[3] point towards several "Energy Belts" that encircle the body at various

---

[1] Yang, *The Root of Chinese Chi Kung*, p. 236.
[2] Mantak & Maneewan Chia, *Chi Nei Tsang: Internal Organs of Chi Massage* (Huntington, NY: Healing Tao Books, 1990), pp. 39–42.
[3] Wilhelm Reich, *Character Analysis* (New York: Simon & Schuster, 1933)—Reich's research is from a Western perspective, but fits nicely with Traditional Chinese Medicine understandings concerning bio-energy or Qi.

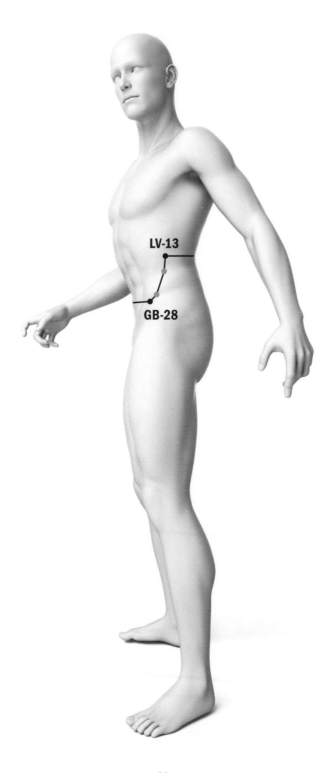

LV-13

GB-28

points. These theories, and supporting research, indicate that this Segmental Theory, which is supported by ancient Taoist teachings, may constitute a complete energetic subsystem. The theories concerning those findings are beyond the scope of this text and are basically from a healing or diagnostic perspective.

Martial attacks aimed at the Girdle Vessel can disrupt the balance of the opponent, which is a structural or biomechanical attack that opens the opponent for additional attacks to other more sensitive energetic targets. The fact that the Girdle Vessel influences the Gall Bladder and Liver Meridians has some energetic significance, but considering the ability of those two meridians to rapidly adjust imbalances it has few martial implications.[4] Generally, the use of the Girdle Vessel to adjust energy in the Gall Bladder and Liver Meridians is more from a healing aspect of Traditional Chinese Medicine.

Girdle Vessel Point Descriptions

LV-13   Chinese Point name: *Zhang Men*;[5] English translation: "Camphorwood Gate;" **Special Attributes:** This point is the Alarm point for the Spleen. It is also the intersection point of the Liver and Gall Bladder Meridians and the Girdle Vessel. It is a bilateral point. It is one of the 36 Vital Points listed in the *Bubishi*; **Location:** At the free end of the eleventh floating rib; **Western Anatomy:** The sixth intercostal artery and vein, and the intercostal nerve are present; **Comments:** This point is of interest to the martial artist. Considering that LV-13 is the alarm point for the spleen makes it a prime target for strikes. Generally, the alarm points are over or near the organ that it is associated. Strikes should be aimed at the energy core of the body or downward at a 45-degree angle at the center of the body. A forceful strike to this point can cause internal injuries to the spleen and other unprotected organs of the abdomen. Likewise, a strike to this area can cause the floating rib to break and with enough force drive it into sensitive organs in the rear of the abdominal cavity. From an energetic perspective this point is excellent. It is the intersection point of the Liver and Gall Bladder Meridians and the Girdle Vessel. A strike will disrupt the energy of those two meridians and upset the Girdle Vessel. Strikes to the Liver and Gall Bladder Meridians will usually cause the legs to bend. This can either drop your opponent to the ground or bend them just enough for follow-up attacks to the neck and head areas.

---

[4] The actual manner that the twelve Main Meridians interact with the Extraordinary Vessels will be covered in later chapters in this book.

[5] Ellis, Wiseman, and Boss, *Grasping the Wind*, p. 300.

GB-28   Chinese Point name: *Wei Dao*;[6] English translation: "Linking Path;" Special Attributes: This point is bilateral and is an intersection point for the Gall Bladder Meridian and the Girdle Vessel; Location: About .5 of an inch below GB-27 and slightly to the inside; Western Anatomy: The superficial and deep circumflex iliac arteries and veins, and the iliohypogastric nerve are present; Comments: Strike in similar manner as GB-27. Given the close proximity of these two points (GB-27 and 28) a single strike will activate both.

GB-27   Chinese Point name: *Wu Shu*;[7] English translation: "Fifth Pivot;" Special Attributes: The point is an intersection point for the Gall Bladder Meridian and the Girdle Vessel. It is also bilateral; Location: About three inches below GB-26 on the inside of the hipbone; Western Anatomy: The superficial and deep circumflex iliac arteries and veins, and the iliohypogastric nerve are present; Comments: This point is an exception to the rule of striking to the energy core of the body. You still need to strike at a 45-degree downward angle, but your aim should be directed towards the outside of the body. This point is located on the hipbone and strikes to the outside will cause the hip to collapse backward. It works to either side, as the point is bilateral (that means it is found on both sides of the body). A strike here will cause the hip to fall back and to the outside, the legs to bend and an energetic fluctuation in the Gall Bladder Meridian. This may be important in follow-up strikes to finish the opponent.

GB-26   Chinese Point name: *Dai Mai*;[8] English translation: "Girdling Vessel;" Special Attributes: It is an intersection point for the Gall Bladder Meridian and the Girdle Vessel. It is bilateral; Location: About 1.5 inches below the free end eleventh on the same level as the navel; Western Anatomy: The subcostal artery and vein, and subcostal nerve are present; Comments: Strikes should be aimed toward the core of the body and downward at a 45-degree angle.

---

[6] Ibid., p. 276.
[7] Ibid., p. 275.
[8] Ibid., p. 274.

Finding yourself inside of the opponent is NOT the preferred place to be!

While protecting your head from attack with one hand, strike GB-27 and 28 with the other hand.

This breaks the balance of the opponent and causes their attacked hip to move backwards, which opens up attacks to their head and neck.

Defensive Counters

Deflect the attacker's arm to the outside as he reaches for your hip. Raise your other arm under the attacker's opposite arm.

Snake your arm over the attacker's triceps area bringing your other hand to reinforce it, as you pivot and lower, which will drop your opponent.

Maintain control of the attacker's arm and prepare for a powerful downward palm strike to the head.

Strike the side or back of the attacker's head depending on what is available. Repeat the same strike if necessary.

Chapter 6

THE **HEEL VESSELS**

The Heel Vessels are a paired system of vessels that control the eyes and mouth, the ascent of fluids in the body and the descent of *qi*, and regulate general muscular activity.[1] They are divided into the Yin Heel Vessel and the Yang Heel Vessel, with both maintaining separate pathways. Their role in the Extraordinary System is vital to the proper function of the body, but from a martial perspective they are of little consequence. Some points along their pathways are shared with sensitive energetic targets and those will be detailed in the point descriptions.

The Heel Vessels are responsible for the energy flow to the legs,[2] as their name implies. Their connections run the length of the body and are bilateral. One set, the Yin Heel Vessel, connects with the various Yin associated Main Meridians and helps to provide energy to the inner aspects of the legs. The other set, the Yang Heel Vessel, connect to the Yang associated Main Meridians. It provides energy to the outer aspects of the legs. As stated above, martial implications of attacking the Heel Vessel3 are somewhat limited to reducing the flow of energy to the legs. Causing energetic imbalances in the legs, enough to cause your opponent to collapse, can be easily performed by attacking the leg meridians directly or by utilizing the Five Element Theory.[3]

The Yang Heel Vessel is connected to the Governing Vessel. The energy that is produced from the burning of fat tissue in the legs is transported up the Yang Heel Vessel to be feed into the Governing Vessel. There it is transported to any of the other Yang associated meridians if they happen to be deficient or to the Thrusting Vessel for storage.

---

[1] Teeguarden, *A Complete Guide to Acupressure*, pp. 69-72.
[2] Yang, *The Root of Chinese Chi Kung*, p. 236.
[3] The Five Element Theory of Traditional Chinese Medicine is covered in Chapter 9. A detailed examination of attacking the twelve Main Meridians in accordance with that theory is planned in future efforts by the author.

The Yin Heel Vessel

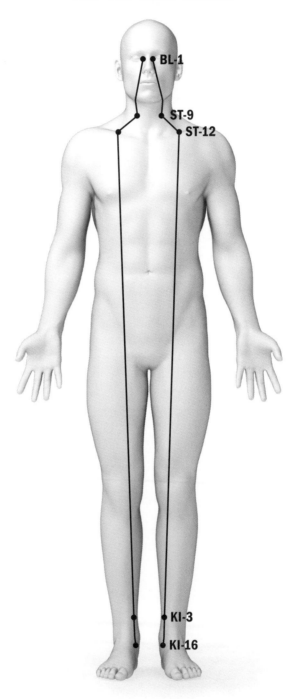

The Yin Heel Vessel starts at KI-6 on the inside of the heel and ascends the inside of the leg until it enters the genital area. From there it continues on an internal path through the abdomen and chest. It emerges again at ST-12 and then continues up the throat, at ST-9, and intersects with the Yang Heel Vessel and the Bladder Meridian at BL-1. It then branches into the brain.[4]

Yin Heel Vessel Point Descriptions

KI-6   Chinese Point name: *Zhao Hai*;[5] English translation: "Shining Sea;" Special Attributes: This bilateral point is an intersection point for the Yin Heel Vessel and the Kidney Meridian. It is one of the 36 Vital Points listed in the *Bubishi*; Location: About one inch below the inside of the anklebone; and is bilateral. Western Anatomy: The posterior tibial artery and vein and the medial crural cutaneous nerve are present; Comments: This point can be struck, with a number of other points, with low sweeping kicks to the inside of the lower leg and foot. Additionally, once an opponent has become prone on the ground this point can be stomped.

KI-8   Chinese Point name: *Jiao Xin*;[6] English translation: "Intersection Reach;" Special Attributes: This bilateral point is the intersection point of the Kidney Meridian and the Yin Heel Vessel; Location: About two inches above the inner anklebone, just posterior to the medial edge of the tibia; and is bilateral. Western Anatomy: The posterior tibial artery and vein and the medial crural cutaneous nerve are present; Comments: Strike in the same manner as KI-6.

ST-12   Chinese Point name: *Que Pen*;[7] English translation: "Empty Basin;" Special Attributes: It is an intersection point of the Stomach Meridian and the Yin Heel Vessel. It is bilateral and is one of the 36 Vital Points listed in the *Bubishi*; Location: At the midpoint of the collarbone, which is about four inches lateral from the centerline of the body; and bilateral. Western Anatomy: The transverse cervical artery, intermediate supraclavicular nerve and the supra-clavicular portion of the brachial plexus are present; Comments: This point is an excellent target when your opponent is at close range. By gripping the col-larbone you can dig your fingers down behind the natural curve of the bone

---

4   Maciocia, *The Foundations of Chinese Medicine*, pp. 362–363.
5   Ellis, Wiseman, and Boss, *Grasping the Wind*, p. 201.
6   Ibid., p. 204.
7   Ibid., p. 67.

and towards the centerline of the body. It is most active when your opponent has their arms raised, given the structural weakness of the body at this location, will drop the majority of attackers. A sharp thrust down into this point will cause your opponents knees to bend.

ST-9   Chinese Point name: *Ren Ying;*[8] **English translation:** "Man's Prognosis;" **Special Attributes:** ST-9 is an intersection point for the Stomach Meridian, Gall Bladder Meridian and the Yin Heel Vessel. It is a bilateral point that sets over the carotid artery. It is one of the 36 Vital Points listed in the *Bubishi;* **Location:** About 1.5 inches to the outside of the Adam's apple on the throat; **Western Anatomy:** The superior thyroid artery, the anterior jugular vein, the internal jugular vein, the carotid artery, the cutaneous cervical nerve, the cervical branch of the facial nerve, the sympathetic trunk, and the ascending branch of the hypoglossal and vagus nerves are all present; **Comments:** This is one of the weakest points on the human body and regardless of the size and muscular strength of an opponent it is extremely sensitive. Strikes to this point can kill due to the structural weakness of the area. Strikes should be aimed toward the center of the spine on a 90-degree angle. A variety of empty hand weapons can be employed in striking this point. Forearms, edge of hand strikes, punches, kicks, and elbow strikes are all effective.

BL-1   Chinese Point name: *Jing Ming;*[9] **English translation:** "Bright Eyes;" **Special Attributes:** It is an intersection point of the Small Intestine Meridian, Bladder Meridian, Stomach Meridian, Yin Heel Vessel and the Yang Heel Vessel. It is also bilateral; **Location:** About .25 of an inch from the inner corner of the eye; **Western Anatomy:** The angular artery and vein and branches of the oculomotor and ophthalmic nerve are present; **Comments:** Strike this point slightly upward and towards the centerline of the head. This point is fairly difficult to strike in a combative situation due to the location. Forceful strikes to the eye socket area can activate this point, as well as traumatize the eye and possible breaking the bone structure in the general area.

---

[8] Ibid., p. 64.
[9] Ibid., p. 143.

An opponent has grasped the lapel in an aggressive action.

Move your hands into a defensive position and slip the right hand to the back of the opponent's neck. This will prevent the opponent from moving to the rear.

Then grasp the opponent's collarbone and dig your fingers behind it and towards the center of the body, which attacks ST-12.

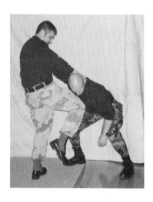

Drive the opponent down into a squat position and deliver a knee lift to the chest or head.

Defensive Counters

Turn your centerline slightly away from the attacker (right) as you bring your lead arm up and to the inside to deflect his reach for ST-12.

Advance towards your attacker as you prepare to strike.

Strike the attacker in the centerline of his face with an Open Palm Strike.

The Yang Heel Vessel

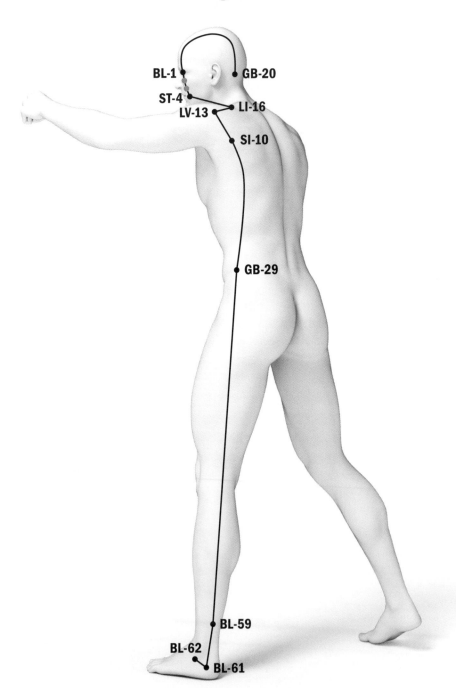

The Yang Heel Vessel starts at BL-62, on the outside of the foot below the anklebone, and ascends the outside of the leg. It continues up the side of the torso to intersect with GB-29 and then across the lateral aspect of the shoulder. It then crosses over the shoulder to the front of the body, up the neck, over the jaw, to intersect with the Yin Heel Vessel at BL-1. From there it runs up the forehead and over the head to GB-20. It finally terminates at GV-16 as it enters the brain.[10]

The Yang Heel Vessels are bilateral and contribute to the function between the Extraordinary Vessels and the twelve Main Meridians by controlling the energy levels of the outer aspects of the legs. It is much simpler to attack the Main Meridians, through use of the Five Element Theory, to drop the energy of the legs. The Yang Heel Vessel has little combative use to the martial artist, but some of the intersection points that it shares with the Main Meridians are excellent targets.

Yang Heel Vessel Point Descriptions

BL-62   Chinese Point name: *Shen Mai*;[11] **English translation:** "Extending Vessel;" **Special Attributes:** It is an intersection point for the Bladder Meridian and the Tang Heel Vessel. It is a bilateral point and is one of the 36 Vital Points listed in the *Bubishi*; **Location:** In the depression directly below the outside aspect of the anklebone; **Western Anatomy:** The external malleolar artery network and the sural nerve are present; **Comments:** This point can be struck, with a number of other points, with low sweeping kicks to the outside of the lower leg and foot. Additionally, once an opponent has become prone on the ground this point can be stomped.

BL-61   Chinese Point name: *Pu Can*;[12] **English translation:** "Subservient Visitor;" **Special Attributes:** It is a bilateral point; **Location:** On the outside aspect of the foot at the bottom end of the heel bone; **Western Anatomy:** The external calcaneal branches of the peroneal artery and vein and the external calcaneal branch of the sural nerve are present; **Comments:** Strike in the same manner as BL-62. It is a bilateral point.

---

[10] Maciocia, *The Foundations of Chinese Medicine*, pp. 363–364.
[11] Ellis, Wiseman, and Boss, *Grasping the Wind*, p. 190.
[12] Ibid., p. 189.

BL-59   Chinese Point name: *Fu Yang;*[13] **English translation:** "Instep Yang;" **Special Attributes:** It is a bilateral point; **Location:** About three inches above the outer aspect of the anklebone and directly on line with BL-58 and 60; **Western Anatomy:** The small saphenous vein, the terminal branch of the peroneal artery, and the sural nerve are present; **Comments:** Strike in same manner as BL-62. It is a bilateral point.

Low sweeping kicks can be employed once position has been gained on the outside of the opponent.

Multiple points are activated with these type of kicks. Similar kicks to the inside of the foot and lower leg can be effective as well.

Defensive Counters

As the attacker (right) launches a low kick to your forward leg, raise that leg and step into the attackers centerline.

If the attacker retreats, throw a forceful forward punch to their CV-4 region.

---

[13] Ibid., p. 186.

GB-29 Chinese Point name: *Ju Liao*;[14] English translation: "Squatting Bone-Hole;" **Special Attributes:** It is an intersection point of the Gall Bladder Meridian and the Yang Heel Vessel. It is a bilateral point; **Location:** About eight inches directly below LV-13 in the depression above the iliac bone; **Western Anatomy:** Branches of the superficial circumflex iliac artery and vein, the ascending branches of the lateral circumflex femoral artery and vein and the lateral femoral cutaneous nerve are present; **Comments:** Strikes to this point should be aimed towards the energy core of the body at about a 30-degree angle. This can cause the hip to collapse towards the opposite side and break the balance of your opponent.

SI-10 Chinese Point name: *Nao Shu*;[15] English translation: "Upper Arm Point;" **Special Attributes:** This is an intersection point for the Small Intestine Meridian, the Yang Linking Vessel and the Yang Heel Vessel. This point is bilateral; **Location:** In the depression of the inferior of the scapula when the arm is raised; **Western Anatomy:** The posterior circumflex humeral artery and vein, the suprascapular artery and vein, the posterior cutaneous nerve of the arm, the axillary nerve, and the suprascapular nerve are present; **Comments:** This point is extremely difficult to strike in a combative situation. A strike, if possible, should be directed towards the center of the body on a 90-degree angle. This is an important point because of the major energetic intersection, but is extremely difficult to strike unless position is gained on the opponent's back.

LI-16 Chinese Point name: *Ju Gu*;[16] English translation: "Great Bone;" **Special Attributes:** It is an intersection point of the Large Intestine Meridian and the Yang Heel Vessel. It is a bilateral point; **Location:** In the depression between the outer aspect of the clavicle bone and the scapular on the top of the shoulder; **Western Anatomy:** The jugular vein, the suprascapular artery and vein, and the suprascapular nerve are present; **Comments:** Strikes should be in a downward manner and will cause the attacked shoulder to drop. Strikes should be forceful and can break the clavicle.

LI-15 Chinese Point name: *Jian Yu*;[17] English translation: "Shoulder Bone;" **Special Attributes:** It is a bilateral point. LI-15 is an intersection point for the

---

[14] Ibid., p. 277.
[15] Ibid., p. 135.
[16] Ibid., p. 51.
[17] Ibid., p. 50.

Small Intestine Meridian, the Large Intestine Meridian, and the Yang Heel Vessel; **Location:** In the depression between the medial head of the deltoid and the humerus bone when the arm is raised; **Comments:** Strikes should be forceful and aimed downward at a 90-degree angle when the arm is in a raised position. Forceful strikes can damage the integrity of attacked shoulder joint. This strike is best when the opponent is controlled at the wrist of the attacked arm.

ST-4   **Chinese Point name:** *Di Cang;*[18] **English translation:** "Earth Granary;" **Special Attributes:** This point is bilateral. It is an intersection point for the Stomach Meridian, the Large Intestine Meridian, the Conception Vessel (according to some sources), and the Yang Heel Vessel; **Location:** About .5 of an inch lateral to the corner of the mouth; **Western Anatomy:** The facial artery and vein, and the facial, infraorbital, and buccal nerves are present; **Comments:** Strikes should be upward at a 45-degree angle towards the center of the head. Strikes to this location can break or damage the teeth and shock the brain.

ST-3   **Chinese Point name:** *Ju Liao;*[19] **English translation:** "Great Bone-Hole;" **Special Attributes:** It is an intersection point for the Stomach Meridian, the Large Intestine Meridian, and the Yang Heel Vessel. This point is bilateral; **Location:** Directly in line with the pupil of the eye and about .75 of an inch from outer edge of the nostril; **Western Anatomy:** Branches of the facial and infraorbital arteries and veins, and branches of the facial and infraorbital nerves are present; **Comments:** It should be struck in the same manner as ST-4.

ST-1   **Chinese Point name:** *Cheng Qi;*[20] **English translation:** "Tear Container;" **Special Attributes:** It is an intersection point of the Stomach Meridian, the Yang Heel Vessel, and the Conception Vessel (according to some sources). This point is bilateral; **Location:** Directly in line with the pupil of the eye and on the ridge of the infraorbital ridge; **Western Anatomy:** Branches of the infraorbital and ophthalmic arteries and veins, branches of the intraorbital, oculomotor and facial nerves are present; **Comments:** Strikes should be upward at a 45-degree angle and aimed toward to the center of the head. Forceful strikes can break the cheekbone and damage the eye.

---

[18] Ibid., p. 59.
[19] Ibid., p. 58.
[20] Ibid., p. 56

After an attempted punch by the opponent, parry the strike and close with the opponent.

Strike with an uppercut strike to ST-4, but follow through disrupts several additional points.

Defensive Counters

As the attacker (right) attempts to launch an uppercut, start deflecting their lead arm to the inside.

Rotate to the inside as your lead arm gains top position.

Reinforce your lead arm and prepare to deliver strike.

Deliver a nailing elbow strike to the attacker's throat, jawline or face.

BL-1   Chinese Point name: *Jing Ming*;[21] **English translation:** "Bright Eyes;" **Special Attributes:** This point is bilateral. It is an intersection point of the Small Intestine Meridian, Bladder Meridian, Stomach Meridian, Yin Heel Vessel and the Yang Heel Vessel; **Location:** About .25 of an inch from the inner corner of the eye; **Western Anatomy:** The angular artery and vein and branches of the oculomotor and ophthalmic nerve are present; **Comments:** Strike this point slightly upward and towards the centerline of the head. This point is fairly difficult to strike in a combative situation due to the location. Forceful strikes to the eye socket area can activate this point, as well as traumatize the eye and possible breaking the bone structure in the general area.

GB-20   Chinese Point name: *Feng Chi*;[22] **English translation:** "Wind Pool;" **Special Attributes:** It is the intersection point for the Gall Bladder Meridian, the Triple Warmer Meridian, the Yang Linking Vessel, and the Yang Heel Vessel. It is also bilateral; **Location:** On the occipital bone on the back of the skull; It is a bilateral point. **Western Anatomy:** Branches of the occipital artery, vein, and nerve are present; **Comments:** GB-20 is an important point for the martial

---

[21] Ibid., p. 143
[22] Ibid., p. 268.

artist. Strikes to this point should be aimed at a 45-degree angle towards the opposite side of the head. When attacks are generated against the Five Element aspects of the twelve Main Meridians GB-20 will weaken significantly. Strikes to this point can easily produce a knockout. Utilizing Five Element attacks, or repeated forceful strikes, can cause death.

GV-16 **Chinese Point name:** *Feng Fu;*[23] **English translation:** "Wind Mansion;" **Special Attributes:** It is the intersection point of the Yang Linking Vessel and the Governing Vessel. It is one of the 36 Vital Points listed in the *Bubishi*; **Location:** About .5 of an inch above GV-15; Strikes to one of these points usually disrupt both given their close proximity. **Western Anatomy:** A branch of the occipital artery and branches of the third occipital and great occipital nerves are present; **Comments:** This is great importance to martial artist. Strike in the same manner as GV-15 for similar effect.

Prepare to deliver a strike to GB-20 after gaining the outside position during an attempted punch.   *Strikes to GB-20 can be repeated multiple times since the opponent is in a tactically weak position.*

---

[23] Ibid., p. 340.

Defensive Counters

As the attacker (right) attempts to gain control of your arm, rotate it over the top of their reaching arm and close distance with them.

Deliver a forceful Open Palm strike to their chin.

Chapter 7

THE LINKING VESSELS

*"Understanding the Linking Vessels is one of the major keys
to unlocking the advanced knowledge of Torite-Jitsu"*
Rick Moneymaker

The Linking Vessels serve a major role in the interaction of the Extraordinary Vessels and the twelve Main Meridians. Whereas the Conception, Governing, and Thrusting Vessels build, transform, and store energy, the Linking Vessels are tasked with the transfer of energy to and from the twelve Main Meridians.[1] They accomplish this through a series of shared acupuncture points with the Main Meridians and do not have any individual points of their own. The Yin Linking Vessel is connected with organs that have a Yin polarity and the Yang Linking Vessel is connected with organs that have a Yang polarity.[2] These two vessels comprise the Linking Vessel Subsystem.

As energy levels change in the various organs the Linking Vessels are responsible for transmitting or extracting energy from them as needed. An example of this function is as follows; Let us assume that the Liver has an overabundance of energy. This imbalance has a number of health related issues that can be traced to several different diseases. The Liver might be in this state of excess due to trauma caused by application of martial techniques. Regardless, the Liver having excess energy means the body needs to correct that problem so that it can properly function. The Liver has a Yin polarity and interacts with the Yin Linking Vessel at LV-14, which is the only point that the two intersect. At that point the Yin Linking Vessel will drain excess energy out of the Liver Meridian. The energy will flow in the Yin Linking Vessel until it connects with the Conception Vessel (the Conception Vessel being the Yin aspect of the "Human Battery" Subsystem) at CV-22 and 23. There the energy will flow down the Conception Vessel until it reaches CV-1. It will enter the Thrusting Vessel at CV-1 and be stored for future use in the "Human Battery." Now consider the

---

[1] Maciocia, *The Foundations of Chinese Medicine*, pp. 364–365.
[2] Larre & Vallee, *The Eight Extraordinary Meridians*, p. 213.

paired Meridian of the Liver — the Gall Bladder Meridian. The Gall Bladder and Liver Meridians are linked together forming an associated couple that represents the Wood Element. The Liver Meridian being the Yin aspect of the element of Wood and Gall Bladder being the Yang aspect of that element. (The Five Element Theory will be discussed in detail in Chapter 9.) The excess energy that is present in the Liver Meridian will "spill over" into Gall Bladder Meridian due to the manner that the two meridians interact. The Gall Bladder Meridian will have a higher level of energy than normal, but less than the affected Liver Meridian. The Yang Linking Vessel will draw the additional energy, which is caused by the Liver excess, from the Gall Bladder Meridian. This will occur at the numerous intersection points that the Yang Linking Vessel shares with the Gall Bladder Meridian. It will be transported by the Yang Linking Vessel to the Governing Vessel (the Yang aspect of the "Human Battery" Subsystem) at GV-15 and 16. The excess energy will then be carried to the Thrusting Vessel to be stored for future use.

The reverse is true if an organ has a deficient amount of energy. In this example the Bladder is low on energy. The Thrusting Vessel will discharge energy from the Energy Core into the Governing Vessel. The Governing Vessel will transport the energy to GV-15 and 16. The energy will then transfer from the Governing Vessel into the Yang Linking Vessel. It will then flow to the acupuncture point that connects to the Bladder Meridian. That point is BL-63 and the energy will enter the Bladder Meridian at that point and correct the deficiency. Additional energy will travel through the Conception Vessel to CV-22 and 23. Those points are the location that the Conception Vessel intersects with the Yin Linking Vessel. Once the energy enters the Yin Linking Vessel it will travel to KI-9. That location is where the Yin Linking Vessel connects to the Kidney Meridian. The Kidney Meridian is the coupled meridian of the Bladder. The Bladder is the Yang aspect of the Water Element and the Kidney is the Yin aspect. The energy will flow through the Kidney Meridian until it helps to adjust the low energetic level of the Bladder. Additionally, the Thrusting Vessel connects directly to Kidney Meridian at KI-11 and KI-21. Adjustments to the Water Meridians (Bladder and Kidney) can be made rapidly from those points.

Hopefully, these examples will assets you in gaining an understanding of how the Linking Vessels function. They are the "middleman" between the "Human Battery" and the twelve Main Meridians. Their role is pivotal in understanding how the body corrects energetic fluctuations. Understanding how the Linking Vessels function is extremely important to the martial artists. If you can understand how the Linking Vessels function and the locations of where they intersect with the twelve Main Meridians, then strikes can be aimed at those points to "seal" the energy. By "sealing" the energy you can stop or greatly hinder the natural body function of correcting energetic imbalances. This has tremendous martial implications and will be examined later in the book.

The Yin Linking Vessel

The Yin Linking Vessel connects the "Human Battery" with all the Yin organs of the body.[3] Understanding how the Yin Linking Vessel functions are vital to the martial artist considering the Yin organs are the most sensitive of the organs. The Chinese consider the Yin associated organs as those vital to life. The Yang associated organs are sometimes referred to as "bowels." On the most part they are what the Chinese refer to as "hollow" and are secondary to the significance of the Yin organs. The following table shows the breakdown:

YIN	YANG
Kidney	Bladder
Liver	Gall Bladder
Heart	Small Intestines
Spleen	Stomach
Lungs	Large Intestines
Pericardium	Triple Warmer

Table 7-1: *Breakdown of Organs according to their polarity.*

Notice the organs, or bowels, that are associated with Yang polarity. We all know of people that have had one of these organs removed, or greatly reduced, due to disease or an accident. Those people have managed to maintain a fairly normal life and can function quite well. Survivors of Colon cancer often lose major portions of the Large Intestine and live for years with only minor inconveniences. This is true for all the organs that are associated with Yang polarity. The exception in the west is the Triple Warmer. The Chinese considered it as an organ of the body, but there is no corresponding entity in Western anatomy. The Triple Warmer is more of an energetic process than an organ, but was associated with Yang polarity due to its interaction with the Pericardium.

---

[3] Larre & Vallee, *The Eight Extraordinary Meridians*, p. 213.

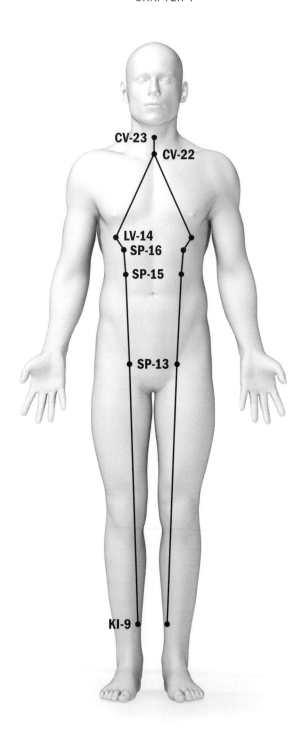

Now notice the organs that comprise the Yin polarity column. All of these are vital to human life. Western medical science has advanced to the point that the spleen can be removed, and life maintained, but that was not the case in China at the time that Traditional Chinese Medicine was being developed. Likewise, a person can survive with only one lung, or one kidney, or a reduced liver, but they can not survive without the function of those organs. The heart stands alone in this group as the most important of these organs. This is echoed by Western medical science and a key component in understanding probabilities in attacking the body from a martial perspective.

Yin Linking Vessel Point Descriptions

KI-9 Chinese Point name: *Zhu Bin*;[4] English translation: "Guest House;" **Special Attributes:** This point is an intersection point of the Kidney Meridian and the Yin Linking Vessel. This point is bilateral; **Location:** About five inches above the inner anklebone, at the border of the lower aspect of the calf muscle; **Western Anatomy:** The tibial artery and vein, the medial sural cutaneous nerve, the medial crural cutaneous nerve, and the tibial nerve are present; **Comments:** This point can be struck, along with a number of other points, with low sweeping kicks to the inside of the lower leg. Additionally, once an opponent has become prone on the ground this point can be stomped.

SP-13 Chinese Point name: *Fu She*;[5] English translation: "Bowel Abode;" **Special Attributes:** This point is an intersection point of the Spleen Meridian, the Liver Meridian, and the Yin Linking Vessel. This point is bilateral; **Location:** About 3.5 inches lateral of CV-2 at the point that leg joins the lower abdomen; **Western Anatomy:** The femoral artery and the ilioinguinal nerve are present; **Comments:** Strikes to this point should be at a downward 45-degree angle aimed at the energy core of the center of the body. Forceful strikes can break the pubic bone causing great pain in the opponent. The femoral artery can also be shocked. Downward aimed punches and hard driving straight kicks to this region can be effective in a combative situation.

SP-15 Chinese Point name: *Da Heng*;[6] English translation: "Great Horizontal;" **Special Attributes:** It is an intersection point of the Spleen Meridian and

---

[4] Ellis, Wiseman, and Boss, *Grasping the Wind*, p. 205.
[5] Ibid., p. 112.
[6] Ibid., p. 113.

the Yin Linking Vessel. This point is bilateral; **Location:** About four inches lateral of the navel; **Western Anatomy:** The tenth intercostal artery, vein, and nerve are present; **Comments:** Strikes to this point should be toward the center of the body on a downward 45-degree angle.

SP-16   Chinese Point name: *Fu Ai;*[7] **English translation:** "Abdominal Lament;" **Special Attributes:** It is an intersection point of the Spleen Meridian and the Yin Linking Vessel. This point is bilateral; **Location:** About three inches directly above SP-15; **Western Anatomy:** The eighth intercostal artery, vein, and nerve are present; **Comments:** Strike in same manner as SP-15.

LV-14   Chinese Point name: *Qi Men;*[8] **English translation:** "Cycle Gate;" **Special Attributes:** It is an intersection point for the Liver Meridian, the Spleen Meridian, and the Yin Linking Vessel. It is also the alarm point of the Liver. This point is bilateral; **Location:** Two ribs below the center of the nipple; **Western Anatomy:** The sixth intercostal artery, vein, and nerve are present; **Comments:** This point is of considerable value to the martial artist. Strikes to this point should be toward the center of the body on a downward 45-degree angle. Forceful strikes can shock or damage the liver. An interruption of the energy core of the body can result. The additional benefits to strikes to this location are the serious implications of the intersection with the Yin Linking Vessel at the sensitive Alarm point of the Liver. Strikes to this point can inhibit the ability to correct energy imbalances of the Liver caused by martial attacks.

CV-22   Chinese Point name: *Tian Tu;*[9] **English translation:** "Celestial Chimney;" **Special Attributes:** this is an Intersection Point of the Yin Linking Vessel and the Conception Vessel. It is listed as a Vital Point in the *Bubishi*; **Location:** On the centerline of the body at the center of the suprasternal notch. That structure is the commonly referred to the "horseshoe notch" at the base of the throat; **Western Anatomy:** the jugular arch and a branch of the inferior thyroid artery are superficially represented. The trachea, or windpipe, is found deeper and the posterior aspect of the sternum, the innominate vein and aortic arch are also present; **Comments:** This point is of particular importance the martial artist as it is the intersection point of the Yin Linking Vessel and the Conception Vessel. The interrelationship between these two vessels will be covered in detail

---

[7] Ibid., p. 114.
[8] Ibid., p. 302.
[9] Ibid., p. 324.

later in the book. Additionally, the structure of the suprasternal notch is an excellent "touch point" for situations when sight is reduced and you find yourself at extremely close range with your opponent.

CV-23 Chinese Point name: *Lian Quan*;[10] **English translation:** "Ridge Spring;" **Special Attributes:** Some Traditional Chinese Medicine textbooks state that this location is an intersection point for the Yin Linking Vessel and the Conception Vessel; **Location:** On the centerline of the throat just above the Adam's apple; **Western Anatomy:** the anterior jugular vein, a branch of cutaneous cervical nerve, the hypoglossal nerve, and branch of the glossopharyngeal nerve are present; **Comments:** Strikes to this point should directly inward, or slightly upward, to bust the structure of the Adam's apple and disrupt the energy flow to the head. Generally, any strike to the throat area will activate a number of sensitive acupuncture points and attacks the structural weakness of this part of the human body.

The Yang Linking Vessel

The Yang Linking Vessel connects the "Human Battery" to all the Yang organs of the body.[11] That connection occurs at the various acupuncture points that the Yang Linking Vessel shares with the various Yang associated bowels. The Yang Linking Vessel connects to each of these bowels at least once along its trajectory. It connects with the Gall Bladder Meridian at ten intersecting points. The Chinese placed great importance on the Gall Bladder Meridian as a "governor of the body." Part of that distinction is because the heavy role that it has in correcting energetic imbalances. Considering the outer surfaces of the body that the Gall Bladder Meridian occurs, it is apparent that the meridian has to be able to adjust rapidly correct imbalances due to the various bumps, strikes, and collisions that occur to the outer aspects of the body.

As a martial artist you have more than likely observed a pressure point technique that strikes the Gall Bladder Meridian, or one of its points. One of the first techniques that I observed like this was a strike to GB-20. I was attending a seminar in Atlanta, Georgia, when the instructor struck an attendee on that point and knocked him out. The strike was fairly light in comparison to

---

[10] Ibid., p. 325.
[11] Larre & Vallee, *The Eight Extraordinary Meridians*, p. 213.

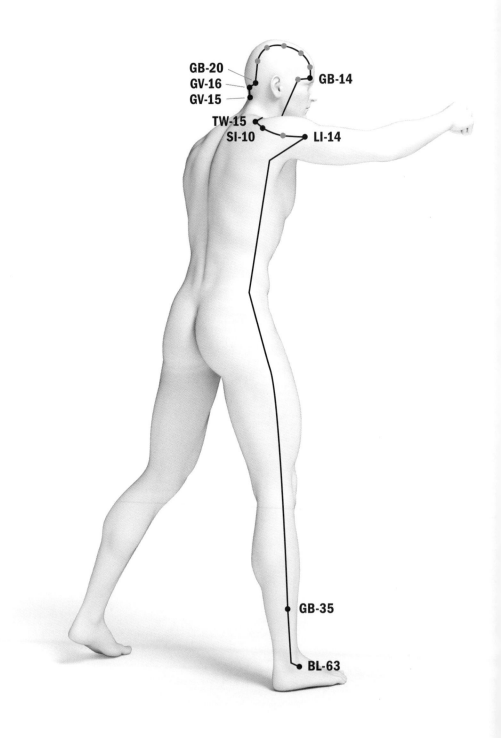

GB-20
GV-16
GV-15

GB-14

TW-15
SI-10

LI-14

GB-35

BL-63

the result. The man went completely out and within a minute was back on his feet and apparently no worse for the experience. One of the reasons for his fast recovery was because the instructor had only hit GB-20 and the body corrected the energy imbalance utilizing the numerous points of intersection with the Yang Linking Vessel. I have observed numerous such knockouts, and stunning techniques, to the Gall Bladder points and in every circumstance the individual that was struck makes a rapid recovery. It took me several years of intense study of Traditional Chinese Medicine to understand why.

Yang Linking Vessel Point Descriptions

BL-63   Chinese Point name: *Jin Men*;[12] **English translation:** "Metal Gate;" **Special Attributes:** This point is an intersection point of the Bladder Meridian and the Yang Linking Vessel. This point is bilateral; **Location:** Slightly to the front of the midpoint of the outer anklebone; Western **Anatomy:** The lateral plantar artery and vein, the lateral dorsal cutaneous nerve, and the lateral plantar nerve are present; **Comments:** This point can be struck, with a number of other points, with low sweeping kicks to the outside of the lower leg and foot. Additionally, once an opponent has become prone on the ground this point can be stomped.

GB-35   Chinese Point name: *Yang Jiao*;[13] **English translation:** "Yang Intersection;" **Special Attributes:** It is an intersection point of the Gall Bladder Meridian and the Yang Linking Vessel. This point is bilateral; **Location:** About seven inches above the outer anklebone on the same level as GB-36 and BL-58; **Western Anatomy:** Branches of the peroneal artery and vein, and the lateral sural cutaneous nerve are present; **Comments:** Strike in the same manner as BL-63.

LI-14   Chinese Point name: *Bi Nao*;[14] **English translation:** "Upper Arm;" **Special Attributes:** It is the intersection point of the Large Intestine Meridian, the Stomach Meridian, and the Yang Linking Vessel. This point is bilateral; **Location:** On the upper arm near the insertion of the deltoid muscle; **Western Anatomy:** Branches of the posterior circumflex humeral artery and vein, the deep brachial artery and vein, the posterior brachial cutaneous nerve, and the radial nerve are present; **Comments:** Strikes to this point can cause damage to

---

[12] Ellis, Wiseman, and Boss, *Grasping the Wind*, p. 191.
[13] Ibid., p. 281.
[14] Ibid., p. 49.

the shoulder joint. They are best if the wrist of the attacked arm is acquired. Energetically, it is a good target due to the three intersecting meridians.

TW-13   Chinese Point name: *Nao Hui*;[15] English translation: "Upper Arm Convergence;" **Special Attributes:** It is an intersection point of the Triple Warmer Meridian and the Yang Linking Vessel. This point is bilateral; **Location:** On the posterior border of the deltoid muscle about three inches from the tip of the shoulder; **Western Anatomy:** The medial collateral artery and vein, the posterior brachial cutaneous nerve, and the radial nerve are present; **Comments:** Strike in same manner as LI-14.

SI-10   Chinese Point name: *Nao Shu*;[16] English translation: "Upper Arm Point;" **Special Attributes:** This is an intersection point for the Small Intestine Meridian, the Yang Linking Vessel and the Yang Heel Vessel. This point is bilateral and extremely difficult to strike in a combative situation. This point is bilateral; **Location:** In the depression of the inferior of the scapula when the arm is raised; **Western Anatomy:** The posterior circumflex humeral artery and vein, the suprascapular artery and vein, the posterior cutaneous nerve of the arm, the axillary nerve, and the suprascapular nerve are present; **Comments:** A strike, if possible, should be directed towards the center of the body on a 90-degree angle. This is an important point because of the major energetic intersection, but is extremely difficult to strike.

TW-15   Chinese Point name: *Tian Liao*;[17] English translation: "Celestial Bone-Hole;" **Special Attributes:** It is an intersection point of the Triple Warmer Meridian and the Yang Linking Vessel. This point is bilateral; **Location:** About two inches below GB-21 on the back; **Western Anatomy:** The descending branch of the transverse cervical artery, a branch of the suprascapular artery, the accessory nerve, and a branch of the suprascapular nerve are all present; **Comments:** Forceful strikes should be toward the energy core of the abdomen on a 45-degree angle.

GB-21   Chinese Point name: *Jian Jing*;[18] English translation: "Shoulder Well;" **Special Attributes:** It is an intersection point of the Gall Bladder Meridian, the

---

[15] Ibid., p. 242.
[16] Ibid., p. 135.
[17] Ibid., p. 243.
[18] Ibid., p. 269.

Triple Warmer Meridian, the Stomach Meridian, and the Yang Linking Vessel. This point is bilateral; **Location:** About midway between GV-14 and LI-16 on the highest point of the shoulder; **Western Anatomy:** The traverse cervical artery and vein, a branch of the supraclavicular nerve, and the accessory nerve are present; **Comments:** This point should be stuck in a downward fashion toward the energy core of the abdomen.

ST-8 **Chinese Point name:** *Tou Wei;*[19] **English translation:** "Head Corner;" **Special Attributes:** This is an intersection point for the Stomach Meridian, the Gall Bladder Meridian, and the Yang Linking Vessel. This point is bilateral; **Location:** About .5 of an inch inside the hairline and 4.5 inches lateral to the Governing Vessel; **Western Anatomy:** Branches of the superficial temporal artery and vein, branches of the auriculotemporal and facial nerves are present; **Comments:** Strikes should be aimed at the center of the head on a 45-degree downward angle.

GB-13 **Chinese Point name:** *Ben Shen;*[20] **English translation:** "Root Spirit;" **Special Attributes:** It is an intersection point of the Gall Bladder Meridian and the Yang Linking Vessel. This point is bilateral; **Location:** About .5 of an inch to the front of ST-8 in the hairline; **Western Anatomy:** Branches of the superficial temporal artery and vein, the lateral branches of the frontal artery and vein, and a branch of the frontal nerve are present; **Comments:** Strikes should be aimed at the center of the head at a downward 45-degree angle.

GB-14 **Chinese Point name:** *Yang Bai;*[21] **English translation:** "Yang White;" **Special Attributes:** It is an intersection point of the Gall Bladder Meridian, the Large Intestine Meridian, the Stomach Meridian, and the Yang Linking Vessel. This point is bilateral; **Location:** About one inch above the midpoint of the eyebrow; **Western Anatomy:** Branches of the frontal artery, vein, and nerve are present; **Comments:** Strike in same manner as GB-13.

GB-15 **Chinese Point name:** *Tou Lin Qi;*[22] **English translation:** "Head Overlooking Tears;" **Special Attributes:** It is an intersection point of the Gall Blad-

---

[19] Ibid., p. 263.
[20] Ibid., p. 262.
[21] Ibid., p. 263.
[22] Ibid., p. 264.

der Meridian, the Bladder Meridian, and the Yang Linking Vessel. This point is bilateral; **Location:** About two inches directly above GB-15 just inside the hairline; **Western Anatomy:** The frontal artery and vein, and branches of the frontal nerve are present; **Comments:** Strike in similar manner as GB-13.

GB-16 Chinese Point name: *Mu Chuang;*[23] **English translation:** "Eye Window;" **Special Attributes:** It is an intersection point of the Gall Bladder Meridian and the Yang Linking Vessel. It is bilateral; **Location:** Directly posterior to GB-15; **Western Anatomy:** Branches of the superficial temporal artery and vein, and branches of the medial and frontal nerves are present; **Comments:** Strike in a similar manner as GB-13.

GB-17 Chinese Point name: *Zheng Ying;*[24] **English translation:** "Upright Construction;" **Special Attributes:** It is an intersection point of the Gall Bladder Meridian and the Yang Linking Vessel. This point is bilateral; **Location:** About 1.5 inches posterior of GB-16; **Western Anatomy:** Branches of the superficial temporal and occipital arteries and veins, and branches of the frontal and great occipital nerves are present; **Comments:** Strikes should be towards the center core of the head.

GB-18 Chinese Point name: *Cheng Ling;*[25] **English translation:** "Spirit Support;" **Special Attributes:** It is an intersection point of the Gall Bladder Meridian and the Yang Linking Vessel. This point is bilateral; **Location:** About 1.5 inches posterior to GB-17; **Western Anatomy:** Branches of the occipital artery and vein and a branch of the great occipital nerve are present; **Comments:** Strike in similar fashion as GB-17.

GB-19 Chinese Point name: *Nao Kong;*[26] **English translation:** "Brain Hollow;" **Special Attributes:** This point is bilateral; **Location:** About three inches above GB-20; **Western Anatomy:** Branches of the occipital artery and vein and a branch of the great occipital nerve are present; **Comments:** Strike in a similar fashion as GB-20.

---

[23] Ibid., p. 265.
[24] Ibid., p. 266.
[25] Ibid., p. 267.
[26] Ibid.

GB-20 Chinese Point name: *Feng Chi;*[27] English translation: "Wind Pool;" Special Attributes: It is the intersection point for the Gall Bladder Meridian, the Triple Warmer Meridian, the Yang Linking Vessel, and the Yang Heel Vessel. It is a bilateral point; Location: On the occipital bone on the back of the skull; Western Anatomy: Branches of the occipital artery, vein, and nerve are present; Comments: It is an important point for the martial artist. Strikes to this point should be aimed at a 45-degree angle towards the opposite side of the head. When attacks are generated against the Five Element aspects of the twelve Main Meridians GB-20 will weaken significantly. Strikes to this point can easily produce a knockout. Utilizing Five Element attacks, or repeated forceful strikes, can cause death.

GV-15 Chinese Point name: *Ya Men;*[28] English translation: "Mute's Gate;" Special Attributes: It is the intersection point of the Yang Linking Vessel and the Governing Vessel; Location: About .5 of an inch within the hairline on the centerline of the neck. This points marks the point in which the Governing Vessel leaves the back and ascends onto the head; Western Anatomy: Branches of the occipital artery and vein and the third occipital nerve are present; Comments: This point is of major importance to the martial artist. Strikes to this point should aimed at about a 30-degree upward angle. Considering that this point is located where the skull and spine connect, it is a structural weak location. Strikes to this point can cause death.

GV-16 Chinese Point name: *Feng Fu;*[29] English translation: "Wind Mansion;" Special Attributes: It is the intersection point of the Yang Linking Vessel and the Governing Vessel. It is one of the 36 Vital Points listed in the *Bubishi*; Location: About .5 of an inch above GV-15; Strikes to one of these points usually disrupt both given their close proximity. Western Anatomy: A branch of the occipital artery and branches of the third occipital and great occipital nerves are present; Comments: This is great importance to martial artist. Strike in the same manner as GV-15 for similar effect.

---

[27] Ibid., p. 268.
[28] Ibid., p. 339.
[29] Ibid., p. 340.

PART II
Laws, Theories, Concepts, and Interactions

## Chapter 8

THE LAW OF YIN/YANG

*"To the frogs in a temple pond
The Lotus stems are tall;
To the gods of Mount Everest
An elephant is small."*
Taoist Poem

The concept of Yin and Yang is the basic underlying principle that Traditional Chinese Medicine is founded. It is simply the concept that was used by the ancient Chinese to describe two opposing forces. Those forces, Yin and Yang, enjoy a relationship that is opposing, but when combined result in harmonious interaction. It is easier to consider Yin and Yang as "complementary opposites." One can not exist without the interaction of the other. They are opposites, but complementary to one another. Yin/Yang has been referred to as a symbolic representation of the universal process that portrays a changing rather than static picture of reality.[1] It is also used to illustrate the different aspects of various processes. This theory is sometimes confusing to the martial artist and the average Westerner alike.[2] Yes, we have all seen the Yin/Yang symbol associated with the martial arts, but few students of the arts have ever studied the concept in detail. Yin/Yang is the root of the Eastern paradigm and understanding it is a perquisite to the more advanced knowledge of martial science.

The Yin/Yang Symbol.

1 Beinfield & Korngold, *Between Heaven and Earth*, p. 50.
2 Ibid.

Yin/Yang is used to describe the various qualities of paired items in relation to one another and that nothing in nature can exist without its counterpart.[3] This is expressed in the following examples. Without day there can be no night, without right there can be no left, without hard there can be no soft, without East there can be no West, without expansion there can be no contraction, without rest there can be no activity. This list can go on forever. Just take a minute and think of the numerous like comparisons that you can make on your own. The complementary opposite characteristics of Yin/Yang should quickly become apparent.

This comparison is even extended to like items, which means that there is no absolute in the concept. Take daytime for example. It is associated with Yang. The counterpart of daytime is nighttime, which is associated with Yin. As the sun moves through the sky during the course of the day it produces shadows. The shadows are associated with Yin, which is in comparison with areas that are receiving full sunshine. The shadows are the Yin within the Yang of the day. At night the moon will sometimes cast light on to the surface of the Earth. That occurrence is considered as Yang, which is in comparison to dark, shadowy areas. It is the Yang within the Yin of night. As the sun and moon move through the sky the positions of the corresponding light and shadow areas will merge and alternate. This represents the cyclic qualities of Yin/Yang. All events in nature, including the interactions of the human body, are cyclic and contain a complementary opposite according in Eastern thought.[4]

Yin/Yang, at the most basic level, is a simple comparison. Taoist philosophy does not separate cause from effect. In their view, everything is in a constant state of metamorphosis. Day is not caused by night, but simple precedes it. Winter is not caused by summer, but the two are linked in the cycle of the seasons. The question of which was first, the chicken or egg, is viewed as accepting them as inseparable agents of the same process. The chicken lays the egg, which the Chinese view as the Yang chicken generates the Yin egg. Likewise, the egg produces a chicken, which is represented as Yin generating Yang. The process of chicken to egg or egg to chicken is mutually supportive. This process is an example of the complementary aspect of the Yin/Yang theory. One can not exists without the other. The egg itself can be examined by this theory as well.

---

[3] Moneymaker, *Torite-Jutsu Reference Manual*, p. 12.

[4] Park Bok Nam & Dan Miller, *The Fundamentals of Pa Kua Chang Volume One* (Burbank, CA: Unique Publications, 1999), pp. 35–38: Pa Kua Chang, or Ba Gua Zhang, is a Chinese internal art that makes specific use of the principles that are associated with Traditional Chinese Medicine. It is an excellent fighting method that utilizes many of the concepts that are outlined in this book.

The shell of the egg is considered Yang, which is hard and protective. The fluid and yoke of the egg are considered as Yin, which is soft and sensitive in comparison to the shell. The harder yoke is considered Yang in comparison to the more liquid Yin fluids. Yin/Yang is simply a means of comparison, which should be a concept that the Western martial artist can grasp.

Yin/Yang Applied to the Body

The Chinese applied their understanding of Yin/Yang to the human body, as well as every aspect of nature. This is an extremely important concept to the martial artist and a major prerequisite to the more advanced aspects of Traditional Chinese Medicine. The concepts that are presented in the Yin/Yang model: cyclic movement, complementary opposition, constant change, etc., are very important to the understanding of how the energetic systems of the body function. Traditional Chinese Medicine utilizes Yin/Yang to represent the various organs and bowels of the body. The concept is used to identify specific characteristics and energetic properties, which are in comparison to one another. Table 8-1 illustrates the Yin/Yang comparison of the twelve Main Meridians.

YIN	YANG
Organs	Bowels
Heart	Small Intestines
Pericardium	Triple Warmer
Lungs	Large Intestines
Liver	Gall Bladder
Spleen	Stomach
Kidneys	Bladder

Table 8-1: *Yin/Yang association of the Main Meridians.*

Remember that the Law of Yin/Yang considers these pairs as complementary opposites. They are not adversarial, but mutually supportive of one another. Each pair is engaged in maintaining an energetic balance between themselves and the rest of the pairs. They assist one another to maintain a state of harmony in which individual pairs help to feed, control and balance the energetic system as a whole. Understanding those relationships allows us to learn how to disrupt that balance, which will cause a collapse of the harmonious energetic state of the body. The disruption of the energetic state of an opponent is the goal of martial artist.

Combatively, we want to cause as much to go wrong as possible. Understanding that a given point lays on a Yang associated meridian, allows us to determine that attacking a point on a Yin associated meridian should have a negative effect on the energy balance of the body. The wrist is an excellent area to illustrate this event. The outer aspects of the arm, wrist and hand are considered as Yang. This is in comparison to the softer inner aspects of the arm, wrist and hand, which are considered as Yin. We will normally connect the Yang and Yin points during a simple wrist grasp on an opponent. The Yang meridians are associated with positive energy and the Yin meridians are associated with negative energy. Think of what happens when you connect a negative wire with a positive wire on an electrical circuit. The resulting shower of energy sparks illustrates what happens to the energies of the body during such a technique.[5] This connection creates an energetic imbalance in the Yin and Yang meridians.

Yin/Yang Applied to Body Structure	
YIN	YANG
Interior	Exterior
Anterior	Posterior
Front	Back
Body	Head
Organs	Muscles
Medial	Lateral
Organs	Bowels

Table 8-2: *Yin/Yang and Body Structure.*

In addition to the Yin/Yang associations of the twelve Main Meridians, the Chinese utilized the same model to describe the structure of the body. It is obvious that the outer surfaces of the body are considered as Yang, which is in comparison to the Yin associated inner body. The back and posterior aspects of the body are Yang, which are in comparison to the Yin associated front and

---

[5] Moneymaker, *Torite-Jutsu Reference Manual*, pp. 12–17 — The examples of a Yin/Yang connection of the wrist is adapted from this source. The majority of Traditional Chinese Medicine textbooks do not cover the martial applications to that science. This manual is one of the few available sources that describe the effects of the laws, theories and concept of Traditional Chinese Medicine from a martial perspective.

anterior aspects. The bowels, or hollow organs, are considered Yang in comparison to the organs, or solid organs, which are considered as Yin. A Yin associated organ has a Yang outer surface and a Yin interior. A Yang associated bowel will have both Yin and Yang qualities, as it is further examined by this model. The comparisons include every aspect of human anatomy. There is nothing magical about the concept of Yin/Yang. It is simply a comparison of the qualities of one item to that of another or itself.

Yin/Yang in Action

Just as the human body can be described within the Yin/Yang model, so can movement and action. This can be used to describe specific martial techniques and the various structural mechanics that are caused by those techniques. Strikes that cause the shoulders of your opponent to roll forward, which places them in a standing fetal-like position, are referred to as a Yin Response. Strikes that cause your opponent to stand erect, often throwing their arms upward are referred to as a Yang Response. It has nothing to do with injection of Yin or Yang energy into the body.[6] It is simply a comparison of the two positions.

Techniques where you move to the rear are Yin, which is in comparison to techniques where you move toward your opponent. Forward movement is associated with Yang. Movement to the rear is associated with Yin. Again, this is just a comparison of the two and there is nothing secret or magical about the terms. Do not get confused when you hear them.

Often these terms are used in pressure point seminars and classes. The terminology is sometimes confusing to the student. Instruction should be in terms and concepts that the student can understand, not in cryptic terms that confuse. This book makes an effort to explain Traditional Chinese Medicine, as applied to the martial arts, in a manner that is understandable. Granted, some of the material is from a totally different paradigm than that which we are accustomed and may require additional reading to clarify.

---

[6] According to the Chinese, there is no such thing as Yin energy or Yang energy. There is just energy and during the flow (diurnal cycle) it has Yin and Yang characteristics.

Yin response.

Yang response.

Chapter 9

FIVE ELEMENT THEORY

"In nature, we have the four seasons and five energetic transformations of wood, fire, earth, metal, and water."
Nei Jing: Chapter 5

We will now examine how the Extraordinary Vessels interact with the twelve Main Meridians in a more detailed fashion. Hopefully, you have gained a better understanding of the Extraordinary Vessels in the previous chapters. If you still feel a little shaky concerning the material take the time to study it again. You will also need to have a sound understanding of the concepts of the Five Element and Yin/Yang Theories, in relation to Tradition Chinese Medicine. A brief explanation of the Five Element Theory will be presented, but a detailed examine of the interactions of martial applications will not.

The Five Element Theory is one of the cornerstones of Traditional Chinese Medicine. It is a further division of the Yin/Yang Theory. It will be assumed that the reader has a sound understanding of Yin/Yang Theory, which on the most basic level is a method used for comparison. The Chinese observed the interactions of the human body during the development of Traditional Chinese Medicine. That development occurred, according to some sources, for close to five thousand years. They applied the names of the five elements, according to Chinese tradition and logic, to meridians and organs in an attempt to simplify their ability to understand their interactions. The names of those five elements are Wood, Fire, Earth, Metal, and Water. When they applied the element of Wood to the Liver, they did not imply that that organ was made of wood. Their intention was to imply that the Liver interacted with the other organs in a manner that was represented by the element of "wood" in traditional logic. Interactions with the other elements were then applied to their understanding of this model as Traditional Chinese Medicine continued to develop.

Chinese traditional thought, which has roots in the Taoist philosophies, state that the five elements follow a Cycle of Creation and a Cycle of Destruction. Again, English translation of the terms leaves a lot to be desired. The

Cycle of Creation works fine for the average Westerner in grasping the intent of the theory. It could just as easily be considered the Cycle of Nourishment, but the more commonly used term will be utilized in this book. The term of "Destruction" for the counterpart of the Cycle of Creation can cause the Western mind to focus on the negative aspects of the word. The word "control" suits this process better than the word "destruction." The Cycle of Control, rather than the term of "Destruction," allows the Westerner to gain an easier understanding of the interaction of this aspect of the theory.

The Cycle of Creation states that the Water Element nourishes the Wood Element. An example of this is the rain/water that nourishes a tree/wood. The Wood Element nourishes the Fire Element. Think of adding a log/wood to a campfire. The Fire Element nourishes the Earth Element. Visualize the ashes of the fire mixing with the soil/earth. The Earth Element nourishes the Metal Element. Think of how various metals are found with the ground/earth. The Metal Element nourishes the Water Element. Consider the condensation/water on the side of a metal container on a hot day. That completes the cycle of interaction from a creation or nourishing perspective.[1] It is depicted in the illustration below.

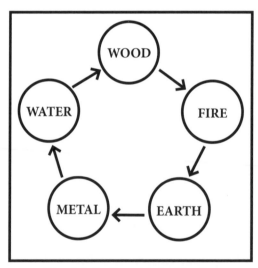

Figure 9-1: Five Element Cycle of Creation.

---

[1] Moneymaker, *Torite-Jutsu Reference Manual*, pp. 23–33; Park Bok Nam, *The Fundamentals of Pa Kua Chang*, pp. 53–56; Yang, *The Root of Chinese Chi Kung*, 197–198: Dr. Yang illustrates another cycle theory in this reference source. It is the Demeaning Cycle, but it is more of a tool used from the healing perspective of Traditional Chinese Medicine.

The Cycle of Control, or Destruction, is the counter to the Cycle of Creation. Chinese teachings maintain that there must always be balance within a system for everything to work properly. If all the organs of the body were in a constant state of nourishment the body would be completely out of balance. The Cycle of Control explains how the five elements can control one another, thus creating a balanced healthy organism. The Cycle of Control states that Water Element controls the Fire Element. That is easy enough to understand. Think of pouring water on a fire. The Fire Element controls the Metal Element. Visualize a blacksmith that is using fire to melt metal. The Metal Element controls the Wood Element. Think of a metal axe that is cutting a tree/wood. The Wood Element controls the Earth Element. Think of how the roots of a tree/wood penetrate the soil/earth. The Earth Element controls the Water Element. Think of how the soil/earth dams up a lake/water. That competes this cycle of interaction from a controlling or destructive perspective.[2] See Figure 9-2.

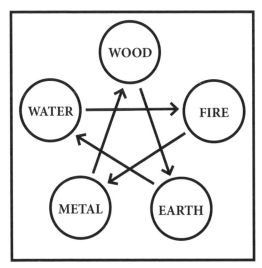

Figure 9-2: Five Element Cycle of Control.

The Chinese grouped the various organs of the body, as they understood them, into the Five Element model. The amazing science of acupuncture, which was developed over the last three thousand years, utilizes that model to treat many forms of sickness and disease. Likewise, the martial artist can use the same model to enhance their combative abilities. The interactions of the Five

2 Maciocia, *The Foundations of Chinese Medicine*, pp. 15–34; Beinfield & Korngold, *Between Heaven and Earth*, pp. 39–44, 85–127.

Element Theory has expanded the combative aspects of the martial arts in the Western world. But, the vast majority of the applications have been focused on the easier understood interactions of the twelve Main Meridians.

ORGAN	ELEMENT
Stomach	Earth
Spleen	Earth
Heart	Fire
Small Intestine	Fire
Bladder	Water
Kidney	Water
Pericardium	Fire
Triple Warmer	Fire
Gall Bladder	Wood
Liver	Wood
Lung	Metal
Large Intestine	Metal

Table 9-1: *Elemental Value of the Organs.*

We can further breakdown the method used by the Chinese by showing the polarity of each organ within the Five Element model. This corresponds with the concept of the "Ten Stems," which is examined by Matsumoto and Birch.[3] In a future effort by this author, the interactions of twelve Main Meridians will be explored from a martial perspective. Those interactions are highly dependent on the Five Element Cycles of Creation and Control. The additional information that is gained from understanding the processes of those two cycles, in accordance with the Ten Stems, is noteworthy. Information pertaining to the Ten Stems will be examined in a cursory manner in this book. The interested student can study the material and gain some understanding of this additional breakdown of the two cycles.

---

[3] Kiiko Matsumoto & Stephen Birch, *Five Elements and Ten Stems* (Brookline, MA: Paradigm Publications, 1983), p. 175.

ORGAN	ELEMENT	POLARITY
Stomach	Earth	Yang
Spleen	Earth	Yin
Heart	Fire	Yin
Small Intestine	Fire	Yang
Bladder	Water	Yang
Kidney	Water	Yin
Pericardium	Fire	Yin
Triple Warmer	Fire	Yang
Gall Bladder	Wood	Yang
Liver	Wood	Yin
Lung	Metal	Yin
Large Intestine	Metal	Yang

Table 9-2: *This shows the organ, or associated meridian, element, and polarity of each of the twelve organs.*

Table 9-2 illustrates the breakdown of each meridian into the associated element and the associated polarity of that element. This may seem a little confusing, but it is actually very simple. Remember that we learned earlier that each of the five elements has a Yin and Yang aspect and that the Main Meridians are broken into six sets of two. This is all that the above table is representing. The element of Earth has a Yin aspect, which is the Spleen Meridian, and a Yang aspect, which is the Stomach Meridian. Likewise, all the other Main Meridians are grouped in a similar manner. Take a look at the next table. It might depict this concept in an easier manner to comprehend.

	EARTH	METAL	WATER	WOOD	FIRE	
Yang	Stomach	Large Intestine	Bladder	Gall Bladder	Small Intestine	Triple Warmer
Yin	Spleen	Lung	Kidney	Liver	Heart	Pericardium

Table 9-3. *Breakdown of each of the twelve Main Meridians by element and polarity.*

You will notice that the Fire Element has four meridians instead of the two, which are common to the rest. The interrelationship of the Fire Meridians will be discussed later in this book. The focus of this section will be on the accepted manner that the "Ten Stems" interact from an energetic perspective. It can be stated that the Ten Stem theory, which is a further division of the Five Element Theory, asserts that the Yin associated Meridians create or nourish the other corresponding Yin Meridians. The same is true with the Yang associated Meridians. What this means on the most basic level is that the Yin associated organs, which are the Liver, Heart, Spleen, Lungs and Kidneys, nourish each other in the Cycle of Creation. That means that the Gall Bladder, Small Intestines, Stomach, Large Intestines and Bladder follow the same pattern of nourishment with the Cycle of Creation.

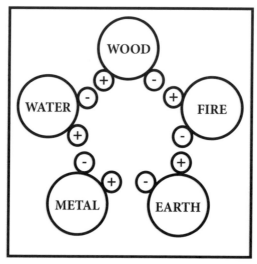

Figure 9-3: Basic Ten Stem Theory. The (+) and (-) indicate Yang and Yin associated Meridians.

The Ten Stems of the Five Element Theory can best be represented in the above diagram. It shows the basic configuration of the concept. In dealing with the Cycle of Creation just think of connecting the Yin associated meridians, which are depicted with the minus sign in Figure 9-3. Follow the Cycle of Creation for the Yang associated meridians, which are depicted with the plus sign, in the same manner. The Cycle of Control operates in a slightly different manner, as you have already determined from Figure 9-2. The major difference, once the more advanced Ten Stem theory is added, is that the Yang aspect of an element controls the Yin aspect of that same element. That Yin aspect of the element is also controlled by the corresponding Yang element in the Cycle of Control.[4] This is more than a little confusing to most students and it will be covered in volume two in much greater detail.

---

[4] Matsumoto & Birch, *Five Elements and Ten Stems*, pp. 27–32.

The basic Cycles of Creation and Control will be utilized during this book. It will be sufficient to explain the interactions between the Extraordinary Vessels and the twelve Main Meridians, which are the major focus of this text. The full potential of Ten Stems Theory is realized in energetic disruptions and imbalances within the twelve Main Meridians. The method that the Extraordinary Vessels interacts with the Main Meridians is fairly basic in comparison, but an area that has been greatly overlooked by martial artists—until now.

Chapter 10

ELEMENTAL BODY TYPES

"In the fabric of each individual life there are certain main threads and themes."
Jeremy Ross

A s Traditional Chinese Medicine was developing, the diagnostic qualities of that discipline started observing individuals that exhibited certain physical and mental characteristics. Those characteristics happen to correspond with what the Chinese referred to as the Five Elements. Thus, a school of knowledge was developed, basically for diagnostic purposes,[1] which addressed those associated characteristics in a manner that was easy for the Chinese to understand and within the Taoist framework that Traditional Chinese Medicine was formed. The result is what is referred to Elemental Body Types or Elemental archetypes.

Traditional Chinese Medicine combines the traits common to physical sickness and disease with all manner of emotional and mental health. There is no division between the disciplines as there is in the west. Some of the observations that reinforced this belief with the Chinese were that specific mental and emotional constitutions were noticed to occur, and correspond, with specific physical body types of individuals. That observation was critical in establishing an association between those specific body types and the broadly excepted Five Element Theory.[2]

Other observations were noticed that supported their understanding of Taoist logic, as this line of thought developed over the years. Certain like energetic imbalances were noticed to occur in individuals that shared specific physical traits.[3] For instance, tall and lanky individuals were observed to have

---

[1] Maciocia, *The Foundations of Chinese Medicine*, pp. 320–327.

[2] Jeremy Ross, *Acupuncture Point Combinations* (New York: Churchill Livingstone, 1995) — This text has extensive examination of the five elemental types in regard to their emotional and mental states. It does not cover the physical associations of the various elements, but is an excellent source for supporting information regarding their psychological constitutions.

[3] Michio Kushi, *Book of Oriental Diagnosis* (Tokyo, Japan: Japan Publications, 1980) — This excellent diagnostic book covers numerous traits that are associated with the energetic constitution of individuals. It does not cover Elemental Body Types specifically, but is of value in understanding the diagnos-

excessive energy in their Wood associated meridians. Strong and stocky individuals were noticed to have excessive energy in their Earth associated meridians. A picture of basic human energetic states was developed as this diagnostic tool advanced by years of observation. The result is what is referred to as Elemental Body Types. This knowledge is important to the martial artist. No one expects that the martial artist will commit the energetic weaknesses of the five basic elemental body types to memory. Instead, consider that the information concerning the Elemental Body Types is a prerequisite to more advanced material.

Wood Body Types

Wood type people are generally tall and have a slender body. They are broad shouldered and often have a darkish face and skin tone. Wood types usually are fairly well muscled, but not in a massive way. They commonly have strong bones and are physically stronger than they might appear. A common characteristic is that they have an extremely straight back and rarely walk "hunched."[4]

One association that I have made that simplifies Wood body types is thinking of them as basketball players. When you watch a NBA game on television notice the physical characteristics of the players. They are generally tall, lanky, well muscled (but not massive), and they walk very upright. This is a quick mental tool to utilize when thinking about Wood body types. Just think of a basketball player.

Energetically, a Wood type has an abundance of energy in their Wood associated meridians, which are the Liver and Gall Bladder. This means that they will be extremely strong in those meridians. Once during a seminar, in a field test, I struck a Wood type on GB-31 to observe the effect. There was slight response, but nothing akin to the standard response common in the majority of people. I have found them to be sensitive in the Metal meridians, which are responsible for controlling the Wood meridians.[5]

---

tic techniques of Traditional Chinese Medicine.

[4] Maciocia, *The Foundations of Chinese Medicine*, p. 320; Moneymaker, *Torite-Jutsu Reference Manual*, pp. 40–41.

[5] Harriet Beinfield & Efrem Korngold, *Between Heaven and Earth – A Guide to Chinese Medicine*, (New York: Ballantine Books, 1991), pp. 160–175 — This book focuses on the psychological aspects of the elemental body types, but contains excellent descriptions of the natural energetic imbalances of each of the five archetypes.

Fire Body Types

Fire type people generally have a reddish face, a small pointed head or pointed chin, and they usually have either curly hair or are balding. Another interesting common trait is that they often have small hands. They will generally walk fast and appear to be very energetic.[6] I have often observed that they are quick to anger and when angry they flush red in their upper chest and face. That is indicative of the excessive Fire energy that is in their body. They are a little harder to classify with a group like basketball players for association. Many Fire types often have a "beer gut" and are often extremely focused on material wealth.

Fire types are extremely sensitive to almost any form of pressure point techniques. I have observed several Fire types being knocked completely out during demonstrations by only slight strikes to points. From an energetic standpoint they are at a great disadvantage and according to the Chinese they often die at a young age.[7]

Earth Body Types

Earth type people generally have a darkish complexion and a strong, stocky body. They usually have a rather large head, strong powerful thighs, and wide jaws. They often walk by barely lifting their feet off the ground. On the most part they are fairly easy going individuals and are hard to make angry.[8]

Think about football players for a moment and more specifically the large guys that play on the line. They are perfect examples of Earth types. You will find many big Earth types in the sport of rugby as well. They are big, strong, thick, and have powerful thighs. Most of them have large heads. This is an easy way to think of Earth Body types.

Energetically, Earth types have an excessive amount of energy in their Earth associated meridians. Unfortunate for them is that makes them very weak in the Wood meridians, which have the task of controlling the Earth meridians. The Wood meridians, which consist of the Liver and the Gall Bladder, are excellent targets on Earth types. Considering that the Gall Bladder runs on the outer sides of the body makes an Earth type vulnerable to strikes to GB-31, GB-20, and a host of other Gall Bladder points. The reaction that they

---

[6] Maciocia, *The Foundations of Chinese Medicine*, p. 320; Moneymaker, *Torite-Jutsu Reference Manual*, pp. 40–41.

[7] Beinfield & Korngold, *Between Heaven and Earth*, pp. 176–189.

[8] Maciocia, *The Foundations of Chinese Medicine*, p. 320; Moneymaker, *Torite-Jutsu Reference Manual*, pp. 40–41.

have to strikes on this meridian is extreme in comparison to other elemental body types.[9]

Metal Body Types

Metal type people generally have broad and square shoulders. They have a triangle shaped face and a strong-built body, but are rarely heavily muscled. They tend to be lean and will usually have a strong voice.[10] Another character-istic that is common to Metal types is a large nose.

The best group that I know of that can be associated with Metal types is runners. They tend to exhibit the majority of these physical qualities more so than any other group.

Think about the things you associate with metal. One of the things that you might associate with it is armor. Energetically, Metal types are wearing a suit of armor. Often pressure point strikes will have little to no effect on Metal types. Their weakness will be in the Fire meridians, but even then it is sometimes difficult to get a response.[11]

Water Body Types

Water type people generally have a round face and body. They are often fat and have soft-white skin. They will sometimes have a longer than normal spine. They tend to move slow and easy and can sometimes be considered as lazy.[12]

The association that comes to mind for Water types are fat office workers. I am sure that you have seen these types on numerous occasions. They are ex-tremely hard to anger and are traditionally associated as being good negotiators.

On the most part you will never have to worry about facing a Water type individual in a self-defense situation. Confrontation is just not in their charac-ter. Remember that water flows around obstacles, which is a trait of the Water Type. Energetically, they are very strong in the Bladder and Kidney meridians. That makes them weak in the Earth meridians. Unfortunately, those meridians run on the front of the body and since most water types are excessively fat those

---

[9] Beinfield & Korngold, *Between Heaven and Earth*, pp. 190–203.

[10] Maciocia, *The Foundations of Chinese Medicine*, pp. 320–321; Moneymaker, *Torite-Jutsu Reference Manual*, pp. 40–41.

[11] Personal research notes from the Dragon Society International Research Group, 1994 to 2004; Beinfield & Korngold, *Between Heaven and Earth*, pp. 204–217.

[12] Maciocia, *The Foundations of Chinese Medicine*, p. 322.

points are hard to disrupt with strikes.[13]

Conclusions on Elemental Body Types

An excellent exercise is to go to a mall, sporting event, or some other location that has a large gathering of people. Take a seat and start noticing the various examples of Elemental Body Types that are found in the crowd. It will not take you long to start recognizing specific examples of the five elemental types. Some will be textbook examples. Others will exhibit characteristics of more than one element. You might notice an Earth Body Type that has strong secondary Fire characteristics. It might be a Wood Body Type that exhibits strong secondary Metal characteristics. The more you do this exercise you will notice that there are numerous combinations of the elements that are observable in any large group of people.[14]

From a martial perspective this can seem maddening. How can you be expected to know the energetic weaknesses of all the various combinations of elemental body types and expect to respond and attack those weaknesses in a self-defense situation? The answer to that question is in Chapter 13.

An interesting "trick" of pressure point instructors while conducting seminars is to pick a uke[15] of a specific elemental body type for demonstration purposes. If a thick-legged, stocky individual is chosen for a technique that attacks the Gall Bladder meridian, which will be highly sensitive in this Earth Body Type, they will respond to the energetics of the technique in a more dramatic manner than other body types. If the instructor picks a Wood type for a technique to the Gall Bladder it will have less of an effect on them due to their strength in that meridian. Considering this information you will rarely see an instructor pick a Metal type for demonstration purposes.

Additionally, when considering the constitutions of the five archetypes you will rarely be faced with a self-defense situation against a Water Body Type. They tend to be more passive than the other elemental types and you will rarely find them in any physical activity like taking martial arts classes or other contact sports. You will more than likely face a Wood, Fire or Metal type in a street encounter given their constitutions. The taller Wood types tend to enjoy alco-

---

[13] Beinfield & Korngold, *Between Heaven and Earth*, pp. 218–231.

[14] Maciocia, *The Foundations of Chinese Medicine*, p. 322; Beinfield & Korngold, *Between Heaven and Earth*, pp. 131–159.

[15] *Uke* is a Japanese term that is used to represent the person that a martial technique is to demonstrated. They are traditionally of a lower rank than the person executing the technique.

hol, which affects their Liver — the Yin Wood meridian, and can be aggressive during that time. Fire types are known for having quick tempers and it can easily get out of control in an encounter. Metal types tend to suffer from the "Little Man" syndrome. They are generally smaller in stature than the other elemental types and the more Yang versions tend to be aggressive.[16] Earth types can be a handful when they are mad, but on the most part they are slow to anger. These examples will hopefully help you gain some insight to the advanced aspects of the diagnostic abilities of Traditional Chinese Medicine, which transcends the physical treatment of disease into the mental and emotional constitutions of the individual. Again, this information should be considered as perquisite material from a martial perspective. The exception being if you are good enough to be able to pick specific elemental body types for demonstration purposes. This is not realistic from a combative viewpoint, but is a good utilization of the material.

---

[16] Personal research notes from the Dragon Society International Research Group, 1994 to 2004.

Chapter 11

EXTRAORDINARY VESSEL INTERRELATIONSHIPS

*"Knowing ourselves and knowing our opponents can be the
one hundred secrets of our winning one hundred fights."*

Sun Tzu

A s you have learned by now, the Extraordinary Vessels have a number of intersection points with the twelve Main Meridians. The primary function of those connections is the transfer of excess or deficient energy from the twelve Main Meridians to the "Human Battery" or the energetic core. At first examination the system seems complex and difficult to understand. We will now break down those connections in a manner that should simplify the two subsystems.

First, we will illustrate how the "Human Battery," which consists of the Thrusting, Conception, and Governing Vessels, is connected to the twelve Main Meridians. From the presentation of the trajectories of the Thrusting Vessels in Chapter 4, we can determine that it connects to the Main Meridians at points ST-30, KI-11, and KI-21. In Chapter 2 the trajectory of the Conception Vessel is outlined. From that we can see that it is connected to the Main Meridians at the termination point, which is ST-1. It is also connected to some of the Main Meridians at CV-2, 3, 4, 10, 12, 13, 17 and 24. The Governing Vessel, presented in Chapter 3, connects to the Main Meridians at BL-12 (see Figure 11-1).

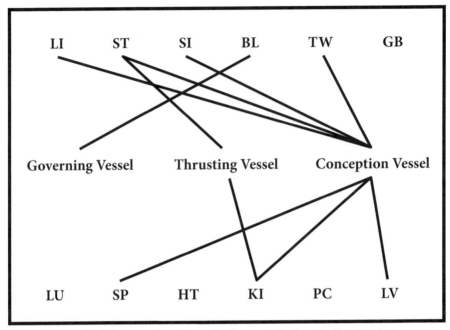

Figure 11-1: The connections between the "Human Battery" and the Main Meridians.

One of the obvious conclusion from this diagram is that the "Human Battery" Subsystem, which consists of the Thrusting, Conception, and Governing Vessels, has direct contact with the twelve Main Meridians. The Conception Vessel connects at intersections with the Spleen, Stomach, Small Intestine, Liver, Large Intestine, Kidney and Triple Warmer. This is curious due to the Conception Vessel being associated with the yin meridians. Contributing energy is exchanged through the four Yang associated meridians, which are the Stomach, Small Intestine, Large Intestine and Triple Warmer meridians, to assist in correcting energetic imbalances in their yin associated coupled meridian. The Thrusting Vessel connects to the Stomach Meridian and the Kidney Meridian. The connection to the Kidney Meridian is to aid in the regulation of energy of the Kidneys, which are paramount in the Chinese idea of energetic function. The Governing Vessel is directly connected to the Bladder Meridian to asset in maintaining a proper energy balance in the two Water Element Meridians, the Kidney and Bladder Meridians. The connections between the Girdle Vessel and the Heel Vessels with the twelve Main Meridians are illustrated in Figure 11-2.

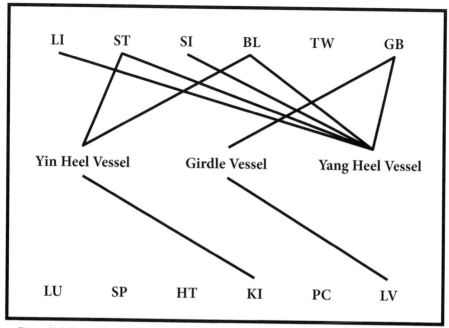

Figure 11-2: The connections between the Heel Vessels and the Girdle Vessel and the Main Meridians.

Some conclusions from the illustration are that the Girdle Vessel is only directly connected to the Liver and Gall Bladder Meridians. This is supported by one of the functions of that vessel. That function is to help regulate the energy level of the coupled Wood Element Meridians, those being the Liver and Gall Bladder. It has no other direct connection to the twelve Main Meridians. The Yin Heel Vessel, with the primary responsibility of supplying the yin aspects of the legs with energy, is connected with the Yin Kidney Meridian, the Yang Stomach Meridian, and the Yang Bladder Meridian. These three meridians all have a major role in the energy of the legs. The Yin Heel Vessel does not connect with any of the other Main Meridians. The Yang Heel Vessel is responsible for supplying energy to the yang aspects of the legs. It is directly connected to the Large Intestine, Stomach, Small Intestine, Bladder, and Gall Bladder Meridians. One of the more obvious facts that can be derived from the two preceding diagrams are that the majority of the connections between the Extraordinary Vessels and the twelve Main Meridians are those that connect to the Yang associated meridians. Why is this? Because given the very nature of the Yang organs, or bowels, they are more resilient to energetic fluctuations than the more sensitive Yin organs. The Yang organs are more robust than the Yin organs. They can take more abuse, be that physical trauma or energetic fluctua-

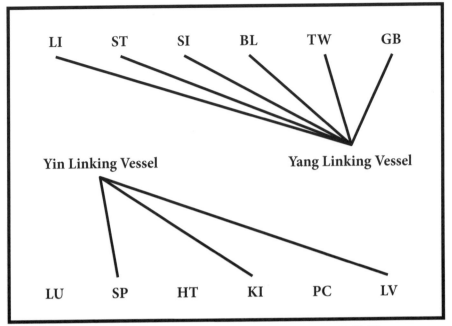

Figure 11-3: The connections between the Linking Vessels and the Main Meridians.

tion, than the Yin organs. This is an important key for the martial artist in understanding which of the twelve Main Meridians, and their associated organs, should be attacked. This is further supported in the next diagram, which shows the connections between the Linking Vessels and the twelve Main Meridians.

This illustrates that the Yang Linking Vessel connects to each of the Yang associated Main Meridians. Those are the Large Intestine, Stomach, Small Intestine, Bladder, Triple Warmer, and Gall Bladder Meridians. This enables the Yang Linking Vessel to quickly make energetic adjustments to these meridians. Remember that the Yang associated meridians are more robust and can handle fast adjustments to their energy levels. They are not as vital to the function of the body as the Yin associated organs. The Yin Linking Vessel connects to just the Spleen, Kidney and Liver Meridians. It does not have a direct connection to the Lung, Heart, and Pericardium Meridians. The spleen, kidney, and liver are important organs to the life functions of the body, but they are secondary to the lungs and the heart. The pericardium is closely related to the function of the heart and will not be considered separately at this point. The ability to breath and the function of the heart are essential to life. If one stops the rest of the body will die. The ancient Chinese knew this too and as Traditional Chinese Medicine developed overall thought grew around that knowledge. The manner that they utilized to describe the interactions of the various organs and bowels, and the energetic system that supports them, reflect the need for delicate manipulations when influencing the energy of the heart and lungs.[1]

How does the energetic system of the body adjust the energy of the heart and lungs? The answer will require the student to have an understanding of how the coupled pairs, or Yin/Yang pairs, of the twelve Main Meridians interact. Knowing how to attack that system will require the student to understand the function of the Extraordinary Vessels. Knowing what the desired energetic state of those organs will require the student to look outside the Eastern paradigm for a moment. The next chapter will deal with a branch of Western science that will help unlock that answer.

---

[1] Personal research notes from the Dragon Society International Research Group, 1994 to 2004. The information that is presented in this chapter is from research by the author into the function and interrelationships of the Extraordinary Vessels and the twelve Main Meridians. Those interrelationships are supported by many of the textbooks that have been cited thus far, but the exact manner that they are represented in this chapter was personally developed to visually illustrate the often confusing interactions.

## Chapter 12

BODY ALARM REACTION

"Not only will men of science have to grapple with the sciences that deal with man, but — and this is a far more difficult matter — they will have to persuade the world to listen to what they have discovered."
Bertrand Russell

S tress. It is a subject that has received a great deal of attention in research and for excellent reason. It is something that effects each and every one of us in varying degrees. In fact, it effects every living organism on the face of the Earth. Dr. Hans Selye forwarded the study of stress, and the effects it has on living organisms.[1] He is considered by many as the vanguard of stress theory and a pioneer in addressing the causes of stress-related diseases. Selye defined stress as "the nonspecific response of the body to any demand made upon it." His research has led to a greater understanding in how human beings respond to all kinds of stress. It is his theories, and those expanded by his colleagues, that have influenced this attempt to incorporate them into martial science.

Selye's research found that stress causes specific changes in the structure and chemical composition of the body. Those changes can be accurately predicted and confirmed by experimentation and observation. Some of the predictable changes are due to actual damage to the body. Other changes are the body's attempt to defend itself. This is referred to as adaptive reactions. Selye grouped all these predictable changes into what he coined as the General Adaptation Syndrome.[2] The General Adaptation Syndrome is further divided into three stages: the Alarm Reaction Stage, the Resistance Stage, and the Exhaustion Stage.[3] The initial Alarm Reaction Stage represents the physical manifestation of the body's "call to arms" of its defense mechanisms. Additionally, the

---

[1] James V. McConnell, *Understanding Human Behavior* (New York: Hot, Rinehart and Winston, 1974), p. 320.

[2] Ibid., p. 320–322; James C. Coleman, James N. Butcher and Robert C. Carson, *Abnormal Psychology and Modern Life*, (Glenview, IL: Scott, Foresman and Company, 1984), pp. 154–156 .

[3] McConnell, *Understanding Human Behavior*, p. 320.

body is considered to be in a state of shock during the initial moments of the Alarm Reaction Stage.[4] If the stress stimulus remains the body will enter into the Resistance Stage. The body will eventually move in the Exhaustion Stage if it can not continue to resist the stress stimuli. Each of these stages has different and unique characteristics that are predictable in everyone. Though his model was developed as an explanation for the effects of the stress of disease, it is equally adaptable in explaining the effects of stressful situations like the threat of potential physical harm. Understanding the Alarm Reaction Stage of Selye's General Adaptation Syndrome is of great importance in unlocking the secrets of why we are predictable. If we can predict our reactions to stress, caused by the potential of physical harm as in a combative situation, then we can adjust our training methods to develop a more realistic and effective response.

So what does this have to do with the martial arts? Plenty. Understanding that the human body reacts to stress in a predictable manner gives us insight into any potential opponent and ourselves. Given a highly stressful event, like an actual self-defense situation, the vast majority of people will exhibit certain changes to our normal physical state. Those predictable changes are referred to as *Body Alarm Reaction*.[5] This can be defined as the predictable reactions that occur to the human body when there is a perceived chance of physical harm. The reactions occur rapidly and unconsciously to varying degrees depending upon individual conditioning. Those reactions to the stimulus of stress have a direct influence on our ability to defend ourselves. It can also provide clues on the same physical reactions that are occurring within a potential opponent. If we examine and understand these predictable reactions then we can adjust our training to overcome many of the negative aspects of the phenomenon. We can use Traditional Chinese Medicine as a model to predict the effects of our combative methods on the human body. Likewise, we can use the model of Body Alarm Reaction to predict the effects of stress on our ability to defend ourselves. In observing many different styles of martial arts, it is apparent that the majority of them do not take these physical reactions to stress into account in their training methods. If we can analyze a specific technique under the scrutiny of this proven area of scientific study, then we better determine its chances of success. Those techniques that relay on principles that conflict with, or totally ignore, these predictable human responses to a harmful situation can

---

[4] Ibid., p. 320.

[5] Body Alarm Reaction is a term used within the Dragon Society International, which is the martial arts organization that is headed by Tom Muncy and Rick Moneymaker. It is commonly referred to as BAR by the members and instructors of that organization.

be exposed and discarded. Likewise, techniques that demonstrate and account for these reactions can be embraced and incorporated into our training methods. In doing this we increase our chance of success and survival.

Once a potential threat is recognized, as in someone exhibiting aggressive behavior, your body will automatically initiate a "call to arms" of its various defensive mechanisms. Depending on how you interpret that potential threat will greatly influence the degree in which you body responds. It will respond according to the perceived level of threat from the aggressive person. It is obvious that you will have a greater Body Alarm Reaction to the threat of aggression from an armed six-foot five inch, two hundred and fifty pound thug than that of a ten-year-old child. The greater the perceived threat is equal to the greater level of Body Alarm Reaction. The degree in which the body alarms can also be influenced directly by conditioning and training. If you are regularly exposed to large aggressive attackers you will develop a level of conditioning that, to varying degrees, will lesson your Body Alarm Reaction to that specific stress stimulus. That is as long as you can successfully defend yourself against larger aggressors. As soon as an unconditioned element is presented, two large aggressive attackers rather than one for instance, your body will automatically increase its "call to arms."[6]

Most martial artists do not take this into account. They are comfortable working out in their well lit, carpeted, air conditioned dojos. They train enough to develop skills that they believe will enable them to defend themselves "on the street." Many of them have never been in an actual self-defense situation. Their experience, conditioning, and training revolve around the rules and etiquette of controlled sport-oriented sparring. Their martial lineage, no fault of their own, are often in styles that put more emphasis on performance and visual appeal than actual combative effectiveness. We have all heard of some high ranking martial artist, with umpteen years of experience, getting beaten in a street fight. Not considering the effects of Body Alarm Reaction in their training is a major cause of this embarrassing, and potentially life-threatening, outcome.

---

[6] Hans Selye, *The Stress of Life* (New York: The McGraw-Hill Companies, Inc., 1956), pp. 36–38, Selye goes into great detail concerning his extensive research on stress and specifically the "call to arms" phase of General Adaptation Syndrome; Personal research notes from the Dragon Society International Research Group, 1994 to 2004. The information in this chapter is the result of research by the author. The application of Dr. Selye's findings to martial science is presented for the first time to martial artists. It is based on proven responses to stress, though not specifically aggressive encounters, which have been documented by numerous Behavioral Psychologists. Additionally, this is the first time that the effects of Body Alarm Reaction have been examined under the laws, theories and concepts of Traditional Chinese Medicine.

"Call to Arms"

Once you recognize the threat of aggressive behavior, your body will start a chain reaction of events that are completely automatic in nature. You will not have the ability to stop this from occurring. Your mind will be too involved in handling the potential threat for you to realize that you are slipping into Body Alarm Reaction. Given the society that we live in today, the majority of people that will read this book have never experienced the stress of an actual combative situation. The closest that most have come to this type of life experience is during another potentially life threatening event. For this example we will use a near miss of a severe automobile accident. Depending on where you live, and you individual driving habits, you may have had several such experiences. Think about the physical reactions that you had to this sudden threat of physical harm. According to the model of Body Alarm Reaction you would have exhibited some, if not all, of the reactions listed in Table 12-1.

Body Alarm Reactions
Increase in blood pressure and heart rate
General increase in muscle tension
Increase in respiratory rate
Higher state of mental alertness
Tunnel Vision (over focus on threat)
Auditory exclusion
Impaired sense of time
Decrease in blood flow to non-essential body functions
Elimination of body waste

Table 12-1: *Physical Reactions during BAR.*[7]

Now, if you will, consider the manner that those same reactions would hinder your ability to defend yourself in an actual self-defense situation. As your endocrine system dumps adrenaline into your bloodstream it will produce several physical reactions. You will have a general tightening of the muscles of the forearm, as well as the entire muscular system. This will have a noticeable

---

[7] Rick Moneymaker, *Master Series Handout*, 1995 — Professor Moneymaker was the first instructor in the United States to teach the effects of Body Alarm Reaction to martial artists. He has developed a series of exercises that demonstrate some of the basic responses to martial artists. Peter Consterdine and Geoff Thompson have contributed to the martial application of Body Alarm Reaction in the United Kingdom.

effect on your ability to perform techniques that require using your hands to manipulate joints, grasp, or otherwise "handle" your opponent. Imagine attempting to perform the simple task of pouring a cup of coffee the moment after a close call automobile crash. The physical effects of the stress, in this case the "shakes," will make this very difficult to accomplish. You body will react in the same manner during an actual self-defense situation. This is predictable and WILL occur in the vast majority of human beings, martial artists included, when subjected to these types of stresses.[8] Those of us that have had actual street self-defense situations have experienced many of these reactions first hand. In retrospect, if our training had been geared to account for Body Alarm Reaction, we would have probably received less physical damage from our attackers.

As your mind recognizes a potential threat to your well being, your body will start to react to this stress in a number of ways. One of the first reactions to potential physical harm is the secretion of large amounts of the hormone adrenaline into the bloodstream. Adrenaline is one many hormones that are "dumped" into the body during Body Alarm Reaction.[9] Their functions are intended to be biologically protective. Unfortunately, the changes they produce can actually inhibit our ability to physically defend ourselves. The intent of the body's automatic "call to arms' is to provide the increases in strength and energy to either fight or run away from the threat. This is sometimes referred to as the "Fight-or-Flight" syndrome. It is a product of our evolution to develop mechanisms that allowed us to survive various physical threats.

As the body continues down the path of automatic response the effects of the massive hormone "dump" will manifest itself in several different reactions. There will be an increase in both blood pressure and the heart rate.[10] This is designed to increase the blood flow to the brain and the muscles, which will be placed under increased activity levels if you either defend yourself or run away. As blood flow increase to the brain and muscular system, they are the most important to survival at this particular moment, there is a decrease of blood flow to the digestive system, kidneys, liver, and skin. There will be an increase in the respiration rate to assimilate additional oxygen into the system. The increase of blood flow to the brain will induce a higher state of mental alertness and sensory perception. This is with the intent to aid our ability to mentally assess the situation at hand and to decrease our reaction time. It can have some negative effects

---

[8] Selye, *The Stress of Life*, pp. 36–38.

[9] James V. McConnell, *Understanding Human Behavior* (New York: Hot, Rinehart and Winston, 1974), p. 319.

[10] Peter Consterdine, *Streetwise* (Leeds, England: Protective Publications, 1997), pp.155–168.

like tunnel vision, auditory exclusion, and an impaired sense of time. There will be an increase in the level of extra energy in our blood with the higher amounts of cholesterol, fats, and blood sugar. In case we might be injured, our body also raises the level of platelets and blood clotting factors to help prevent hemorrhage. One other reaction, one that has serious implications for the martial artist, is that there will be a general increase in muscular tension. This aspect of Body Alarm Reaction alone has limiting effects on several martial skills. One in particular that we should recognize is that muscular tension equates to reduction of speed. So realistically, if we are in Body Alarm Reaction we can expect to be slower than when we are in a normal relaxed state. We can expect to have reduced ability to defend ourselves due to these automatic responses that are intended to provide assistance, but in actuality can greatly hinder that ability.[11]

Training Adjustments

So how do we adjust our martial training, and possibly more important—our mindset, to account for how Body Alarm Reaction effects our ability to execute techniques under the stress of a combative situation? Unfortunately, the manner in which many of the modern sport-oriented martial arts interpret their techniques is not realistic.[12] As the martial arts evolved in Western society it began to move farther and farther away from the original combat-oriented systems from which they were born. The result is that there are many styles that promote teachings and training methods that are founded on the myth that they are street effective. In fact, many of these teachings and training methods are counter-productive to self-defense. Many students of these systems have been "sold" the idea that these methods will work for them "if they ever have to use them."[13] Not all techniques fall into this category, but enough do that it is necessary to illustrate the differences.

Let's say that an obviously aggressive person[14] has surprised you. This individual exhibits enough aggressive behavior that your internalized automatic

---

[11] Coleman, Butcher and Carson, *Abnormal Psychology and Modern Life*, p. 155 — note that the physical reactions of Body Alarm Reaction have been documented through exhaustive research by numerous Behavioral Psychologist.

[12] Montaigue, *Advanced Dim-Mak*, pp. 309–313.

[13] Interview with Professor Rick Moneymaker, 2001.

[14] McConnell, *Understanding Human Behavior*, pp. 98–110, McConnell provides some interesting information concerning violence and the factors that are known to produce violence. Some theorists suggest that we are born with an aggressive instinct that we must somehow learn to control. Additional information is represented concerning the Triune, or reptilian, brain and the role it plays in aggressive behavior. Erle Montaigue has forwarded this theory in martial science.

responses are activated. You start slipping into Body Alarm Reaction. As this individual escalates their aggression your body will increase its descent into the predictable reactions of stress. As the individual launches a right hand punch to your head — you must react or be hit. In the milliseconds that your brain is interpreting the stimulus of the incoming right hand punch, many of the effects of Body Alarm Reaction are already taking place. Adrenaline, and other hormones, have been and are still being secreted into your bloodstream. Their increased levels have initiated an increase in your blood pressure. Your heart rate is rising to anaerobic levels and your respiratory rate has increased noticeably. The arteries and capillaries that fed your digestive tract, liver, kidneys, and other non-essential (in relation to this physical threat) organs and bowels are constricting to decrease the amount of blood that is flowing to them. Clotting factors and platelets numbers are rising in your blood to aid against the potential threat of hemorrhaging. An increase of blood flow to the brain had made you keenly aware of this threat by putting your senses on "high alert." You may start perceiving the experience in an altered state of time: i.e. the events may seem to occur in slow motion. Because of the threat you may get "tunnel vision" and/or "tunnel hearing." Your muscular system will experience a general tightening that will decrease your reaction speed and inhibit your ability to perform. In extreme case, depending on your conditioning and the perceived level of threat, your bladder and bowels may empty to remove their harmful waste from your body in the event of injury.

At some point during those milliseconds your brain fires off the impulses to cause your body to react to this threat. Your arms rise up in front of your head and chest in a reflective response to the incoming punch. Your reaction time is slower due to the muscular tightness of your upper body. You might have trained yourself to perform hundreds of blocks to this type of an attack. Those blocks may have been engrained to focus on a very exact strike to the belly of the biceps with a two-knuckle strike. Having performed this technique hundreds, if not thousands, of times in the dojo, you fully expect it to work. It does not. Instead, your left forearm meets the forearm of the attacker. You have probably trained to step into the attacking arm for this type of an attack, as well. The technique is not successful, either due to the combined effects of the dynamics of the attack or the reduction in your physical capabilities due to Body Alarm Reaction. In fact, as you pick yourself up off the floor you might realize that nothing worked as it was "supposed" to work. Your many years of training failed when you actually needed it the most. Why? The reason is that you did not account for the effects of Body Alarm Reaction. Your training had been centered around the make-believe world of self-defense techniques that work in the dojo, but fail on the street.

Taking into account that we will experience general muscle tightening during an actual self-defense situation allows adjusting our training methods to compensate. Rather than practice making an initial reactive block with pinpoint accuracy, you train to make the initial block with a large surface. That surface should be the area between the elbow and the tips of the fingers. The idea that you will be able to execute a pinpoint two-knuckle strike in the initial stages of a real self-defense situation is fairy tale. The blocking surface will need to be the large area of the lower forearm. During training your focus should be on making contact with incoming punches with the eighteen-inch section of your arm, rather than a smaller blocking surface like your knuckles. The same holds true in the manner that you execute kicks. Successful use of the small four-inch striking surface of the ball of your foot is dramatically less than striking with the twelve-inch surface of your shinbone. When training for combative, high stress situations it is necessary to incorporate the use of the larger striking and blocking surfaces during the initial Body Alarm Reaction stage. All further escalations of violence will depend on other reflectively trained responses. Actually believing that you will react to the initial attack with pinpoint accuracy is totally unrealistic. That train of thought is common in the majority of self-defense techniques that are taught in martial art schools. That is the reason that many "street fighters" view the martial arts as a joke. They

Many martial arts schools teach blocking with small surfaces. This is unrealistic in actual encounters die to the effects of BAR.	A more realistic perspective is to utilize the major surfaces of the body for blocking and striking.

have learned that all the "fancy karate stuff" just doesn't work on the street. That is a lesson that many martial artists have learned the hard way.

Training Effect

Our perception of the threat has a direct and dramatic effect of the rate and severity that Body Alarm Reaction will occur. By continual exposure to certain aspects of an attack, or visual perception of an attacker, we can reduce the speed and degree that we fall into automatic body response. By doing realistic self-defense drills we can condition ourselves to the threat of a "haymaker" punch. The more we practice against a specific threat our brain and body becomes well conditioned to that particular stimulus. The more realistic the practice, by increasing speed and intensity, the greater the conditioning level to a realistic attack. This is referred to as *Training Effect*. An individual that has never practiced any self-defense technique against a "haymaker" punch will ascend into a higher state of Body Alarm Reaction than someone that practices against them. Likewise, someone that trains against full speed, high intensity "haymaker" punches will be in a less state than someone that trains at half-speed.

Training Effect can give any martial artist a false sense of security. By developing a high level of skill in the execution of a particular technique, one can be lulled into the falsehood of believing that they have moved beyond the "hold" of Body Alarm Reaction. What they do not realize is that by introducing an *Unconditioned Element* into the situation that they will automatically slip into Body Alarm Reaction to some degree. The addition of an unconditioned element can occur at any time during a self-defense encounter. Let us assume that someone is attacking with a "haymaker" punch. You have spent many hours perfecting a technique to defend against such an attack and are confident on your ability to execute it properly. You have incorporated the knowledge of what occurs during Body Alarm Reaction into the technique. You have practiced this technique at full speed and from every conceivable angle. It works and you know that it works. You feel confident about the technique and have successfully conditioned yourself to this type of attack — you think. Now as this actual attack is taking place, all that is required to send you into full-blown Body Alarm Reaction is the introduction of an unconditioned element. It can be a slip on wet pavement during the initial execution. It can be an overly large and aggressive attacker. Someone that is much larger, and more frightening, than the training partners that you have worked with in honing this technique. It can be the addition of another potential attacker that is the friend, or colleague, of the one that you are facing. It can be any number of events or circumstances that will cause you to start slipping into Body Alarm Reaction. It is necessary to understand that any one of us can become a victim of this automatic response, even if we have been incorporating the knowledge into our training methods.

We are also prone to fall into Body Alarm Reaction due to our perception of visual threats. Our visual recognition of a potential threat has a direct bearing on the initial onset of Body Alarm Reaction. For instance, if our social exposure does not include members of other races or of lower social status, then just by being exposed to an attacker from one of these groups can cause you to initiate Body Alarm Reaction. Let us say that you train at a dojo in the affluent section of town. Your instructors and fellow students are predominately upper class Caucasians. Your training methods incorporate the effects of Body Alarm Reaction against various types of initial attacks. Through years of training you develop a false sense of security concerning your ability to "deal" with these automatic body reactions. This false sense of security has fooled you into thinking that you will be able to successfully defend yourself with little or effect of those reactions. By simply adding the visual stimulus of an aggressive attacker that is of a different race, or dressed in "gang" clothes, you start falling into Body Alarm Reaction. In both of these examples the addition of an unconditioned element causes the onset of Body Alarm Reaction. It can, and possible will, effect everyone when faced with an actual self-defense situation. By accepting this into our mindset and training allows us to train against it and incorporate solid self-defense principles. Not the "fairy tale" techniques taught by so many martial arts schools.

Combat Mindset

Developing a mindset that understands and seeks methods to avoid the pitfalls of Body Alarm Reaction is very difficult for many martial artists. Some may have spent many years training in dogmatically followed systems that are unrealistic in their application of self-defense techniques. Their life experiences may not include ever having been in an actual "street fight." Even with years of martial arts training under their belts they are unable to see the folly of their ways. Ask yourself, when confronted with a seemingly complicated self-defense technique, could you perform that technique under stress? Can you perform that technique while experiencing Body Alarm Reaction? Can you perform it when you are slower due to general muscular tightening? Can you perform the technique at "combat speed" in the controlled environment of the dojo? Much less in the uncertain environment of the street. Can you take into account the many unknown, unconditioned elements that might contribute to your Body Alarm Reaction level? Take the time to ask yourself these questions. Analysis all of your self-defense techniques to determine if they are applicable to the way that you will need to defend yourself during an actual encounter. Remember that developing the combat oriented mindset may require you to question the established teaching and training methods of your particular system.[15] The combat mindset martial artist knows that they will receive contact during a street fight. They understand and train against the unpredictability of those situations. They train with techniques that "get the job done" with speed and efficiency utilizing gross motor skills. Their training is centered on realistic fighting techniques that apply many levels of knowledge to determine combat effectiveness. The combat mindset martial artist incorporates their knowledge of the predictable reactions of the stress of a combative situation into their training. They do not fall into a false sense of security because they understand that Body Alarm Reaction, just like Murphy's Law,[16] will show up when you least expect it.

An Eastern Perspective

The majority of this book is concerned with taking Eastern thought, theories, and concepts and examining them from a Western perspective. The reverse is true in the examination of the theories of Body Alarm Reaction. This branch of Behavioral Psychology will be examined from an Eastern perspective to determine any energetic associations that can be derived and utilized by the martial artist.

We know that Dr. Selye's research led to the formation of what we now consider Body Alarm Reaction. That research was not available to the creators of Traditional Chinese Medicine, but the reactions that occur during stress can be applied to that system. We can take each of the reactions that are associated with Body Alarm Reaction and apply them to the Chinese model of the functions of the body.

First, let us look at the energetic implications of an increase in blood pressure and heart rate. As the body recognizes a potential threat it starts to descend into Body Alarm Reaction. The Heart meridian is given a "jolt" of extra energy that elevates the normal energy level of that organ. That extra "jolt" of energy

---

[15] Consterdine, *Streetwise*, pp. 203–240.
[16] Murphy's Law — If it can go wrong, it will go wrong.

comes from the Extraordinary Vessel Subsystem, specifically the "Human Battery." The extra energy that the Heart receives causes it to increase in the rate of pumping and level of blood pressure. There is also an increase in the respiratory rate as extra energy is pumped into the Lung Meridian. As defensive qi, or energy, is pumped through the body there is an increase in muscular tension and a slow down of the rate that the capillaries are feeding the skin. This is another function of the Metal associated meridians. Selye observed that the digestive organs decrease in function. This marks the energetic system decreasing the energy to the Large Intestine, Bladder, Kidney, Liver, Gall Bladder, Stomach, Spleen, and Small Intestine Meridians. Energy is pumped into the brain that causes tunnel vision, impaired sense of time, and auditory exclusion. All of these energetic reactions stem from the Extraordinary Vessels and understanding that will play an important role as we examine the methodology of attacking that subsystem.[17]

Considering that the organs and bowels are given Elemental qualities we can examine the effects of Body Alarm Reaction from that model. We can observe that there is an increase in the Fire and Metal associated meridians and decreases in the Wood, Water, and Earth meridians. This is represented in Table 12-2.

EARTH	METAL	WATER	WOOD	FIRE
<	>	<	<	>

Table 12-2: *Energetic Qualities of Body Alarm Reaction.*

This should be a major clue to the martial artist that is seeking to understand which organs are most prone to energetic attack in a combative situation. Should the organs that are associated with Wood be the primary focus of an attack? They are obviously at a lower state than normal. Maybe the Earth associated organs? Or Water? Possibly the Fire or Metal associated organs since they are in an excess? The next chapter will answer the question.

---

[17] Personal research notes of the author. Several Traditional Chinese Medicine practitioners have substantiated the information that is presented in this chapter concerning the energetic effects of Body Alarm Reaction. This is the first time that the laws, theories and concepts of Traditional Chinese Medicine have examined the effects of Body Alarm Reaction to the knowledge of the author. Both Rick Moneymaker and Peter Consterdine have worked with the effects of Body Alarm Reaction from a martial viewpoint, but have not published any examination of the theory from an Eastern perspective.

Chapter 13

PRIMARY ENERGETIC TARGETS

"Men occasionally stumble over the truth,
most just pick themselves up and hurry off as if nothing happened."
Winston Churchill

Hopefully, you have gained a higher understanding of the more advanced aspects of Traditional Chinese Medicine, and their application to martial science, from the wealth of information presented thus far in this book. The functions and interactions of the Extraordinary Vessels, interrelationship of the Five Element Theory with the twelve Main Meridians, and Body Alarm Reaction are all necessary prerequisites in understanding the primary energetic targets of the body. In earlier chapters, information was offered that should give you a solid foundation of each of those three areas of study. The information that will be presented in this chapter will "tie" together all of that data and present to the reader a reasonable explanation of why certain organs are primary energetic targets. Understanding which of the organs are the most vulnerable to energetic disruption allows the martial artists to tailor their specific training methods to attack the most sensitive areas of the body. This will give them a higher probability of success in the event that they find themselves in an actual self-defense situation. Actually, the information that was discovered through this research goes beyond a simple self-defense situation.

Martial Arts?

The word "martial" has been used in relation to the "martial arts" for years. The definition of the word is "warlike" or "having to do with war." The vast majority of the arts, as practiced in the west today, are very far removed from anything that is "warlike." The information what can be gleaned from this book will give the martial artist the ability to understand how to kill their opponent. It puts the "martial" back into the martial arts and holds a high degree of responsibility.

Martial artists, through the information that is shared in this book, cannot use this information lightly. It is for "life-or-death" circumstances. The original *Bubishi* was written with the intent of training warriors for unarmed combat.[1] The information that is presented in this book gives the student the knowledge, accumulated over thousands of years, of how to quickly kill or maim an opponent in battle. Once that information is understood, it is easy to "tone down" the application of that knowledge to just defend oneself. If placed in a situation where it is necessary to kill an opponent this knowledge is extremely valuable. Understanding how to effectively strike someone in a manner that attacks the sensitive organs of the body and shuts down the ability of the energetic system to correct those attacks is serious business. It should not be taken lightly.

Elemental Aspects of the Extraordinary Vessels/Main Meridian Points

The Extraordinary Vessels are not associated with the Five Element Theory as are the twelve Main Meridians. The Main Meridians are basically grouped in five pairs, which consist of a Yin and Yang aspect, of each of the five elements.[2] The exception to this is the Fire meridian, which has two pairs of associated organs. The Liver and Gall Bladder meridians are the yin and yang aspects of the Wood element. The Kidney and Bladder meridians are the yin and yang aspects of the Water element. The Lung and the Large Intestine meridians are the yin and yang aspects of the Metal element. The Spleen and Stomach meridians are the yin and yang aspects of the Earth element. The Heart and Small Intestine meridians are the yin and yang aspects of the Fire element. Also, the Pericardium and Triple Warmer meridians are associated with the Fire element.[3] Table 13-1 illustrates these associations.

Polarity	EARTH	METAL	WATER	WOOD	FIRE
Yin	Spleen	Lung	Kidney	Liver	Heart
					Pericardium
Yang	Stomach	Large Intestine	Bladder	Gall Bladder	Small Intestine
					Triple Warmer

Table 13-1: *Polarity and Five Element values of the twelve Main Meridians.*

---

[1] McCarthy, *The Bible of Karate: Bubishi*, pp. 107–111. McCarthy covers some interesting historical accounts of Chinese warriors and the development of Vital Point Striking.

[2] See Chapter 9 for additional information concerning the Five Element Theory.

[3] Kiiko Matsumoto & Stephen Birch, *Five Elements and Ten Stems* (Brookline, MA: Paradigm Publications, 1983), p. 53.

A moment is needed to consider the functions of the Pericardium Meridian and the organ itself, as it is considered in Traditional Chinese Medicine. The pericardium is closely related to the heart and according to the Chinese it functions as an external covering of the heart muscle and protects it from energetic fluctuations.[4] The role of the Pericardium as the "Heart Protector" is of importance to the martial artist. From an energetic point of view the two, heart and pericardium, should be considered as one unit. This is when dealing with the destructive energetics of the various combative disciplines and not the healing aspects of Traditional Chinese Medicine.

Now we will breakdown all the points that the Extraordinary Vessels communicate with the twelve Main Meridians, or intersection points, by their elemental values. This should show some interesting conclusions.

| EARTH | | METAL | | WATER | | WOOD | | FIRE | | | |
Yin	Yang	Yin	Yang	Yin	Yang	Yin	Yang	Yin		Yang	
SP-13	ST-1		LI-14	KI-6	BL-1	LV-13	GB-13			SI-10	TW-13
SP-15	ST-3		LI-15	KI-8	BL-12	LV-14	GB-14				TW-15
SP-16	ST-4		LI-16	KI-9	BL-59		GB-15				
	ST-8			KI-11	BL-61		GB-16				
	ST-9			KI-21	BL-62		GB-17				
	ST-12	LU			BL-63		GB-18	HT	PC		
	ST-30						GB-19				
		No Points					GB-20	No Points	No Points		
							GB-21				
							GB-26				
							GB-27				
							GB-28				
							GB-29				
							GB-35				

Table 13-2: *Extraordinary Vessel Intersection Points by Element.*

Table 13-2 illustrates that the Gall Bladder Meridian plays the most important role in the exchange of energy between the Extraordinary Vessels. Notice that the Gall Bladder has fourteen intersecting points with the Extraordinary Vessels. That is the most of any of the twelve Main Meridians. The Gall Bladder Meridian was referred to as the "General of the Body" because it was believed

---

[4] Maciocia, *The Foundations of Chinese Medicine*, pp. 103–104.

to regulate all the other Yang associated organs (Stomach, Large Intestines, Bladder, and Small Intestines). From a Western perspective, the Gall Bladder stores bile that is produced by the Liver. It then releases that bile into the Small Intestines to assist digestion. The Gall Bladder and the Liver are closely linked in the function of the digestive system. If the Liver is producing an irregular amount of bile the Gall Bladder will be affected. Likewise, if the Gall Bladder is not releasing or storing bile properly then the Liver will be affected. Through the Yin/Yang linking of the Gall Bladder and the Liver Meridians the Extraordinary Vessels (the "Human Battery") can quickly adjust energetic imbalances in both of these organs. The Gall Bladder is linked to the Liver on its internal trajectory. This is reflected in the fact that Liver only intersects the Extraordinary Vessels at two locations. Those are Liver points 13 and 14. The manner that the Extraordinary Vessels adjust the energy level of the Liver is primarily through those two points, but secondarily through all the intersecting points of the Gall Bladder. The Gall Bladder Meridian assists in making rapid adjustments to the Liver.

Many times at numerous Pressure Point Seminars individuals are stunned or knocked out by strikes to the Gall Bladder Meridian. Part of this is due to the easily accessible location of the meridian on the outer portion of the body. Those that conduct the seminars know that the Gall Bladder is associated with the Wood Element. Generally, by applying the Cycle of Control, or Destruction, to three of the elements a stun or knockout often happens. When someone throws a punch or grasps you, and the ensuing block, parry, or other such technique is executed, then the Fire and Metal associated meridians of the arms are activated. This generally opens the opponent's body in such a way as to present a target on the Gall Bladder Meridian. When struck it completes three steps in the Cycle of Control and the resulting stun or knockout occurs. Strikes to the Gall Bladder Meridian, which are executed in this controlled manner, are fairly safe from a energetic standpoint. One of the main reasons for this is the manner that the Extraordinary Vessels are interconnected with the Gall Bladder Meridian. The imbalance that is created by the strike is quickly corrected and the person returns to a normal state.

The meridians that are associated with the Earth Element are second in the number of point locations that they intersect with the Extraordinary Vessels. The Stomach Meridian intersects with the Extraordinary Vessels a total of seven times at ST-1, ST-3, ST-4, ST-8, ST-9, ST-12, and ST-30. These points allow the Extraordinary Vessels to correct energy imbalances in the Stomach Meridian. The paired meridian of the Stomach Meridian, the Spleen Meridian, is connected to the Extraordinary Vessels at SP-13, SP-15, and SP-16. This allows the Extraordinary Vessels to directly correct Spleen energy imbalances, but only at those three points. However, they do adjust the energy levels of the Spleen through the paired Stomach Meridian, in the same manner as the relationship between the Gall Bladder and the Liver.

The Bladder Meridian, which is associated with the element of Water, is third in the number of connections with the Extraordinary Vessels. It intersects the Extraordinary Vessels at BL-1, BL-12, BL-59, BL-61, BL-62, and BL-63. The Yin aspect of the Water element pair is the Kidneys. The Kidney Meridian intersects the Extraordinary Vessels at KI-6, KI-8, KI-9, KI-11, and KI-21. Through these connects the Extraordinary Vessels correct imbalances in these two meridians. Given the energetic importance of the Kidneys, according to Traditional Chinese Medicine, it can be adjusted more rapidly than the other Yin associated organs.

YANG					
EARTH	METAL	WATER	WOOD	FIRE	
ST-1	LI-14	BL-1	GB-13	SI-10	TW-13
ST-3	LI-15	BL-12	GB-14		TW-15
ST-4	LI-16	BL-59	GB-15		
ST-8		BL-61	GB-16		
ST-9		BL-62	GB-17		
ST-12		BL-63	GB-18		
ST-30			GB-19		
			GB-20		
			GB-21		
			GB-26		
			GB-27		
			GB-28		
			GB-29		
			GB-35		
YIN					
EARTH	METAL	WATER	WOOD	FIRE	
SP-13	LU	KI-6	LV-13	HT	PC
SP-15		KI-8	LV-14		
SP-16	No Points	KI-9		No Points	No Points
		KI-11			
		KI-21			

Table 13-3: *The Extraordinary Vessel Intersection Points by Element divided by Yin/Yang associations.*

Table 13-3 shows that the vast majority of the intersection points between the Extraordinary Vessels and the twelve Main Meridians are with the Yang associated meridians. What does that tell us about the choice of potential targets from an energetic standpoint? It illustrates that the Yang associated meridians can quickly correct the energy imbalances of strikes, and various diseases from a healing perspective, in comparison with the more sensitive Yin associated organs. This is substantiated by what Traditional Chinese Medicine states about the constitution of the Yang meridians. They are more robust than the Yin meridians, which means that they can handle more abuse from an energetic standpoint.

The table also clearly illustrates that the Yin associated organs have only ten intersection points that directly connect to the Extraordinary Vessels. This is in comparison to the thirty-three intersections of the Yang meridians. The Spleen Meridian has three intersecting points. The Kidney Meridian has the most with five intersection points. The Liver Meridian has only two intersection points. The Lung Meridian, which is associated with the Metal Element, has no direct intersection points with the Extraordinary Vessels. Likewise, the Heart and the Pericardium Meridians, both of which are associated with the element of Fire, and do not have any direct intersection points with the Extraordinary Vessels.

It can be determined through a simple process of elimination that the most energetically sensitive organs of the body are the Heart and Lungs. The Pericardium is linked to the function of the heart and is basically considered as an extension of that organ. Referring to the Table 13-3, it is obvious that the Lung Meridian does not have a direct link to the Extraordinary Vessels, but that adjustments are made to its energetic level through the associated Large Intestine Meridian. That meridian shares only three intersection points with the Extraordinary Vessels and aids in the adjustment of the Lung Meridian at a much slower rate than the organs associated with Water, Earth, and Wood. Those meridians, and their associated organs, can be adjusted rapidly in comparison to the meridians that are associated with Metal and Fire. The Lung Meridian also draws energy from the air that we breathe. The Chinese called this "air qi" and when the heart is beating, and there is no obstruction, there is ample supply of "air qi" available to the body. Constant and fast tweaking of the energy level of the Lung Meridian is therefor not required. Any tweaking that is required is through the associated Yang Metal meridian, which is the Large Intestine Meridian.[5]

The Pericardium Meridian does not share any intersection points with the Extraordinary Vessels. It is adjusted through the Triple Warmer Meridian at TW-13 and 15. Likewise, the Heart Meridian does not share any intersection points with the Extraordinary Vessels. It is adjusted through the Small Intestine Meridian, which is the coupled Yang aspect of the Fire element.

Now consider that all the above mentioned points are <u>bilateral</u>. That means that they occur on both sides of the body. The numbers of exchange points between the Extraordinary Vessels and the twelve Main Meridians is represented in the following table.

EARTH		METAL		WATER		WOOD		FIRE			
Yin	Yang	Yin	Yang	Yin	Yang	Yin	Yang	Yin		Yang	
SP	ST	LU	LI	KI	BL	LV	GB	HT	PC	SI	TW
6	14	0	6	10	12	4	28	0	0	2	4

Table 13-4: *Bilateral examination of intersection points between the Extraordinary Vessels and the twelve Main Meridians.*

This illustrates that the twelve Main Meridians have numerous intersection points with the Extraordinary Vessels. This is considering that the twelve Main Meridians are bilateral. The sheer number of potential targets to "seal the energy" in specific elemental associated meridians is staggering. It is also an indicator of which of the associated elemental energy meridians are the most likely targets from a martial perspective. It can be determined that certain elements are more prone to energetic disruption by developing a probability model. In this model we are looking for the least number of possible points that can connect to the Extraordinary Vessels. Those meridians with the least numbers have the highest value from a martial perspective. The Extraordinary Vessels connect with the twelve Main Meridians at eighty-six points on the human body. This is the total of the points in Table 13-4. Thirty-seven percent of those points are associated with the Wood element, which consists of the Liver and Gall Bladder Meridians. Twenty-five percent are associated with the Wate element, which are the Kidney and Bladder points. Twenty-three percent are associated with the Earth element, which consists of the Spleen and Stomach points. That leaves the Metal and Fire associated points which each having seven percent. This is represented in Table 13-5 with further breakdown into their polarity.

---

[5] Yang, *Muscle/Tendon Changing & Marrow/Brain Washing Chi Kung*, p. 191.

Element	Polarity	Meridian	Total Points With EV	% of 86
EARTH	YIN	SP	6	7%
	YANG	ST	14	16%
METAL	YIN	LU	0	0%
	YANG	LI	6	7%
WATER	YIN	KI	10	12%
	YANG	BL	12	14%
WOOD	YIN	LV	4	5%
	YANG	GB	28	32%
FIRE	YIN	HT	0	0%
	YANG	SI	2	2%
	YIN	PC	0	0%
	YANG	TW	4	5%

Table 13-5: *Percentage of Extraordinary/Main Meridian points by element and polarity.*

This is further broken down into a clearer illustration of Yin points to Yang Points. The results should indicate which of the targets have the least ability of correcting energetic imbalances.

Element	Polarity	Meridian	Total Points with EV	% of 86	% by Polarity	% within polarity
EARTH	YIN	SP	6	7%	24%	30%
	YANG	ST	14	16%	76%	21%
METAL	YIN	LU	0	0%	24%	0%
	YANG	LI	6	7%	76%	9%
WATER	YIN	KI	10	12%	24%	50%
	YANG	BL	12	14%	76%	18%
WOOD	YIN	LV	4	5%	24%	20%
	YANG	GB	28	32%	76%	43%
FIRE	YIN	HT	0	0%	24%	0%
	YANG	SI	2	2%	76%	3%
	YIN	PC	0	0%	24%	0%
	YANG	TW	4	5%	76%	6%

Table 13-6: *Percentage of Extraordinary/Main Meridian points by polarity.*

Table 13-6 clearly shows that the more sensitive Yin associated organs are not as capable as the Yang associated organs in being corrected for energetic imbalances. Roughly seventy-six percent of all points of Extraordinary Vessels connect with the Main Meridians are associated with Yang organs. This leaves just twenty-four percent that connect to the more sensitive Yin associated organs. Within the Yin associated organs the Kidney meridian connects with fifty percent of all Yin associated points. The Spleen meridian connects with thirty percent of all Yin associated points. The Liver meridian connects with twenty percent of all Yin associated points. That leaves the Lung, Heart and Pericardium meridians with NO direct connections to the Extraordinary Vessels. That deserves repeating. The Lung, Heart and Pericardium meridians DO NOT have any direct connections with the Extraordinary Vessels. These three meridians are most susceptible to energetic disruptions from a probability standpoint. That is of great importance to the combative martial artist.[6]

The Primary Target

From analyzing the preceding information it should be apparent that the Heart Meridian is the primary target from an energetic standpoint. This holds true from the Western perspective as well, but as martial artists we generally do no think of attacking the heart. Western anatomy states the heart is the most protected of the organs. It is located with the safety of the ribcage, which protects it from even forceful strikes. Western medical science has conditioned us, as Westerners, to think that the heart can only be attacked by directly striking the chest area that it is situated under. As noted earlier, it is possible to disrupt the beating of the heart by forceful strikes to centerline of the body at CV-17. Additionally, the structure of the ribcage can be broken from extremely forceful strikes and the possibility exists that bone splinters could penetrate the heart muscle, or supporting arteries and veins, causing death. Given the protected location of the heart it is extremely difficult to achieve that type of result from attacks aimed at its physical location.

Traditional Chinese Medicine views the heart in a different manner than Western medical science. The Chinese classic *Su Wen* states: "The Heart is the basis of life" because it was believed that the Heart affects all the other organs. Likewise, all the other organs affect the Heart, but it is better protected from extreme energetic imbalances that can occur in the other organs of the body. The Pericardium is considered as the "Protector of the Heart" to the Chinese.

---

[6] It should be noted that the Conception and Governing Vessel do have direct contact with the majority of the Main Meridians, but those contacts play a secondary role in adjusting energetic imbalances to the associated organs and bowels. Even the Conception and Governing Vessel do not connect directly to the Lung, Heart and Pericardium Meridians. The Alarm Points for the Pericardium and Heart are on the Conception Vessel, but these points are more of a diagnostic nature and do not reflect a point in which energetic exchange occurs.

When the Pericardium and Heart are combined they comprise a complete functional unit rather than two separate entities. The Pericardium has the function of shielding the Heart from major energetic fluctuations and imbalances. Just as the heart is anatomically the best protected of the organs, it is also the best protected energetically. Dr. Yang Jwing-Ming, a noted martial artist and author, has stated that the Heart and Pericardium are the two most vital organs of the body. Because of their importance their energy levels must be extremely accurate in comparison to the other organs.[7] His conclusions help to validate the information presented in this book. Yang Jwing-Ming also states that if the Heart and Pericardium were directly connected to the Main Meridians it would be possible for excessive *qi* to flood into them when the body is reacting from an emergency. A "flood" of energy could cause a serious malfunction in those two vital organs. The late Erle Montaigue emphasized the importance of the Heart meridian in Dim-Mak techniques. He has stated that most Dim-Mak strikes affect the heart in a manner that weakens the body.[8] The term "weakens" should not be thought of as making things energetically deficient. Think of it as causing energetic imbalances to the body.

The information presented thus far indicates that the Heart is the primary target from an energetic standpoint. The next question to answer is what energetic state is the Heart most susceptible to attack from a combative viewpoint? Is it better to attack the heart when it is deficient of energy or when it is in excess? To answer this we will need to examine what we learned about Elemental Body Types. Additionally, we will need to examine what we have learned about Body Alarm Reaction. By combining the information, which was presented earlier, on those subjects we are able to solve the deficient/excess question.

One Body Type

We discussed the five basic Body Types that are associated with the Five Element Theory of Traditional Chinese Medicine in Chapter 9. Examples were given of the characteristics that make up each of the different variations. Wood types are associated with a tall, lanky basketball player. Earth types are associated with more stocky football players. Metal types are associated with marathon runners. Fire types are associated with balding, quick-tempered individuals. Water types are associated with soft, sometimes fat, businessmen. Now go to a public place

---

[7] Jwing-Ming Yang, *Muscle/Tendon Changing & Marrow/Brain Washing Chi Kung*, p. 191.
[8] Montaigue, *Advanced Dim-Mak*, p. 114.

and observe all the people that are walking around. I have done this exercise many times in the past at malls, sporting events, etc. You will pick out individuals that exhibit specific characteristics that are associated with each of the elemental body types. Additionally, you will observe many, the majority in fact, that are predominately one elemental type, but exhibit strong characteristics of another element. Earth types that show signs of the Fire element. Wood types that exhibit signs of the Metal element. It goes on and on in every conceivable combination that you can imagine. After a while you will ask yourself, "How in the world can I expect to keep so much information in my head and effectively be able to defend against all of them." You don't. Let's take a look at a simplified model of each of the basic elemental body types. The ">" character will indicate that that element energy is in abundance. The character ">>" will indicate an energy element that is in excess. The "<" character will indicate that it is deficient. The character "<<" will represent an energy element that is in a highly deficient state. The "-" character will represent a neutral position.

WOOD BODY TYPE				
EARTH	**METAL**	**WATER**	**WOOD**	**FIRE**
-	<	>	>>	>

Table 13-7: *Wood Body Type Energetic Values.*

Table 13-7 illustrates the basic energetic qualities of a Wood Element Body Type individual. The meridians that are associated with the element of Water, which are the Kidney and Bladder meridians will be in slight excess. This will cause excess in the Wood associated meridians, which are the Liver and Gall Bladder meridians. The Water associated meridians are those that "feed" the Wood meridians. Take notice of the Five Element Cycle of Creation for reference. Considering that the Wood element meridians nourish the Fire meridians they (Fire associated meridians) can be slightly evaluated or neutral. The Earth associated meridians will be in a neutral state in comparison to the other elements. The Metal associated meridians will be in a deficient state. This is because they are responsible in controlling the energetic levels of the Wood meridians. Referred to the Five Element Cycle of Control for details on this process. The Metal meridians are low of energy and can not control the Wood meridians properly. This will cause excess in the Wood meridians during the development of the body at the fetal stage. The result is a Wood Element Body Type.

FIRE BODY TYPE				
EARTH	METAL	WATER	WOOD	FIRE
>	-	<	>	>>

Table 13-8: *Fire Body Type Energetic Values.*

Table 13-8 illustrates the basic energetic qualities of a Fire Element Body Type individual. The meridians that are associated with the element of Wood, which are the Liver and Gall Bladder meridians, will be in a slight excess. This is due to their giving energy to the Fire meridians during the Five Element Cycle of Creation. The Wood meridians are basically over-feeding the Fire meridians and causing them to be in an excessive state. The excessive energy in the Fire meridians spills over into the Earth meridians as the energy continues to flow according to the Cycle of Creation. The Metal meridians are neutral in comparison to the other elements. The Water meridians will have to be in a deficient state according to the laws that govern the Cycle of Control. The result is a Fire Element Body Type individual.

EARTH BODY TYPE				
EARTH	METAL	WATER	WOOD	FIRE
>>	>	-	<	>

Table 13-9: *Earth Body Type Energetic Values.*

Table 13-9 illustrates the basic energetic qualities of an Earth Element Body Type individual. The meridians that are associated with the element of Fire, which are the Heart, Small Intestine, Pericardium, and Triple Warmer meridians, will be in slight excess. This is because of their position in the Cycle of Creation. They are over-feeding the Earth meridians and causing the excessive state. The Wood meridians are responsible for controlling the energy level of the Earth meridians. Take notice of the Cycle of Control for details. They have to be deficient since they are not controlling the energy levels of the Earth meridians. The Water meridians are neutral in comparison to the other elements. This is the basic energetic state of an Earth Element Body Type individual.

METAL BODY TYPE				
EARTH	METAL	WATER	WOOD	FIRE
>	>>	>	-	<

Table 13-10: *Metal Body Type Energetic Values.*

Table 13-10 illustrates the basic energetic qualities of a Metal Element Body Type individual. The meridians that are associated with the element of Earth will be in slight excess since they are those that "feed" the Metal meridians. This is according to the Cycle of Creation. The excess energy of the Metal meridians will "spill" over into the Water meridians and cause slight excess in them. The Water meridians are fed by the Metal meridians in the Cycle of Creation. The Wood meridians will be neutral in comparison with the other elements. The Fire meridians will be in a deficient state due to the fact that they are not controlling the Metal meridians. The result is a Metal Element Body Type individual.

WATER BODY TYPE				
EARTH	METAL	WATER	WOOD	FIRE
<	>	>>	>	-

Table 13-11: *Water Body Type Energetic Values.*

Table 13-11 illustrates the basic energetic qualities of a Water Element Body Type individual. The Metal meridians will be in slight excess. This is due to their position in the Cycle of Creation. They are responsible for feeding energy to the Water meridians. The excessive state of the Water meridians will "spill" over into the Wood meridians, which are fed by them in the Cycle of Creation. The Fire meridians will be neutral in comparison of the other elements. The Earth meridians will be in a deficient state due to the fact that they are not controlling the Water meridians properly. This is in accordance with the Cycle of Control. The result is a Water Element Body Type individual.

Now add in all the various combinations of elemental body traits that you can think. What are the basic energetic qualities of a predominately Earth body type that has strong characteristics of Metal? What are the energetic qualities of a predominately Wood body type that exhibits additional characteristics that are associated with Fire? The possibilities are endless and preclude the martial artist from being able to effectively utilize this information in a combative sense. There are too many possible combinations to remember and too many energetic states that could be attacked. It is maddening!

The key to understanding how this knowledge can be utilized is in the information that was presented on Body Alarm Reaction in Chapter 12. Remember that Body Alarm Reaction not only has effect on you — it has the same effect on your opponent. Your opponent will go through the same automatic energetic changes during an aggressive encounter. They can not help it anymore than you can. The automatic responses that are associated with Body Alarm

Reaction are common to all human beings. It is the human reaction to potential harm that drives this automatic response and no one is immune, which includes aggressive opponents. We will now show a table of the basic energetics that occurs during Body Alarm Reaction. The same key will be used as in the above tables on the five Elemental Body Types.

Body Alarm Reaction				
EARTH	METAL	WATER	WOOD	FIRE
<<	>>	<<	<<	>>

Table 13-12: *The energetic qualities of Body Alarm Reaction.*

Table 13-12 illustrates the energetic reactions that occur during Body Alarm Reaction. First, let us look at the energetic implications of an increase in blood pressure and heart rate. As the body recognizes a potential threat it starts to descend into Body Alarm Reaction. The Heart meridian is given a "jolt" of extra energy that elevates the normal energy level of that organ. That extra "jolt" of energy comes from the Extraordinary Vessel Subsystem, specifically the "Human Battery." The extra energy that the Heart receives causes it to increase in the rate of pumping and level of blood pressure. There is also an increase in the respiratory rate as extra energy is pumped into the Lung Meridian. As defensive qi, or energy, is pumped through the body there is an increase in muscular tension and a slow down of the rate that the capillaries are feeding the skin. Selye observed that the digestive organs decrease in function. This marks the energetic system decreasing the energy to the Large Intestine, Bladder, Kidney, Liver, Gall Bladder, Stomach, Spleen, and Small Intestine Meridians. Considering that the organs and bowels are given Elemental qualities we can examine the effects of Body Alarm Reaction from that model. We can observe that there is an increase in the Fire and Metal associated meridians and decreases in the Wood, Water, and Earth meridians. The energy levels are excessive in comparison to the normal state of an individual. This is necessary because of the rapid manner that the various functions are needed at the time that Body Alarm Reaction occurs.

The next table will illustrate what happens to the basic energetic qualities of the five Elemental Body Types. The same key will apply to this table as that used in the previous ones.

Body Alarm Reaction Applied to Elemental Body Types					
	EARTH	METAL	WATER	WOOD	FIRE
BAR Body Alarm Reaction	<<	>>	<<	<<	>>
EARTH	>>	>	-	<	>
Earth in BAR	-	>>>	<<	<<<	>>>
METAL	>	>>	>	-	<
Metal in BAR	<	>>>>	<	<<	>>
WATER	<	>	>>	>	-
Water in BAR	<<<	>>>	-	<	>>
WOOD	-	<	>	>>	>
Wood in BAR	<<	>	<	-	>>>
FIRE	>	-	<	>	>>
Fire in BAR	<	>>	<<<	<	>>>>

Table 13-13: *Energetic Qualities of Body Alarm Reaction (BAR) applied to the Basic Energetic Qualities of the Five Elemental Body Types.*

Table 13-13 is a little confusing. It shows how the energetic qualities of Body Alarm Reaction affect the normal energetic states of the Five Elemental Body Types. The basic energetic state of an Earth body type is given, which is excess in the Earth meridians, abundance in the Metal meridians, neutral in the Water meridians, deficiency in the Wood meridians, and abundance in the Fire meridians. (This is shown in Table 13-9) The energetic response that occurs during Body Alarm Reaction is added to the normal energy state of the Earth Body Type. The results are that the Earth meridians drop to a neutral state; Metal meridians climb to an extreme excess; Water meridians drop to a highly deficient state; Wood meridians drop to an even higher level of deficiency; and Fire meridians climb to an extremely excessive state. The same method is utilized for each of the other Elemental Body Types. The next table is added for clarification. It will illustrate the altered energetic qualities of the five Elemental Body Types during Body Alarm Reaction.

Energetic Changes of the Five Elemental Body Types during BAR					
	EARTH	METAL	WATER	WOOD	FIRE
EARTH	-	>>>	<<	<<<	>>>
METAL	<	>>>>	<	<<	>>
WATER	<<<	>>>	-	<	>>
WOOD	<<	>	<	-	>>>
FIRE	<	>>	<<<	<	>>>>

Table 13-14: *The Basic Energetic Qualities of the Five Elemental Body Types after application of Body Alarm Reaction.*

Table 13-14 illustrates that all five of the Elemental Body Types have underwent a radical shift in their energetic states due to the effects of Body Alarm Reaction. The Wood Body Type is now in an energetic state in which the Wood meridians are in a neutral state. This is counter to its normal state of excess, which was balanced out by the flooding of energy from the Wood meridians during Body Alarm Reaction. The Wood type will be in a deficient mode in the Earth and Water meridians due to the same reactions. The Metal meridians will be elevated, as will be the Fire meridians, which are extremely excessive. By examining the table it can be determined that ALL of the elemental body types will be neutral, deficient, to extremely deficient, in the Earth, Water, and Wood meridians during Body Alarm Reaction. Likewise, ALL of the elemental body types will be excessive, to extremely excessive, in the Metal and Fire meridians.

From this interpretation we can now theorize the energetic state of ANY opponent that we might face when considering the energetic effects of Body Alarm Reaction. That opponent will be in a deficient state of energy in the Earth, Water, and Wood meridians. They will be in an excessive, to extremely excessive, state in the Metal and Fire meridians. Table 13-15 illustrates that opponent.

Opponent Energetic State				
EARTH	METAL	WATER	WOOD	FIRE
<<	>>>	<<	<<	>>>

Table 13-15: *The Basic Energetic Qualities of ANY Opponent.*

The extremely confusing energetic qualities of the Five Elemental Body Types, and their numerous possible combinations, can now be discarded. By the application of the energetic qualities of Body Alarm Reaction we establish an energetic state that can be utilized in a combative sense. When a martial artist faces an aggressive opponent they do not have to remember anything concerning the Five Elemental Body Types. There is only one energetic state when faced with a combative situation. That is an opponent who is in a deficient state in the Wood, Water, and Earth meridians and an excessive energetic state in the Metal and Fire meridians.

Deficient or Excessive?

The question of attacking the Heart in a deficient or excessive state is now solved. The information presented on the energetic qualities of the Elemental Body Types and the effects of Body Alarm Reaction to those five basic constitutions solved the last unanswered question. It is obvious that the Fire associated meridians, which include the Heart, is to be attacked while it is in an excessive state of energy. Think about the implications of attacking the lungs while they are in an excessive state. What will it produce? If the Lungs are working excessively then they will be rapidly drawing in oxygen. By attacking them in a manner that accelerates that function they simply draw in additional oxygen. Energetic problems with the lungs are when they are in a deficient state. Human beings have serious health problems when the lungs are not able to draw the correct levels of oxygen needed for proper function of the body. That is indicative of a deficient energetic state. The lungs are a two-part organ with one on each side of the body. The possibility of "blowing out" a lung, or both of them, is very low. The heart is a singular organ. It does not have a counterpart that can continue operating in the event that one is damaged or shut down. That makes the heart the prime target from an energetic standpoint. Additionally, the fact that organs should be attacked in an excessive energetic state is substantiated by the information in the original *Bubishi*. What the *Bubishi* did not state was why you are driven to attack the organs while they are in this state. It only gives some examples of methods. The information presented in this book explains why. The only question that remains is HOW do you attack the Heart from an energetic standpoint? That will be covered in the next chapter.

## Chapter 14

SEALING THE QI

"The imperatives of war demand deadly, effective, pre-emptive action."
Peter Consterdine

We have established that the Fire meridians, which include the Heart, Small Intestine, Pericardium, and Triple Warmer meridians are the most vulnerable to martial attack. The information and research that has been presented should validate the Fire meridians as the Primary Energetic Targets of the body from a combative viewpoint. There are numerous other tidbits of martial science that can be derived from the information. The knowledge of understanding which of the elemental energies are deficient or excessive during a combative situation allows the martial artist to tailor their self-defense techniques to gain the best response. If you have been applying Traditional Chinese Medicine to your individual style, then you have already been doing this procedure. Examination of the various techniques of your style, through that Eastern perspective, has opened the proverbial door to an increase in the overall effectiveness of your techniques. Knowing that initial strikes to the arms, while an opponent is punching for instance, will "activate" the Gall Bladder meridian for follow-up attacks. This example follows the Cycle of Control by first attacking the Fire and Metal meridians of the arms and then attacking the Wood meridians for a quick follow-up strike. By disrupting the energy flow of three elements, the Fire, Metal, and Wood energies in this example, of the Cycle of Control you are able to drop most opponents fairly easily.

The understanding what is gained by the detailed examination of the Extraordinary Vessels states that strikes to the inner aspects of the arms (the Yin surfaces) should be with the flow of energy. (See photo on p. 160) This will contribute to the already excessive state of the Metal and Fire meridians, which have increased due to the automatic responses of Body Alarm Reaction. Likewise, strikes to the outer aspects of the arms (the Yang surfaces) should be against the flow of energy. (See photo on p. 160) This will further drive them into a greater excessive state. You are simply starting with a temporary energy imbalance and adding to it. You are not attempting to reverse any of the energetic states that your opponent is already exhibiting. You are instead working with what has been given you and amplifying that condition. By following this simple rule you will increase the excessive state of the Fire and Metal meridians, which are already at an extremely high level, and decrease the deficient state the Wood, Water, and Earth meridians.

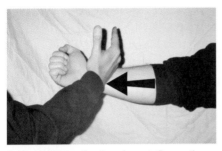

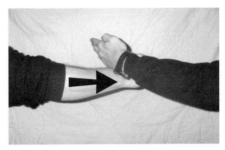

Striking WITH the direction of energy flow on the inner forearm

Striking AGAINST the direction of energy flow on the outer forearm.

Knowing the location of the points that the Extraordinary Vessels intersect with the Fire meridians is the next step in understanding how to attack the fire element. We know that the following are the intersection points of those two paired meridians.

Intersection Points for the Fire Meridians			
HEART	**SMALL INTESTINES**	**PERICARDIUM**	**TRIPLE WARMER**
No	SI-10 x 2	No	TW-13 x 2
Points		Points	TW-15 x 2

Table 14-1: *Intersection Points of the Fire Meridians and the Extraordinary Vessels.*

Table 14-1 shows that the Heart meridian does not have any direct connection points with the Extraordinary Vessels. Nor does the Pericardium meridian, which is closely associated with the heart. Because of the sensitivity of the Yin related Heart and Pericardium, the body makes delicate energy adjustments through their respective coupled organs. Those are the Small Intestine and Triple Warmer meridians. The three intersection points (SI-10, TW-13, and TW-15) are all located on the Yang Linking Vessel of the Extraordinary Vessel Subsystem. Energy imbalances to the Pericardium are made through the Triple Warmer meridian. Because the Pericardium and Triple Warmer are linked together at the internal aspects of their trajectories, energy that is found in the Triple Warmer can be transferred to the Pericardium. This allows for the Extraordinary Vessels, through the Yang Linking Vessels, to make adjustments to the Pericardium. Those energy adjustments are small in comparison to directly connected organs and are indicative of the delicate nature of the Pericardium. The Small Intestine meridian is responsible for correcting energy imbalances to the Heart in the same manner, but rather than intersecting the Yang Linking Vessels at two points (as does the Triple Warmer) it only has one connection at SI-10. Energy adjustments from the Extraordinary Vessels, through the Yang Linking Vessels, enter the Heart/Small Intestine coupled meridians at that intersecting point. The Heart is more sensitive to energy fluctuations than any other organ of the body and this lone connection, to the Yang Linking Vessels, allows for those delicate adjustments. Compare the number of intersection points with the Extraordinary Vessels and the Gall Bladder. The Gall Bladder meridian has fourteen intersection points that allow for rapid energy adjustments. The Liver meridian, which is the yin aspect of the Wood element and coupled with the Gall Bladder, has two intersection points. This is a total of sixteen points that allow for rapid energetic adjustment of the Wood associated Gall Bladder and Liver meridians.

Now consider that all of these points are bilateral. They occur on both sides of the body. There are one on the right side and one on the left side of the body. This further complicates things for the martial artist. If they want to shut off the ability of the Extraordinary Vessels to correct energy imbalances in the Fire meridians then they will have to strike a total of six points to accomplish that task. Or will they?

All the intersection points of the Fire meridians are with the Yang Linking Vessel. That vessel runs the entire length of the body from BL-63 on the foot to GB-20 on the back of the head. This trajectory runs on both the right and left side of the body, but at GB-20 the vessel connects to points 15 and 16 on the Governing Vessel. Those two points are the intersection points between the Yang Linking Vessels and the Governing Vessel. The Governing Vessel runs on the centerline of the body and GV-15 and 16 are critical to the ability of the "Human Battery" in connecting with the Yang associated meridians. That is accomplished through the Yang Linking Vessel. GV-15 and 16 are located within one inch of each other on the back of the head, at the base of the hairline. By striking this point, the ability of the Extraordinary Vessels to correct energetic imbalances of the Yang associated meridians are severed.

What does this mean exactly? It means that a forceful strike or series of strikes, which are aimed at GV-15 and 16, will greatly hinder, or even completely stop, the ability of the body to correct energetic imbalances to the heart.

This concept is referred to as "sealing the *qi*"[1] or "sealing the energy." Remember that in a combative situation that your opponent's body will be in an energetic state in which the Fire and Metal meridians will be in great excess. The Wood, Water, and Earth meridians will be energetically in a highly deficient state during such an encounter. During the encounter you attack the Main Meridians in a manner that accentuates those imbalances. This is through your initial entering technique to the strike that places your opponent in a position where strikes to GV-15 and 16 are possible. Your finishing strike or strikes are focused on those two points, which are no more than one half of an inch from each other. It is a great possibility that the excessive energy of the heart, which can not be corrected by the Extraordinary Vessels after your finishing strike, will result in a heart attack. Think of it this way. Because of the automatic responses of Body Alarm Reaction, the Heart meridian is "flooded" with extra energy by the Extraordinary Vessels. That extra energy places in the Heart meridian in an excessive state. Martial techniques are executed that contribute to this already excessive state. The heart will be overwhelmed with extra energy. It will be beating at a much greater than normal rate. To correct this excessive state the body would normally utilize the connection points of GV-15 and 16 to "pipe out" or "draw off" the excessive energy that is present in the Heart meridian. By striking GV-15 and 16, repeatedly if possible, the connection is disrupted to the point that this can not occur. The result is that the heart is in a major excessive state and it can not correct the imbalance. That can result in arrhythmia. This is the worst possible energetic attack to the delicate Yin associated Heart Meridian. It is the worst possible energetic attack period. The Heart is the most delicate and important organ of the body to energetic fluctuations. Where are no other energetic attacks that have this much of a negative effect on the body. The results of this type of attack are extremely serious and should only be used in life-or-death situations!

There are numerous methods of attack that can be utilized that will enable finishing blows to GV-15 and 16. Even standard pressure point techniques that effect the twelve Main Meridians can produce a Yin response in your opponent. Remember that a Yin response is simply the position in which your opponents shoulder roll forward. This puts them into either a crouched or semi-standing fetal-like position. A finishing blow to GV-15 and 16 will have a lethal effective on your opponent. Compared to a strike to GB-20, which is a favorite knockout point for pressure point fighters, such a blow should be reversed for life-and-

---

[1] Moneymaker, *Torite-Jutsu Reference Manual*, p. 81.

death situations. Study the various self-defense applications of your specific martial system and you will find numerous techniques that can be easily adapted to attacking GV-15 and 16. Your martial abilities will substantially grow now that you understanding that attacks to these "vital points" are lethal.

Additional Sealing Attacks

Combative encounters do not always allow for attacks to the back of the head as finishing strikes. Think about all the numerous possibilities that one might face in a combative situation. Granted, by doing your homework and exploring the possibilities of the various types of attacks you will discover that you can end up in a position that allows strikes to GV-15 and 16 in a number of them. However, there are attacks that place you in the front of your opponent after they have been stunned. Strikes aimed at the intersection point of the Yin Linking Vessel with the "Human Battery" are recommended in those circumstances, which are CV-22 and 23.

Remember what we learned about the Yin Linking Vessels in Chapter 7. We determined that the Yin Linking Vessels are responsible for connecting the Yin associated organs, which are Heart, Lungs, Liver, Kidneys, and Spleen, with the "Human Battery." We were able to determine that due to the delicate nature of the heart and lungs that they were connected to the Extraordinary Vessels through their coupled Yang organs. That leaves the Liver, Kidneys, and Spleen open for energetic attack at the intersection point of the Yin Linking Vessels and the Conception Vessel. The Conception Vessels is the Yin aspect of the "Human Battery" subsystem. The Yin Linking Vessels, which are bilateral, connect to the three remaining Yin meridians at LV-14, SP-13, SP-15, SP-16 and KI-9. Remember that these organs are much better connected to the Extraordinary Vessels than the meridians associated with the Fire and Metal elements. That makes strikes that shut down the Yin Linking Vessels ability to correct energetic imbalances to the Liver, Spleen, and Kidney meridians a secondary target.

The Yin Linking Vessels connect with the Conception Vessel at CV-22 and 23. Like GV-15 and 16 these points are in close physical proximity to one another and forceful strikes to one will usually disrupt both. Strikes to CV-22 and 23 will inhibit the ability of the Extraordinary Vessels to correct the deficient energetic state of these three organs. From a Western anatomy viewpoint, strikes to these points will also attack the windpipe, possibly crushing it, which will cause death in most circumstances. Again, attacks to the Liver, Spleen, and Kidney meridians are secondary to attacks to the Heart.

Conclusion on "Sealing the Qi"

The information that is provided in this chapter is very combative in nature. Only under extreme circumstances, such as life-or-death situations, should techniques that attack these points be utilized in the real world. This information is extremely "martial" and not to be confused with lesser applications of pressure point fighting. Does it work? I can not state that it does with one hundred percent certainty, but consider the following. Do techniques that follow the laws, theories and concepts of Traditional Chinese Medicine work to easily knockout opponents? Yes, if you have ever experienced them or trained with a qualified instructor. Do pressure point techniques allow for easier manipulation of joints and cause the opponent greater pain and discomfort than non-pressure point based techniques? Yes. Do various techniques of Close Combat systems teach attacks to these vulnerable points of the body with the intent of killing their opponent? Yes and strikes to the GV-15/16 and CV-22/23 clusters have killed numerous opponents in unarmed combat. Does the information presented in this book follow the laws, theories and concepts of Traditional Chinese Medicine? Yes. Theoretically, the information that has been presented to the reader works, which is according to all the above stated examples and the information contained within the original *Bubishi*. That ancient document alone indicates that strikes to these points are deadly in a combative situation. Can those that do not understand the thought that it was founded upon dismiss the validity of the accumulated martial knowledge of hundreds of years? They should not, but many do. Those martial artist that have chosen the path of understanding the martial science of Traditional Chinese Medicine will grasp the significance of this research. That group of forward thinking individuals should be considered as the keepers of true martial knowledge, which is not to be confused with the overly commercial belt factory products that are commonplace. Through research and interaction with one another they will usher a new era in the Western martial arts. They will put the "martial" back into the "arts," which is something that has been missing for a long time.

Chapter 15

DEFENSE

"The best defense is a good offense."

Jack Dempsey

The old adage, "The best defense is a good offense," is commonly used in a number of human endeavors ranging from military tactics, business strategy, and in this case, unarmed fighting. This quote is often attributed to Jack Dempsey, the heavyweight boxing champion from 1919 to 1926, but its essence has reverberated through the centuries in one form or the other. This concept can be traced as far back as Sun Tzu (496 BC–544 BC), the revered Chinese military general and tactician. He stated, "Attack is the secret of defense; defense is the planning of an attack." Carl von Clausewitz (1780–1831), author of the classic work, *On War*, stated, "The best form of defense is attack." General George S. Patton, famous for his extreme aggressiveness and ruthless pursuit of his enemy, is quoted as saying, "There is no such thing as a successful defense." What are these great fighters, strategist, and military minds trying to convey to us in their words? On the surface it is quite obvious, but it can become a bit muddied when the concept is applied to real life confrontations.

The flow of techniques are not black and white during a street or combative situation. It is not always as easy as landing your first technique and ending the confrontation immediately. There can be an ebb and flow between offensive oriented techniques and having to utilize defensive ones. Depending on the skill of both combatants this might take several cycles. It is said that you will likely land your first strike on an untrained opponent; it takes two strikes to overcome the vast majority of trained fighters; exceptional fighters will take three or more to be successful defeated. Remember this is not referring to sport fighting, but "your life is on the line" type fighting. In sport fighting you will usually observe long and drawn out exchanges as the fighters utilize strategy and tactics in the controlled environment of the ring. This is much different than being jumped in a dark parking lot or fighting for your life in hand-to-hand combat.

The concept of pure "defense," as we have observed in the quotes earlier, does not lend itself well to favorable outcomes. It is a play on words, as fighting is fighting? Not so much, in my opinion. I view it as understanding the dynamic relationship of fighting technique and having prior training that accounts for the action verses reaction gap. Basically, action is, and always will be, faster than reaction. Thus, the attacker is the one that dictates the fight. They are forcing the encounter with technique after technique that are designed to overcome any defensive techniques initiated by the defender. Much of this exchange, and determining which of the adversaries is victorious, is all a matter of split seconds. That is the gap between action and reaction. That attacker acts; the defender reacts. Military history is saturated with an uneven amount of victorious attackers compared to victorious defenders. It is common to observe the same phenomenon in popular sports, fighting competitions, in the corporate world of big business. The list goes on and on.

So, how do we effectively defend ourselves when we can easily arrive at the conclusion that the defender statistically loses? It is by developing the mentality that once attacked that you immediately counter-attack. That counter-attack has to be ferocious and unrelenting. If someone throws a punch, or otherwise initiates battle with you, putting you, for a split second, on the wrong side of the action versus reaction gap. Your best chance of victory is to deflect, smoother, parry, or otherwise negate their attack and then immediately launch into a vicious counter-attack. Done properly, this forces your adversary into a reactive state, rather than an action one. You turn the table on them and become the aggressor. That is how to effectively conceptualizes being in a defensive situation. Utilizing this method will place you in a greater position to be victorious. Dempsey, Sun Tzu and General Patton would agree.

Humans are very violent animals. As a species, we are capable of high levels of extreme violence. In fact, approaching the subject of unarmed combatives, or any form of combatives, involves the immersion into a field that is inherently violent to the extreme of those extremes. It is one thing to find yourself facing an opponent across a field, or ring, during a sporting match. Those contests still pit skill verses skill, but lack the survival aspects of an unarmed combative encounter. The average person rarely, if ever, ponders any of this and many consider various sporting contests as the apex of human competition. It is not. Finding yourself in a life-or-death struggle against an opponent that is completely intent on ending your life is the greatest of all human competitions. Understanding that and acknowledging that takes some degree of courage in today's society. We have grown accustomed to the ideas of fair play, rules, and good sportsmanship. Those are all wonderful concepts and they each have their place in various forms of competition. So, how would you react in a situation without fair play, rules or sportsmanship? What if someone struck you from behind in the parking lot, knocking you to the pavement in a stunned state, and then continues to strike you repeatedly and there is no referee to intercede? Will this individual's sense of good sportsmanship call on him to stop beating you? What of the rules? Was it fair of him to hit you from behind initially, while you were least expecting to be attacked? Is it fair for him to continue to beat you while you lay defenseless on the ground? They will continue to beat you until *they*, and *they* alone, decide to stop. Remember, there aren't any referees on the street or the battlefield. There are just winners and losers. The winners survive. The losers don't. That is the harsh truth of the universe. So, if you have never given this consideration, please take time to do some serious soul searching and hopefully come to the realization of this truth.

I find myself shaking my head when I hear martial arts instructors tell their students things like, "This is an art of defense," "There is no first strike in this art," or "We honor our opponent." Really? I mean, really? It is as simple as this, if someone is attacking you, intent of causing you physical harm or death, then there is no "honoring" that person. You stop them as quickly and efficiently as possible within the scope of the situation. If you notice them starting to move their shoulder in a way that indicates that are about to launch a punch with that hand, you strike first. When you examine the laws of reaction verses action, and the numerous studies conducted on it, then you should clearly understand that if you are focused on defense, then you are always milliseconds behind your opponent and likely, statistically, you are going to lose. These, too, are laws of the universe and we cannot escape them or wish them away. We live in a society in which there are consequences to our actions, as it should be, and knowing what level of physical response, based on the information known at the time of altercation, is of utmost importance. What level of aggressiveness do you use on an intoxicated patron at a bar that is staggering around and wanting to fight you? What level of aggressiveness do you use on a gang of thugs that have jumped you in a parking lot? I add these two extremes because you are more likely to face one of these examples than find yourself in a life-or-death struggle in a trench on the front lines of a battlefield. Do you understand the Force Continuum that is taught to Law Enforcement Officers? I would suggest that you familiarize yourself with it. Besides being an excellent mental tool to use when faced with potentially violent encounters, it could be invaluable if you ever have to justify your actions to law enforcement or before a judge.

The techniques demonstrated in this book can be very serious when executed. You should have a solid understanding of the law, levels of force needed to mitigate a violent encounter, and most importantly, the moral and ethical foundation of a true warrior. A warrior that has a high level of self-confidence, but isn't arrogant. One that trains their body and their mind for that moment that they might find themselves in a sudden violent encounter. Warriors understand when to hold back the level of their aggression, and likewise, they understand when to unleash it in all its ruthless darkness. Few in today's society walk the true path of a warrior. Most modern warriors are in special operations in the military and within the intelligence community. Others work as overseas contractors. There are some that work in various government agencies, but on the most part average civilians will never be in the role of a true warrior. Can any of us still be thrust into a life-or-death encounter with only our four limbs and, most importantly, our head to survive the situation? Yes, but honestly the odds of being in that kind of situation are extremely low. Given the gravity of such a situation, we should all still train ourselves to be able to increase our chance of surviving. The segment of the population that doesn't train and believes that this type of thing will never happen to them, or their loved ones, falls under the category of those to be protected. Then again, you, as an individual, have the right to turn a blind eye, though morally and ethically wrong to a warrior, in such a situation and let natural selection take its course. I couldn't do that and I'm sure the vast majority of you feel the same way. By examining ourselves and determining that we would not stand by idly while others were attacked, adds additional responsibility and purpose. Our training becomes more serious as we assume the role of the protector of others. It is a noble path, though often lonely and ridiculed, and one of more self-satisfaction than public spotlights. People often ask me why I train. It is really simple. To protect myself, my loved ones and those that cannot protect themselves.

The word *protect* has many associations with the word *defense*. I could easily substitute *defense* for the word *protect* in the reason I train. To *defend* myself, my loved ones and those that cannot *defend* themselves. It still basically carries the same meaning, but there are subtle differences. Defense tends to give the idea of "non-offense" which has been determined through countless real-world encounters to be statistically less effective than assuming an extremely aggressive course with attacked. Words are important in how we think about certain concepts and this is a perfect example. It may seem silly, but start substituting *protect* for the word *defend*. Think of a mother wolf that is protecting her young. She will fight to the death to protect them from harm. That is the level of protection that you should have in your own mind in regards to your loved ones, the weak, and yourself.

This book contains numerous techniques that can cause a fair amount of bodily damage, some even death, if they are performed on another human being. The question on how to defend against these attacks has emerged since I first published this material back in 2003. Not to sound flippant, but I rely on the time proven adage outlined at the beginning of this chapter; the best defense is a good offense. This is a pressure tested concept that has been proven thousands of times in violent encounters all over the world. If someone is attacking you, regardless of what technique they are attacking with, the highest probability of winning that encounter is to immediately attack that person with everything you've got. Kicks, knees, elbow strikes, open palm strikes, chops, punches, etc., thrown rapidly and with as much power you can generate. The key to this kind of defensive theory is that once you initiate your counter-attack, you don't stop throwing techniques until your opponent is incapacitated. Some schools call this a "blitz" type of attack, which is borrowed from American football, but regardless of the name, it is a solid, proven method of counter-attacking. Finding yourself in the position of "getting jumped" by one or more thugs, for instance, would be a perfect example of utilizing this kind of counter-attack.

Remember the action verses reaction gap we covered earlier? I suggest you should take some time and do a little research on what is known about this interaction. Action is always faster than reaction. That just makes common sense, doesn't it? So, if you are waiting on your opponent to make the first move out of some archaic martial arts dogma about not striking first, then you are already behind before the fight starts. To win, you must cause your opponent to react rather that act. They must be the one that is a millisecond behind, always attempting to catch up to what is going on. You must become the initiator, but only after you have determined the level of force needed to control the situation. Once you have determined that, and it is very helpful to rehearse various scenarios prior to actually being involved in them, then it is a matter of always causing your opponent to react during that situation. This concept has been pressure tested numerous times, it works and works very effectively.

Some martial artists have an unrealistic view of their abilities. In fact, most adult males have an unrealistic expectation of how they would react in a street fight. Even trained females, many of them having been lied to by their martial arts instructors, have an unrealistic expectation of how they would fair in a street encounter. First off, physical size and strength matter. They matter a lot. Regardless of the level of training, a bigger and stronger opponent statistically wins. They tend to win even against trained martial artist. That should be a wake-up call to the martial arts community, but it unfortunately is not. Most are content with "playing" with the martial arts or considering it as a hobby. I have attempted to empathize with these types and I am unable to get into that frame of mind. Maybe it is just a form of fitness or social interactions that bring them to class. Who knows? If you are currently approaching your training from such a mindset, please take the time to really consider the reason that you train. Are you chasing trophies, collecting belts, or just building your ego? Are you confident in your abilities in the event you faced a bigger, stronger opponent on the street? What if it was a life-or-death situation and you found yourself protecting someone you love and care about? These two examples should be plenty of food for thought. Maybe it is time to redefine what you consider the martial arts.

PART III

Vital Points of the Original Bubishi

## Chapter 16

THE 36 VITAL POINTS

"There are many people who, by being attached to a martial art and taking apprentices, believe that they have arrived at the full stature of a warrior. But it is a regrettable thing to put forth much effort and in the end become an 'ARTIST'."

Yamamoto Tsenetomo
Hagakure, circa 1716

The original translation of the *Bubishi*, which was presented to the West by Patrick McCarthy in 1987, includes thirty-six points that were considered by its author(s) as vital to the martial artist.[1] That document was intended to teach "warrior arts" to those that might face death in unarmed combat.[2] It was designed to pass on knowledge that was designed to kill or disable an opponent. The original *Bubishi* vindicates the importance of the Extraordinary Vessels in accomplishing that task. That classic document makes specific reference to points what are associated with the Extraordinary Vessels. Both the McCarthy and Alexander/Penland versions present a list of 36 Vital Points, which are associated with the martial use of Traditional Chinese Medicine. There are seventeen points that belong to the Extraordinary Vessels in that list.[3] Those are listed in Table 16-1.

Vital Point	Associated Extraordinary Vessel	Vital Point	Associated Extraordinary Vessel
CV-1	Conception, Governing, and Thrusting	GV-22	Governing Vessel
CV-4	Conception Vessel	GV-24	Governing Vessel
CV-15	Conception Vessel	GV-26	Governing Vessel
CV-18	Conception Vessel	BL-62	Yang Heel Vessels
CV-22	Conception and Yin Linking Vessels	LV-13	Girdle Vessel

---

[1] McCarthy's translation is examined in this text. George Alexander and Ken Penland published a translation of the *Bubishi* in 1993. McCarthy's work is considerably better researched and is the focus of the dissection of the 36 Vital Points that are listed in that ancient document. The two translations appear to be from different sources and some of the vital points vary. From McCarthy's research it is obvious that the *Bubishi* was introduced to Okinawa from China. Given that many of the historic karate masters of Okinawa traveled to China for martial training, it is extremely possible that different versions of the *Bubishi* were introduced.

[2] Flane Walker & Richard C. Bauer, *The Ancient Art of Life and Death* (Boulder, CO: Paladin Press, 2002), pp. 13–15.

[3] See the Overview concerning the *Bubishi* vital points that are analyzed in this section.

Vital Point	Associated Extraordinary Vessel	Vital Point	Associated Extraordinary Vessel
CV-24	Conception and Governing Vessels	KI-6	Yin Heel Vessels
GV-1	Governing Vessel	ST-9	Yin Heel Vessels
GV-14	Governing Vessel	ST-12	Yin Heel Vessels
GV-16	Governing and Yang Linking Vessels		

Table 16-1: *Extraordinary Vessels points found in the original Bubishi.*

That is roughly forty percent of the 36 Vital Points that are listed in the *Bubishi*.[4] This should indicate the importance of understanding the function of this energetic subsystem to the inquisitive martial artist. Additionally, by breaking down the Non-Extraordinary Vessel points in their Five Element associations more insight can be obtained. Table 16-2 illustrates the Elemental comparison of the non-Extraordinary Vessel Points. It shows that out of the remaining points that thirty-four percent of them are associated with the Fire and Metal elements. Those elemental associations have figured into the information presented in this text.

EARTH	METAL	WATER	WOOD	FIRE
ST-9	LU-3	KI-6	LV-3	HT-1
ST-12	LU-8	BL-40	LV-4	HT-5
	LI-10	BL-43	LV-11	SI-16
		BL-51	LV-13	TW-2
		BL-62	GB-3	TW-17
			GB-24	
			GB-31	

Table 16-2: *Elemental breakdown of the Non-Extraordinary Vessel points listed in the original Bubishi.*

Table 16-3 breaks down the above Non-Extraordinary Vessel vital points by their associated Main Meridian. This will indicate some other possible trends for consideration.

ST	SP	HT	SI	BL	KI	PC	TW	GB	LV	LU	LI
ST-9		HT-1	SI-16	BL-40	KI-6		TW-2	GB-3	LV-3	LU-3	LI-10
ST-12	NA	HT-5		BL-43		NA	TW-17	GB-24	LV-4	LU-8	
				BL-51				GB-31	LV-11		
				BL-62					LV-13		

Table 16-3: *Main meridian breakdown of the Non-Extraordinary Vessel points listed in the original Bubishi.*

---

[4] McCarthy, *The Bible of Karate: Bubishi*, p. 114.

It is interesting to note that there are no vital points listed for the Pericardium and Spleen meridians. Interestingly, it was discovered during this research that two of these points are considered as Master Points by Traditional Chinese Medicine. Master points are a set of eight points that are associated with acupuncture treatment of the Extraordinary Vessels. The two points that are confirmed Master points in the above table are BL-62 and KI-6. The Bladder point is associated with treatment of the Yang Heel Vessel. The Kidney point, KI-6, is associated with the treatment of the Yin Heel Vessels. Both of the Heel Vessels play only a minor role with correcting the energetic imbalances of the twelve Main Meridians. They do however play an important role in ensuring that energy is being provided to the legs. They might have been included to represent martial attack points to disrupt the energy of the legs. The Master points will be addressed later in this chapter.

It is unfortunate that the original *Bubishi* did not describe the methods of attacking these thirty-six points. Given the fact that they were listed provides a starting point in determine the martial science that went into these point selections. The information that is provided in this book should help to answer some of those questions. McCarthy also references a book written in 1928 by Jin Yiming, which provides similar information as the *Bubishi*.[5] Jin Yiming was a Chinese internal martial artist and approached the combative arts differently than the Okinawans. The Okinawan arts tend to be described as external or hard styles. The internal style that Jin Yiming practiced is considered a soft style, which can be combatively effective regardless of the implications of the word. *The Secrets of Wudang Boxing* contains 36 Vital Points, but again reflects slightly different points than those that are listed in the Okinawan document. The theme of 36 Vital Points appears to have been common among the early martial artists of China and Okinawa. The fact that *The Secrets of Wudang Boxing* and both English translations of the *Bubishi* contain slightly different points reflects the possibility that various schools taught different points. It is difficult to determine the intent of the author(s), but it is obvious that the acupuncture points of Traditional Chinese Medicine were used as the base. All of the documents contain numerous Extraordinary Vessel points and I chose to examine the function of that energetic subsystem to determine any martial applications that might prove valid. McCarthy's excellent translation was chosen for intense examination due to the clarity that they were presented.

Western pressure point practitioners refer to some of the vital points as

---

[5] Ibid., pp. 129–134.

"latch points." They indicates the points that are located around the wrist of either hand. Those are LU-8 and HT-5 out of the above listed original *Bubishi* points. In various techniques it is possible to grasp the arm of your opponent. This can be from the elbow region down to the point that the lower forearm meets the hand. When you slid your hand down the forearm in the direction of your opponent's hand there is a natural point that your hand will stop. At that location you dig your fingers into the wrist of your opponent and subsequently "latch" on to their arm points. Your fingers will activate points LU-8 and HT-5 if you are to the outside of your opponent's attacking arm when this is executed. Additional points are activated in this technique (SI-5, SI-6, TW-4, LI-5, HT-4, HT-6, HT-7, LU-7, LU-9, and PC-7) which do not reflect in the *Bubishi*, but are a matter of fact in the execution. Numerous kata have techniques where the hand returns to your hip in what many schools refer to as "chambering." This technique will throw your opponent off balance as their hand is yanked to your hip. The energetic value of shutting down the energy flow to the attacking hand will cause it to weaken. It also activates the Fire and Metal meridians, which opens the Wood meridian for attack. It also places your opponent in a very bad position to launch counters when executed properly. Follow-up techniques can easily attack any of the Gall Bladder points for either knocking your opponent out or dropping them to the ground. If the goal is to kill or otherwise disable the opponent your finishing strikes should be aimed at GV-15 and 16. That is in accordance with the information provided in this text.

The application of techniques to the 36 Vital Points is indicative of Pareto's 80-20 Law. This law is a statistical relationship that has been observed in numerous larger sized systems. Those systems can be any large system such as business models or trends within a population. If it is applied to martial science it implies that twenty percent of the techniques produce eighty percent of results. It can also imply that twenty percent of acupuncture points produce eighty percent of effective martial attacks. Pareto's Law is a useful concept for the martial artist. It allows them to analyze their techniques from a statistical viewpoint to determine which of them should be the core of their training.[6] The author(s) of the *Bubishi* listed the points that they considered vital from a combative viewpoint. They did the homework and the field-testing and gave the answer. It is up to us to determine the manner that the listed points are to be attacked.

An examination of the thirty-six points that were listed in the original *Bubishi* follows. Seventeen of the points have already been listed in Part I of this book.

---

[6] Rick Clark, *Pressure Point Fighting* (Boston: Tuttle Publishing, 2001), pp. 16–18.

They are the points listed in Table 16-1. Descriptions and commentary of those points have been added to this section and may contain redundant information.

36 Vital Point Descriptions

GV-22 Being one of several Vital Points that are located on the centerline of the skull, GV-22 has great effect when stuck and causes a shockwave of energetic exchange through the brain. GV-22 is located approximately 4 inches past the front hairline, or the theoretical hairline for those that are balding, on the centerline of the head. An important point to consider is that striking the human skull is similar to striking a bowling ball. It is structurally and inherently very hard in order to protect the brain and consideration must be given in the manner and method it is struck to avoid injuring your own hand. It takes an extremely forceful blow to transfer enough force to produce a shockwave through the brain. Developmental training methods like striking the *makiwara*, a traditional Okinawan training device where the practitioner throws forceful strikes onto a standing wooden post, is an excellent method to develop the hands for strikes to such hard surfaces as the skull. Many trained fighters will lower their chin during a fight and this assists in moving GV-22 into a prime location for attack. The strike, when executed, should travel on a line that is on a 90-degree angle in relation to the surface of the skull. Visualize driving a nail into this point with a hammer and you'll get the idea of the proper angle of your strike. From an occidental viewpoint, there are a network of branches of the Superficial Temporal and Frontal Arteries and veins at this point. Additionally, a branch of the Frontal Nerve is also present. Hard strikes can cause damage to these delicate structures and potential of rupturing the associated blood vessels. This would be superficial, as the energetic shockwave that sweeps through the brain would be the most dramatic aspect of the strike. Depending on the amount of force exchanged in the execution it could likely greatly stun, or momentarily disorient, your opponent or induce unconsciousness. The energetic shockwave from a strike would have a dramatic effect of the brain itself, but would also cause a wave of disruption to the "human battery." If the opponent is prone, due to having thrown them for instance, GV-22 would be an excellent point to deliver a forceful kick. Remember that rapid and repeated strikes to the point cause exponential damage to not only the protective structure of the skull, possibly cracking it, but compounds the energetic transfer into an opponent' brain and energetic system. Defensively, guarding your centerline is generally a paramount concern in the vast majority of combative systems.

There are numerous techniques and counters to strikes that are launched toward centerline targets. An examination of your specific fighting method should identify many of them.

GV-24   Another centerline point on the head, GV-24 sets just slightly posterior of the hairline and about three inches more forward to the forehead than GV-22. The largest difference between these two points is that GV-24 is an Intersection Point and GV-22 is not. The Bladder Meridian and the Stomach Meridian intersect with the Governing Vessel at this location. This makes a strike to this point even more disruptive to the overall energetic system of the body. Consider the structure of the human skull and think of the center of the location of the brain. A strike to this point should be at a 45-degree angle towards that center point, which is different than the 90-degree angle strike recommended for GV-22. The slight change in angle allows for different striking methods to be utilized, which is also assisted with the physical point location being closer to the face at the upper forehead region. Opponents that take the lowered chin head position, as do many trained boxers, martial artists, and full-contact competitors, places this point in a vulnerable position. Again, as with GV-22, strikes to this point must be powerful. This region of the skull is one of the hardest parts. Think of how some systems use this area to head-butt, or ram their opponent. So, it tough and light strikes just won't cut it. Strikes to this point require force. A lot of force. One of my favorite techniques to attack this point is a heel of palm strike that is thrown very similar to a standard chopping motion. Mechanically, it allows the strike to be land at the preferred 45-degree angle. Additionally, this type of strike can be trained to issue a tremendous amount of force, which is very much needed, given the hard structural aspects of the skull. A forceful strike to GV-24 causes an energetic shockwave to move through the brain and the 45-degree angle drives the skull into the neck vertebrae. All of which can have a traumatic effect, either stunning or disorienting your opponent, if not producing unconsciousness. Defending against strikes to your centerline are inherent in the majority of martial arts systems and with training should become second nature.

GB-3   This vital point is located near the lower aspects of the temple area of skull, along the Zygomatic Arch, and is directly forward of the ear. It is bilateral, meaning it is found on both sides of the head, which is unlike any of the centerline points that only occur once. It is not directly associated with any of the Extraordinary Vessels, but is an Intersection Point for the Gall Bladder Meridian, Triple Warmer Meridian, and the Stomach Meridian. This makes it valuable to martial artists, since Intersection Points provide the ability to disrupt multiple meridians with a single strike. It makes attacking them economic from a time and motion standpoint. In a standard defense of being grabbed at the waist, with your arms free, slapping the ears forcefully will allow activation of this point with the meaty part of your hand. It is one of several points in this region of the skull and other would likely be activated while striking it given their proximity and size of the surface you are striking with.

EYES   If you asked a non-martial artist what are vital points on the human body, most of them would include the eyes. This is just basic common sense, as the eyes allow us to see our environment and determine any possible threats. If you happen to be struck in the eye it would inhibit your ability to effectively defend yourself. This is as true today as it was at the time that the author(s) were putting together what became the *Bubishi*. Though the eyes are not pressure point per se, these organs are extremely sensitive to attack. Flicking, poking, or thrusting into the eyes directly will greatly inhibit your opponent's ability to see you in a combative situation. In fact, many of the old school Western hand-to-hand instructors of the World War II area were adamant in attacking the eyes. Likewise, it is common place in many martial arts systems, especially the ones that are truly combative and not sport oriented. Quick flicks of the wrist, with the fingertips striking the eyes, is a method that most opponents aren't expecting. Thrusting your fingers into the eyes, either all or singularly, is another effective technique. More extreme is thrusting one finger into the inner corner of the opponent's eye and then jerking forward and to the outside. This technique will dislodge the eye from its socket and should only be used in extreme circumstances. Defending against eye attacks is built into each of us, as we instinctually know their importance. If you recognize an eye attack from your opponent, dropping, raising and/or turning the head will many times save you from eye injury.

EARS   The ears are not generally considered as pressure points, but can be excellent targets in a combative situation. Cup-handed slaps will produce pain and disorientation in an opponent. There are a number of points that are near the ear structure and attacks to the ear will more than likely activate multiple points in that area. Additionally, the ear can be grasped and then ripped off by pulling the top portion of the ear forward and down. It can be attacked with kicks if the opponent is prone at the later stages of an encounter.

TW-17   This bilateral point is an Intersection Point for the Triple Warmer Meridian and the Gall Bladder Meridian and is not associated with or directly connected to any of the Extraordinary Vessels. Anytime there is an Intersection Point that is attacked, it causes energetic disruption to multiple meridians, which from a combative use of TCM knowledge is a good thing. Basically, you get more "Bang for the buck" when striking Intersection Points. Now, the unusual thing about this particular Intersection Point is that the two meridians are energetically allergic to one another. The Triple Warmer meridian is associated with the element of Fire and the Gall Bladder is associated with the element of Wood. Strikes that are aimed at the ears will generally activate this point. Considering the massive energetic exchange of a strike to the area near the ear, just the distributive nature of the energetic transfer would activate TW-17. It can also be used to control an opponent by firmly grasping their head with one arm and driving a knuckle or fingertip into the point for compliance. Force should be applied towards to the tip of the nose for best effect. This type of control technique is commonly taught to Law Enforcement Officers as part of their training in dealing with a passive, but non-compliant, protesters, for instance. Defensively, attacks to the side of the head can generally be effectively blocked using the shoulder, arm, or movement of the torso.

GV-26   A centerline point that happens to also be an Intersection Point for the Governing Vessel and the Large Intestine Meridians. Its location, between the upper lip and the base of the nose, makes it especially vulnerable to upper-cut and open-hand palm strikes, which given biomechanics are thrown on the preferred 45-degree angle that is recommended, and most advantageous, in attacking this vital point. Smashing an open palm strike into the mouth and nose region will strike GV-26 and several other points. I prefer a rapid string of strikes to the same generally area, especially after taking the calculated chance of gaining that position. Each individual strike causing not only more physical damage to your opponent, but you blast wave after wave of energetic shockwaves through his system, in this case their head and brain. Additionally, this point can be pinched between the thumb and forefinger with great effect and utilized as a control technique on a non-complaint subject. Avoiding centerline attacks, like stated in above vital point descriptions, should be an important part of your combative training. Letting an opponent gain access to your centerline, opening you up to strikes to some of the most sensitive regions of the body, is a real concern. Learning how to counter such attempts in vital to your own well-being.

CV-24 The Chinese refer to this point as *Cheng Jiang*,[7] which does not mean much until you translate it out of pinyin. The translation of the Chinese term for the point, "Sauce Receptacle," is illustrative in that if one were to drip sauce from their mouth while eating it would accumulate at this point of their chin. While the vast majority of the Chinese names for acupuncture points makes little logical sense, this one allows us to paint a clear picture of it in our mind. It is located on the centerline of the head at the slight depression on the upper aspect of the centerline of the chin. Like many of the points that are detailed in the *Bubishi*, this is an Intersecting Point for the Stomach and the Large Intestine Meridians. Some TCM textbooks state that this is the location that the two centerline vessels, the Governing and Conception, intersect at this point, but the majority do not make that claim. Striking this point is most effective when aimed downward at a 45-degree angle. A hammer fist strike to this point, with enough force, will not only cause an instant knockout, but can dislocate the jaw. Likewise, such a strike will activate several other pressure points in the same general area. Ensuring that you are capable of defending your centerline will greatly increase your odds of falling victim of such an attack in a street altercation. Revie your specific systems techniques to determine which ones effectively counter centerline attacks.

SI-16 This point is not directly connected to the Extraordinary Vessels, but is one of the Small Intestine Meridian points that is associated with the Fire element. The Chinese refer to this point as *Tian Chuang*[8] or "Celestial Window." It is located on the outer neck on the border of the sternocleidomastoid muscle and directly posterior to LI-18. The ascending cervical artery, the cutaneous cervical nerve, and a portion of the great auricular nerve are present. This point is bilateral. An easy method to think of this point is that they are located where the bolts stick out of Frankenstein's monster's neck. Strikes should be at about a 45-degree angle towards the center of the neck. When striking the neck there are numerous points that will be activated. This disrupts the energy and blood flow to the head and can cause a knockout. Repeated strikes to this point can cause structural damage to the throat. One of my favorite attack method to points on the side of the opponent's neck is using the forearm as a striking surface. The length of the forearm, roughly eleven inches, which allows a large striking surface to accommodate the loss of accuracy and the dynamics of a

---

[7] Ibid., p. 326.
[8] Ibid., p. 139.

self-defense situation. Basically, using the forearm to strike with increases the likelihood of landing the strike. Effort should be made in your individual training to seek techniques that increase your odds of successfully landing strikes. A forearm strike to the neck, in comparison to a chop strike or punch, provides a much larger striking surface. Shrugging the shoulder, bobbing and weaving, in addition to standard blocking maneuvers, are excellent defensive tactics to avoid being struck on points on the side of the neck.

ST-9   This point is a bilateral point that is found on both sides of the neck and is located about 1.5 inches to the outside of the edge of the Adam's apple of the throat. The fact that the point lays directly over the carotid artery allows strikes to have an immediate reaction to the flow of blood to the brain and head in general. It has a cryptic name in Chinese, *Ren Ying,*[9] which means "Man's Prognosis" and provides no clues to its location or use from a martial standpoint. Its proximity to the carotid artery allows this point to be one of the weakest points on the human body and regardless of the size and muscular strength of an opponent it is extremely sensitive. The superior thyroid artery, the anterior jugular vein, the internal jugular vein, the carotid artery, the cutaneous cervical nerve, the cervical branch of the facial nerve, the sympathetic trunk, and the ascending branch of the hypoglossal and vagus nerves are all present. Just the structurally aspects of all these sensitive and vital nerves, arteries and veins should place it high on the list of potential targets. I personally consider it as one of the most important Vital Points because of this alone. Additionally, ST-9 is an intersection point for the Stomach Meridian, Gall Bladder Meridian and the Yin Heel Vessel. Strikes to this point can kill due to the overall structural weakness of the area. Strikes should be aimed toward the center of the spine on a 90-degree angle. A variety of empty hand weapons can be employed in striking this point. Forearms, edge of hand strikes, punches, kicks, and elbow strikes are all effective. The same defensive tactics outlined under the SI-16 should be employed against attacks to this extremely vital point.

CV-22   This is one of the two most important acupuncture points to the martial arts that is concerned with the hostile actions of life-or-death combatives. It sets in the horseshoe notch located at the extreme upper part of the chest structure and at the centerline of the front of the neck. Resting under it is the trachea, or commonly known as the "windpipe," and a hard and vicious strike

---

[9] Ibid., p. 64.

to this point can cause the surrounding tissue to swell, which can shut off the body's ability to pull oxygen into the lungs. A hard strike to this point can be deadly. Attacking this point should only be done in the most extreme life-or-death situations. Energetically, the Conception Vessel and the Yin Linking Vessel intersect at this point. The implications of that, from a Traditional Chinese Medicine perspective, is included in this book. Additionally, the structure of the suprasternal notch is an excellent "touch point" for situations when sight is reduced and you find yourself at extremely close range with your opponent. This allows for utilization of this point in a self-defense situation that is not as extreme as full force strikes, as only a finger or two are inserted and rolled to the backside of the notch causing pain for the opponent. Note that this still may produce swelling of the surrounding tissue that can result in serious medical situations. The term "seal the *qi*" of the Extraordinary Vessels is applied to this point, as it inhibits the body from correcting energetic imbalances in the Yin associated organs. Structurally, it can inhibit the body from taking in much needed oxygen and should only be attacked during situations when you fear for your own life. It is not to be used in demonstration or for sport-oriented martial arts. It is just too risky. I hesitate to use the term "kill technique," but if it is to be applied, it would to a forceful strike to CV-22. As stated numerous times in the description of other centerline points above, standard martial art defensive techniques that protect your centerline from attack(s) should be abundant in your specific art and should be trained to ensure that you can adequately defend yourself.

ST-12   This point is an Intersection Point for the Yin Heel Vessels and the Stomach Meridians. It is bilateral, found on both sides of the body, and is located about four inches lateral of the centerline of the body, about midpoint of the collarbone. The Chinese pinyin translation for this point is *Que Pen*,[10] and means "Empty Basin," which provides a clue of the physical structure of the body associated with this point. This point is an excellent target when your opponent is at close range. By gripping the collarbone, you can dig your fingers down behind the natural curve of the bone and towards the centerline of the body. It is most active when your opponent has their arm raised and given the structural weakness of the body at this location. I consider this point one as being utilized to gain positional dominance over an opponent, as it will quickly cause the opponent to bend at the knees and expose other areas for follow-on

---

[10] Ibid., p. 67.

strikes. Additionally, hard chops or hammerfist to the collarbone, besides breaking it and aiding in disabling the arm on that side, will trigger this point causing the same automatic bending of the knees. Taking split second advantage of their compromised body position is one of the reasons that I feel this point was included in the *Bubishi*, which is not to mention the systemic effect of the energetic system. This point is usually gained when an attacker launches a punch towards your head that is effectively defeated and their attacking arm is captured. This allows for a quick attack on ST-12 with your other hand that causes the opponent to buckle at the knees. Defensively, retracting your punching arm rapidly should negate the ability of someone from capturing it and thus does not allow for attack to this point.

GV-16   This Vital Point is the Yang version of CV-22. While CV-22 allows "Sealing the Qi" by attacking the windpipe, this point sets over the location that the spinal column connects to the skull and is another of the extremely vulnerable points of human anatomy. In fact, there are several acupuncture points in close proximity. The easiest way to think of these points is just attacking the back of the neck of the opponent. Given the energetic exchange of the strike, or the preferred numerous striking method, allows for several of them to be activated. GV-16 is an Intersection Point for the Governing Vessel and the Yang Linking Vessels. How these two Extraordinary Vessels work to correct energetic imbalances caused by strikes is covered in detail in Chapter 14. Anatomically, from a Western perspective, provides that this location is where the brainstem connects to the spinal column. It is an extremely sensitive point of attack and can not only cause unconsciousness, but can cause structural damage to this vital brain/spinal column connection, which can cause paralysis. So, how would you effectively attack points on the back of the neck? It is next to impossible while your opponent is in a fighting stance and directly in front of you. This point becomes easily accessible once you have established positional dominance, having initiated a Yang response in their body position. Basically, you have struck them in such a way that folds them at their waist and presents the back of their head for attack. A forceful chop type strike, forearm strike, or stomp kick if they are prone and face down, will allow easy access to this point. Again, if the door is open, just keep throwing the same technique repeatedly to the same location until they are no longer a threat. Like CV-22, this point is a finishing technique and only should be applied in life-or-death situations. It is not to be used in demonstrations or for sport-oriented martial arts. Strikes to this point can be deadly and I feel were included in the *Bubishi* because of the high likelihood of killing your opponent. The *Bubishi* was written in a time when the use of deadly force, in the case of unarmed combat, was a real threat. This knowledge is added with a great degree of hesitation, but without providing a clear examination of the lethal aspects of these strikes, it would lessen the overall understanding of this historic document. Defending yourself to not allow an opponent to gain tactical positioning to your back is of utmost importance. This is common within the vast majority of arts and should be one of the focuses of your training. It is my hope that the reader starts to gain an understanding of the obvious weaknesses of the human body through reading this work, as there are many. Besides the serious implications of attacking these Vital Points, it is my hope that they gain a strong understanding of the original intent of the martial pioneers that developed these fighting traditions. Remember; with great knowledge and power there must be greater control.

GV-14 Located on the last cervical vertebra and the first thoracic vertebra, this Vital Point lays on the spinal column and attacks to it, with enough force, can compromise the structurally integrity of this highly important component of the nervous system. GV-14 sets at approximately level of the shoulders, but is on the centerline of the back. It is an Intersection Point of the six Yang Meridians (Large Intestines, Stomach, Small Intestines, Bladder, Triple Warmer, and the Gall Bladder meridians) and the Governing Vessel. Strikes to this location must be very forceful due to the protective nature of both the Yang meridians and the anatomical strength of the underlying spinal column. This point is accessible when the opponent has been dropped, or thrown, as is facedown prone on the ground. Stomping kicks are extremely effective in this case or tip of the boot kicks, if the opponent is situated on their side and their back is pointed towards you. It is very difficult to achieve access to this point if your opponent is standing, facing towards you, in a fighting stance. I consider that it was added to the *Bubishi* for when the opponent has been put on the ground, but not totally submissive in a live-or-die combative situation. Being capable of defending yourself in order to not be thrown on the ground, and thusly attacked, only comes from serious long term study of any number of fighting arts. If you find yourself on the ground, it is best to roll to your back, rather than present your back to your opponent, and attempt any number of techniques to negate your aggressor's attacks. Otherwise, leaving your back open to an attack to GV-14, or any other of the numerous Vital Points of the back and neck region, is ill advised. Hard strikes to this point can cause paralysis or considerable damage to the spinal column. It should only be used in life-or-death situations and is not intended for demonstrations or sport-oriented martial arts.

CV-18   Given the close physical proximity of this point with the highly sensitive CV-17 a strike aimed at one will more than likely have effect on both points. CV-17 is the point that basically sets over the actual physical location of the heart and was curiously omitted from the *Bubishi* by its author(s). Because it is so close to CV-17, the effect of a strike to that point will likely affect CV-18 as well. For more information see page 38.

CV-15   Yet another of the centerline points that make it into the *Bubishi's* 36 Vital Points. It is located on the Conception Vessel and is about seven inches above the naval at the bottom of the xiphoid process. It shares the same Western anatomy characteristics as CV-12, 13, and 14. It is the connecting point of the Conception Vessel and is called the Luo Connecting Point for its relationship with other areas of the chest and abdomen. Strikes to this point should be downward at a 45-degree angle for best energetic results, but an upward strike can effectively knock the air out of the lungs. Forceful strikes may also break the xiphoid process itself. Just taking a slightly slanted stance with the upper body places your centerline in a more difficult position for your opponent's attack. Numerous martial arts techniques that help defend your centerline are found throughout the various systems.

HT-1   This point is difficult to access, as it is well protected by the structure of the human body. HT-1is a bilateral Vital Point that is located in the armpit at the junction of the inner arm with the torso. It is associated with the Heart Meridian and is the point that the internal aspects of that meridian leaves the inner torso and emerges close to the surface of the skin. It does not have a direct connection to any Extraordinary Vessels, but is highly sensitive to attack. Traditional Chinese Medicine state that this is a no-needle point in many related textbooks. On the surface, this point would appear to be a difficult one to access during an altercation, but it is accessible. HT-1 becomes easily accessible if the opponent's arm is raised, which occurs in the short instances that they are throwing a punch. A quick finger thrust or one-knuckle fist strike can easily activate it, but it requires a fair amount of precision to land. Combat science teaches us that precision generally diminishes during an altercation, but I add the above variant for those that would be willing to put in the training time for achieve such a strike. Just remember that the likelihood of landing such a technique during an actual altercation is remote, even with copious amounts of practice. A more realistic attack to HT-1 is when you have used your opponent's arm to take them to the ground. Once established, as a generally rule of thumb, it is advised that if you have established control over an opponent's arm that you should maintain that control until you deliver a blow that ends the fight. So, with that in mind, one of my favorite attacks to HT-1 after driving an opponent to ground while having established and maintained arm control, that you jerk the arm towards yourself as you throw a kick into this Vital Point. The type of kick will be dependent on the positioning of your opponent. If he is bladed on the ground (laying on one side with the arm you control in the air) a hard side kick or stomp works well. If the opponent starts turning, or squaring his shoulders towards you as he hits the ground in an attempt to regain his feet, then a forceful forward, or straight kick, can work. I would suggest working with a training partner to determine the various configurations that a downed opponent would react when you maintain control of one of their arms. Notice that I did not advise that you kick your training partner in HT-1, which is ill advised since it theoretically can cause disruptions to the heart and according to Traditional Chinese Medicine theory even death. Again, this technique is not for demonstration or sport-oriented martial arts, but mature and thoughtful training practice can provide a wealth of knowledge on how best to attack a Vital Point, even if it is not actually struck. Not allowing an opponent the opportunity to gain control of one of your arms is critical in understanding the defense against a HT-1 attack.

BL-43   Located on the back, just three inches lateral to the lower border of the fourth thoracic vertebra on the medial edge of the scapula, this bilateral point is associated with the Bladder Meridian. It does not directly connect to any of the Extraordinary Vessels. I consider its inclusion in the *Bubishi* as being one of a more structural attack. If you have gained a position on your opponent's back, forcefully striking this point will cause the attacked side to jerk forward, which will slightly turn the opponent and place you in perfect position to attack the opponent's rear centerline. Many of those centerline points have already been discussed in this chapter. Additionally, if you opponent is prone on their stomach then stomping this point can produce serious injuries to the scapula, which might result in damage to the point that it is no longer useful combatively. The attacks appear to follow more structural attack than an energetic one. Even after interviewing several practicing acupuncturist and TCM doctors, the energetic weaknesses of this point are not at the same level of the vast majority of other Vital Points. The most important insight from a defensive perspective is to not allow an opponent to gain position on your back. Numerous techniques counter an opponent's movement to accomplish such a tactic.

BL-51 This vital point does not directly intersect with any of the Extraordinary Vessels. Located about three inches lateral to the lower part of the first lumbar vertebra on the spinal column. Branches of the first lumbar artery and vein and a branch of the twelfth thoracic nerve are present on this bilateral point. It sets at the lower aspect of the ribcage on the back. Strikes should be toward the head at a 45-degree angle. Striking the ribcage in this manner is best in causing breaks. Secondly, strikes will disrupt the energy of the Bladder meridian. Given the close physical proximity of other points in the area it can be interpreted that this is more of a structural target added to cause damage to the ribcage. Forceful or repeated strikes can possibly drive bone fragments into the deeper underlying organs. A martial artist should be well-trained on not giving their back to an opponent, which would be necessary for them to attack BL-51, or any of the other Vital Points found on the back.

GV-1 This Vital Point sets just below the coccyx bone on the end of the spinal column. It is the intersection point for the Kidney Meridian, Gall Bladder Meridian, and Governing Vessel, which makes it a prime energetic target. Remember that strikes to intersection points have greater energetic effect on the body. Strikes to this point should be upward at a 45-degree angle. This places the force of the blow as being aimed at the energy center of the body. From a martial perspective, this point is generally difficult to hit, but situations when you move to the back of your opponent open the possibility of knee strikes aimed in the coccyx bone. These types of strikes are extremely effective in dropping an opponent. Hard knee strikes to this region not only shock the energy core of the body, but also shocks the entire nervous system with the connection of the coccyx bone to the spine. Besides immediately dropping an opponent, as they can no longer continue the fight from the energetic blast up their spinal column, it can cause the bowels and the bladder to empty. As stated numerous times, it is unwise to allow your opponent to gain position on your back. There are just too many devastating strikes that can be landed with little recourse. Your martial arts training needs to account for this. So, if you are training a lot of spinning type moves, or moves that put you into a position that would compromise you position by presenting your back, then you should seriously reconsider those techniques or methods.

CV-4   A properly thrown strike into this Vital Point will cause your opponent to fold forward into a Yin body posture, which will allow easy access to several follow-up points. An easy way to remember this vital point is to think of striking an opponent just below the belt line, but not their genitals. Boxers some time refer to this area as the "bread basket." It is located about three inches below the navel on the centerline of the body. CV-4 is the alarm point for the Small Intestine Meridian and an intersection point of the Spleen, Kidney, and Liver Meridians. Strikes to this point should be at a downward 45-degree angle, if possible, and can break the pubic bone causing great pain in the opponent. Downward aimed punches and hard driving straight kicks to this region can be effective in a combative situation. Striking this point can be conducted very deceptively, as the majority of opponents will not be expecting a strike aimed to a low region of the body. It is instinctive for a male to protect the genitals from attack, usually by twisting the hips to the side or narrowing the legs. CV-4 can still be accessible even if they twist their hips to avoid a genital strike. Once struck with adequate force, the body folds forward and exposes numerous points on the neck and back for additional attacks. A strike to this Vital Point attacks the energy center of the body and has a massive draining effect on an opponent. Defensively, protecting your centerline can not be expressed strongly enough.

CV-1   "Meeting of Yin" is the English translation of the Chinese name for this point and it hints at its unique attributes. It is difficult to access from a combative sense, but if the opportunity presents itself, a strike to this Vital Point is devastating to an opponent. There is no other location on the body where the Governing Vessel, Conception Vessel, and the Thrusting Vessel intersect. From an energetic perspective, a strike there sends a kinetic energy shockwave into both the front centerline and back centerline Extraordinary Vessels. More importantly, it send a shockwave straight into the energy core of the body at the top of the Thrusting Vessel. This vessel is particular difficult to strike directly, though forceful strikes to CV-4 and ones aimed at the core along the abdomen and lower back will disrupt it, but lack the directness of a CV-1 strike. Nature has assisted us by the anatomical placement of this point by locating it between the genitals and the anus. Given this location, though it is devastatingly effective, it is only a viable target in extreme instances. If you are faced with an opponent that attempts to deliver high kicks at you, this point can be accessed, with the correct timing, with a straight kick or low arching upward strike. Land one kick or strike here and I would bet a stack of money that the fight would be over instantly. Another way to access this Vital Point is if your opponent is on the ground and you gain control of one of their legs. Jerking the leg violently towards yourself as you forcefully kick into the area between their legs will likely land a blow to this point. How to best defend against an attack to CV-1? Combat oriented martial arts, almost across the board, repeatedly state that high kicks are suggested for serious situations. The likelihood of failure is too high when the chips are down and your life depends on the outcome. I have heard it stressed numerous times that no kick should be above the waist. The reason is not to hurt the egos of martial artists that can kick beautiful and precise high kicks, which appear impressive to the general public, but to protect this Vital Point in particular. The higher the leg is raised, the more accessible this point becomes. If you are still holding on the idea that you are going to head kick someone on the street, you need to seriously consider to stop approaching kicks with that mindset. They are just too dangerous. Not to the opponent, but to you. CV-1 can easily be placed in the top five Vital Points due to the devastating effect it has on an opponent.

GB-24   Though this point does not directly intersect with any of the Extraordinary Vessels, it is the intersection point for the Gall Bladder and Bladder Meridians. Additionally, it is the Alarm Point for the Gall Bladder meridian. In some Traditional Chinese Medicine textbooks it is listed as intersecting the Yang Linking Vessel. The vast majority does not and it was not included as such in this book. This point is of considerable value to the martial artist. Strikes to this point should be toward the center of the body on a downward 45-degree angle. Forceful strikes can shock or damage the gall bladder. An interruption of the energy core of the body can also result if the strike is thrown at the correct angle and towards the core of the body. The additional benefits of strikes to this location are the serious implications of it being the sensitive Alarm point of the Gall Bladder. Strikes to this point can inhibit the ability to correct energy imbalances of the Gall Bladder caused by martial attacks. One forceful strike to this location will generally activate LV-14, which is close in physical proximity and the alarm point of the Liver. Two for the price of one, as the old saying goes. This will cause the Wood associated meridians to be in an extremely disrupted energetic state. Striking this point is referred to as a "body shot" or "liver punch" in Western boxing. Several online sources have videos of numerous TKO's that were thrown to this point. This is an excellent point for the martial artist due to its ability to drop an opponent easily. Beware; to be successful when striking this requires a great deal of power. Light taps just will not work. Dropping the elbows to cover these points is one of several defensive tactics that are employed to protect not only these points, but many others that are present on the front of the body.

LV-13   This bilateral point is located on the torso and lays on the Liver Meridian. It is the Alarm point for the Spleen, which is utilized in TCM diagnosis. When an Alarm point is out of balance, merely touching the associated Alarm Point will cause a negative reaction in a patient. From a martial perspective, Alarm Points should be prime targets for attacks since often they are located directly over the organ that is represents. The Spleen is the organ associated with LV-13 and attacks should be towards the energy core of the body and downward at a 45-degree angle to get maximum effect. . A forceful strike to this point can cause internal injuries to the spleen and other unprotected organs of the abdomen. Likewise, a strike to this area can cause the floating rib to break and with enough force drive it into sensitive organs in the rear of the abdominal cavity. From an energetic perspective this point is excellent. It is the intersection point of the Liver and Gall Bladder Meridians and the Girdle Vessel, as it is the Intersection Point for these vessels. A strike will disrupt the energy of those two meridians and upset the Girdle Vessel. Strikes to the Liver and Gall Bladder Meridians will usually cause the legs to bend. This can either drop your opponent to the ground or bend them just enough for follow-up attacks to the neck and head areas. Guarding against body strikes, be they punches or kicks, should be a commonly taught part of the curriculum in the vast majority of martial systems.

LV-11   This Vital Point does not directly intersect with any of the Extraordinary Vessels and, I believe, is included in the Bubishi because of it being a structural attack point, more so than a highly vulnerable energetic point. The Chinese refer to this point as *Yin Lian*,[11] which translated from pinyin means "Yin Corner." This point is bilateral and located on the upper part of the inner thigh, fairly close to the pelvic crease. Branches of the medial circumflex femoral artery and vein, the genitofemoral nerve, a branch of the medial femoral cutaneous nerve, and a branch of the obturator nerve are present. This point is in close physical proximity to several intersection points and other energetically sensitive points, but does not stand out for its own energetic qualities considering it is not an Alarm Point or Intersection Point. Either of which would qualify it as having a higher energetic value. Strikes should be aimed at

---

[11] Ibid., p. 299.

the center of the leg on about a 45-degree angle. Besides the physical result of driving the attacked leg and hip to the rear, a forceful strike would threaten the femoral artery, which runs just under the surface of the skin at this location. My theory of it being more of a structural attack point is based on what happens when this point is forcefully attacked. If the angle is correct, then the opponent will fold at that hip and it will inhibit further offensive action on their part because they will temporarily not be able to advance on that leg, which allows time for rapid follow-on strikes due to their compromised balance. To counter an attack to this point, a strong downward blocking type strike or twist of the hips would be sufficient, which would be similar to any low level attack to the genital region.

LU-3   Another point that does not directly intersect with an Extraordinary Vessel, and is more of a structural attack that can deaden the arm of an attacker. The pinyin for this point is *Tain Fu*,[12] which translates as "Celestial Storehouse" and is basically cryptic to Westerners. LU-3 is bilateral and is located near the center of the bicep muscle of the arm. It sets about five inches above the crease of the elbow. Western anatomy shows the cephalic vein, branches of the brachial artery and vein, and the lateral brachial cutaneous nerve are present at this point. Strikes should be aimed at a 90-degee angle directly towards the center of the arm. Forcefully attacks can tear the tendons and ligaments of the bicep at the insertion point at the elbow and deaden the arm. Energetically, strikes will disrupt the energy of the Lung meridian, which is associated with Metal. Attacks to this point can disable the arm of your opponent causing a marked increase in your ability to overcome the attacker. If struck properly and the arm is deadened, or otherwise useless, fighting a one-armed opponent is dramatically easier and you have substantially higher odds of winning the encounter. I personally like using a forearm or elbow strike on this point, but a strong punch can also be effective, though you face the possibility of the fist rolling off the bicep and not getting maximum energetic exchange. A basic defensive tactic to defend against a strike to this point is retracting your punching arm and proper orientation towards your opponent. Prolonged grappling with the hands can expose this point to an attack from a trained opponent.

LI-10   This bilateral point, which is associated with the Large Intestine Meridian, is easily accessible during most violent encounters. It is located on the

---

[12] Ibid., p. 26.

THE 36 VITAL POINTS

meaty mound of muscle that is located about three inches down from the elbow crease on the outer aspect of the arm.

Anytime that an opponent punches or reaches for you, this point is basically offered on a silver platter. LI-10 should be considered as a structural attack point, but it also serves as an easy means to utilize the Five Element Theory of Traditional Chinese Medicine since a hard strike will primarily activate the Metal and secondarily activate the Fire. This leaves only a strike to a wood point to achieve a three step Five Element strike sequence and the predictable body alignment of the opponent after a LI-10 strike presents several to choose, with GB-20 being notable. An examination of Western anatomy shows that branches of the radial recurrent artery and vein, the posterior antebrachial cutaneous nerve and radial nerve are present. It does not have a direct intersection with any of Extraordinary Vessels or have any characteristics that would place it as a strong energetic target. What is lacks energetically, it makes up for in its ability to put hinder an attacking arm useless and placing the opponent in a highly compromised position for follow-on attacks. Strikes should be "cutting" in nature and aimed to strike just above the point and travel in the direct of the opponent's hand. Strikes in this manner will cause the opponent to drop their elbow and shoulder, jut their chin slightly forward and away from the attacked side. This throws their balance down and forward and, in essence, negates their offensive action towards you. This allows easier access to follow-up attacks on points of the neck and head. Forceful strikes can cause the arm to numb and reduce the likelihood of additional attacks. The Chinese pinyin name for this point is *Shou San Li*,[13] which is another cryptic name. Note: the Chinese names for the points are added since anyone training in the Chinese Martial Arts could likely hear them referred to as such by Chinese instructors. Same defensive advice as for LU-3 (listed directly above) in remembering to retract the punching arm and being wary of extended grappling with hands.

HT-5   This point, and the next one, LU-8, are located on the wrist and generally when one is activated the other is as well. HT-5 is bilateral and is the Intersection Point of the Heart and Small Intestine Meridians. Considering that the heart is associated with Fire, according to TCM Five Element Theory, activation of this point, along with LU-8, allows for two steps of the Cycle of Control, as LU-8 is associated with Metal. When two of the elements of the cycle are activated, as in a simple wrist grab in this case, it places the third element in the

---

[13] Ibid., p. 45.

cycle in a hyper-sensitive state. HT-5 is physically located about one inch above the wrist crease, towards the body, on the lower, inner aspect of the forearm. From a Western anatomy perspective, it sets above the ulnar artery, the medial antebrachial cutaneous nerve and the ulnar nerve, which assist in control of the hand. Earlier in this chapter, I discussed "latch" points and these two, HT-5 and LU-8, are the prime examples. Being an Intersection Point between the Heart and Small Intestine Meridians has great implication on the function of the Small Intestine Meridian function in correcting energetic imbalances to the sensitive Heart Meridian. These points are activated when you take control of an opponent's wrist. The key is developing good hand and finger strength, which should allow a strong crushing like grip with your fingers digging into these points. Numerous kata contain a technique often referred to as "chambering" a punch, which can be interpreted as grasping an opponent's wrist and violently jerking it towards your own waistline. In doing so, if you are digging into HT-5 and LU-8 with your fingers, it will not only cause energetic activation of these two points, but throw your opponent off balance as they stumble forward, usually bending at the waist and presenting various Vital Points on the neck and head for follow-up striking. HT-5 does not directly intersect with any of the Extraordinary Vessels, but are still wonderful additions to your toolbox because of their easy manipulation and access. Activation of these two points will cause a further inability of correcting energetic imbalances of the heart. Avoid having an attacker grab your wrist is of utmost importance from a defensive standpoint. Once their grip is established, and they launch into attack, allows them to easily place you into a compromised position from which you will be easy prey to an assortment of attacks. It is better to not allow an opponent to establish control of your wrist to begin with. Various wrist reversals should also be practiced to overcome a stronger opponent that might grasp your wrist.

LU-8   This point is coupled with HT-5 (listed directly above) and is also bilateral. It also does not have a direct connection to the Extraordinary Vessels and falls under the same description of a "latch" point, as does HT-5. It is located at the crease of the wrist on the radial side. Depending on how you grasp someone's wrist, either the fingers or the thumb will likely activate this point and its "latch" mate, HT-5. Activation of this point through grasping or striking will drain energy from the hand and is excellent in causing an opponent to release from a grasp to you. Striking this point, rather than activating it by grasping, should be at a 45-degree angle towards the center of the wrist. Done forcefully, there are few opponents, even those with tremendous hand strength, which will be able to maintain a grip. See the detailed description of HT-5 for additional information on these two points.

LI-4 This Vital Point is located at the center of the where the first and second metacarpal bones meet. Western anatomy states that the radial artery and supporting network, the radial nerve and the palmar digital proprial nerve are present. This point is bilateral and is associated with the Large Intestine Meridian, but does not intersect with any of the Extraordinary Vessels. This point can be struck or grasp. If an opponent has grasp onto your lapel, for instance, by placing your hand over your opponents will allow you to dig your fingers into this point. Energetically, it will disrupt the energy of the Large Intestine Meridian and considering that your other fingers will activate the Fire associated meridians on the outer aspect of the hand, will drain the energy from their grip. This should easily allow you to gain a release of the grasp and allow you to maintain control of their attacking hand. Defensively, avoid any prolonged contact with an opponent in which your arm and hand are touching their torso. Striking and quickly retracting are commonsense methods of avoiding having this point attacked.

TW-2 This is the last Vital Point located on the hand or wrist that is presented in the *Bubishi*. It is a bilateral point that is located at the inner base between the little and ring fingers. It should be attacked in a similar manner as LI-4 (listed directly above). It is associated with the Triple Warmer Meridian, which is Yang Fire according to the Five Element Theory. TW-12 does not intersect with any of the Extraordinary Vessels. Note: all the points on the hands and arms are either associated with Fire or Metal. Activation from forceful grasping or striking will cause an energetic disturbance for the associated meridian(s).

GB-31 The *Bubishi* also contains several Vital Points on the legs and feet and this point is one of the primary targets from a combative perspective. It is located on the lateral aspect of the thigh along the imaginary pants seam. If you let your arm extend down your sides then GB-31 will be at the fingertip of your middle finger. Branches of the femoral artery and vein, the lateral femoral cutaneous nerve, and a branch of the femoral nerve are present according to Western anatomy. GB-21 is a bilateral point that does not have a direct connection with any of the Extraordinary Vessels. This point should be struck at a 90-degree angle. A forceful knee strike to this point will collapse the leg of your opponent. It is excellent when you have moved to the outside of their attack and is a prime target after the Fire and Metal meridians of the arms have been activated. Striking GB-31, after activating the arm meridians, will complete three steps of the Cycle of Control. I have personally used this technique during encounters on a number of occasions and it will drop an opponent to the ground. They are generally in great enough discomfort that you can just walk away or continue attacking them at leisure while they are attempting little to no defense. Since you have to be to the outside of the opponent to strike this point, care should be given to not allow an opponent to gain that position from a defensive point of view. Unfortunately, a low strike to this point is hard to detect, as most concentration is on the opponent's upper body and arms. A knee or shin kick can be delivered very rapidly, and somewhat undetected, that could have devastating results. Better to train yourself to not allow opponents to the opportunity to cut to the outside through continual drilling and footwork.

BL-40   The Chinese refer to this point as *Wei Zhong*[14] or "Bend Middle." It is located at the center of the back of the knee in the crease. The femoropopliteal vein, the popliteal artery and vein, the posterior femoral cutaneous nerve and the tibial nerve are present. This point is bilateral. Given the structure of the body the author feels that it was added to the 36 Vital Points of the original *Bubishi* considering that strikes to it will cause the knee to collapse. Energetically, it will disrupt the energy of the Bladder Meridian. Strikes to this point will activate the Bladder points of the back for follow-up attacks.

KI-6   The Chinese refer to this point as *Zhao Hai*[15] or "Shining Sea." It is located one inch below the inside of the anklebone and is bilateral. The posterior tibial artery and vein and the medial crural cutaneous nerve are present. It is an intersection point for the Yin Heel Vessel and the Kidney Meridian. This point can be struck, with a number of other points, with low sweeping kicks to the inside of the lower leg and foot. Additionally, once an opponent is prone on the ground this point can be stomped.

BL-62   The Chinese refer to this point as *Shen Mai*[16] or "Extending Vessel." It is located in the depression directly below the outside aspect of the anklebone. It is a bilateral point. The external malleolar artery network and the sural nerve are present. It is an intersection point for the Bladder Meridian and the Tang

---

[14] Ibid., p. 172.
[15] Ibid., p. 201.
[16] Ibid., p. 190.

Heel Vessel. This point can be struck, with a number of other points, with low sweeping kicks to the outside of the lower leg and foot. Additionally, once an opponent has become prone on the ground this point can be stomped.

LV-3   The Chinese refer to this point as *Tai Chong*[17] or "Supreme Surge." It is located on the top of the foot about two inches from the base of the big toe. The first dorsal metatarsal artery and a branch of the deep peroneal nerve are present. This point is bilateral. Strike this point by stomping the top of the foot. Breaking the small bones of the top of the foot will greatly inhibit your opponent's ability to continue fighting. From an energetic standpoint attack this point will activate the Yin associated Liver Meridian. If the Fire and Metal meridians of the arms have been activated then striking the top of the foot will complete three steps in the Cycle of Control in the Five Element Theory. It will not likely produce a knockout, but can render your opponent helpless in continuing an attack and allow you to continue with additional strikes.

The Diurnal Cycle

The *Bubishi* makes reference to a twenty-four hour cycle of attacking the various meridians.[18] This cycle follows the biorhythmic patterns that are associated with the Traditional Chinese Medicine term known as the Diurnal Cycle. That cycle follows the normal flow of energy through the twelve Main Meridians during the course of a day. That course flows in the following manner.

Meridian	Time of Peak Energy
Stomach	7am – 9am
Spleen	9am – 11am
Heart	11am – 1pm
Small Intestine	1pm – 3pm
Bladder	3pm – 5pm
Kidney	5pm – 7pm
Pericardium	7pm – 9pm
Triple Warmer	9pm – 11pm
Gall Bladder	11pm – 1am
Liver	1am – 3 am
Lung	3am – 5am
Large Intestine	5am – 7am

Table 16-4: *The Diurnal Cycle is listed in the left column. The corresponding peak time of energy is listed in the right column.*

---

[17] Ibid., p. 292.
[18] McCarthy, *The Bible of Karate: Bubishi*, pp. 136–147.

Table 16-4 illustrates the times of the day that the twelve Main Meridians are at their highest energy levels. Traditional Chinese Medicine also includes a timetable of the days of the month and years for certain treatments.[19] Use of this information started emerging as Western martial artists continued to develop their understanding of some Traditional Chinese Medicine concepts. As this knowledge base grew in the west, through exhaustive study of the theories and laws that govern that system, the obvious use of the diurnal cycle can now be explained. The *Bubishi* lists series of attacks to the specific meridians that are designed to disrupt the energy levels of the Main Meridians during their peak levels of energy.[20] It DOES NOT contain any mention of attacks to the Main Meridians while they are in a deficient state. The implications to the martial artist are that attacks should be focused when meridians are in an excessive state of energy imbalance. This is substantiated with the research that is presented in this book. It is interesting to note that out of the twelve points in this section there are only three points that are found in the 36 Vital Points, which are GB-24, LI-10 and CV-1. The other points are not listed in the 36 Vital Points. These bi-hourly points, which are referred to as *Shichen* in the *Bubishi*, are listed in Table 16-5.

Vital Point	Peak Time for Attack
GB-24	11pm – 1am
LV-14	1am - 3am
LU-1	3am – 5am
LI-10	5am – 7am
ST-25	7am – 9am
SP-14	9am – 11am
HT-8	11am – 1pm
CV-6	1pm – 3pm
CV-2	3pm – 5pm
BL-52	5pm – 7pm
BL-14	7pm – 9pm
CV-1	9pm – 11pm

Table 16-5: *Shichen Points for attacking the Main Meridians during their peak energy levels.*

[19] Liu Bing Quan, *Optimum Time for Acupuncture* (Jinan, China: Shandong Science and Technology Press, 1988).

[20] McCarthy, *The Bible of Karate: Bubishi*, 140–145: This section of the *Bubishi* gives specific attack points that correspond to the twelve two-hour periods of the day when energy is at peak levels in the Main Meridians. These points are referred to as *Shichen*, or bi-hourly points.

From a combative perspective it is ridiculous to consider committing to memory all the peak energy levels of the various meridians during a twenty-four hour period. It is even more ridiculous to consider that in a combative situation that you would have the presence of mind to determine the current time, which meridian is in their normal "energy high tide," and be capable of executing a technique to attack that excessive state. Unarmed combat training needs to reduce the amount of "thinking" and engrain specific techniques that have an extremely high probability of success.[21] It is my opinion that attempting to learn how to utilize the diurnal cycle during a combative situation is a waste of time and brainpower. The exceptional individual might be able to master this information to the point of using it effectively in an encounter, but on the whole it is beyond the reach of the average martial artist.

During the short time that the application of Traditional Chinese Medicine to the martial arts has been in the west there have been numerous "dead ends." I was fortunate enough to be asked to conduct research in the advanced aspects of Traditional Chinese Medicine around 1994 by Rick Moneymaker. The group of individuals that he chose for this research team explored numerous Traditional Chinese Medicine laws, concepts, and theories in an attempt to "take things to the next level." The Diurnal Cycle was one of the concepts that were examined extensively and it was determined that it just is not workable from a martial perspective.[22]

The *Bubishi* even states that the student should divide the twelve attacks that utilize the *Shichen* points into A.M. and P.M. techniques.[23] This could assist the student of the martial sciences to better grasp the bi-hourly techniques. If the advice is followed, and the points follow accepted Traditional Chinese Medicine science, then a fair degree of proficiency could be obtained. Still, the idea of knowing the exact time of day that an aggressive encounter might occur is difficult to accept from a combative viewpoint. It is interesting to note that the United States Marine Corps Raiders, of WWII fame and the foundation of Marine Corps Special Operations Command, taught twelve empty-hand killing techniques to its troops. This was after extensive "field testing" of many techniques that proved unreliable. The unreliable techniques were removed from the training program and the result was twelve extremely effective close com-

---

[21] This is validated by the highly successful unarmed fighting techniques that were utilized by the United States Marine Raiders and British OSS during World War II. Unfortunately, these techniques have been removed from military Close Combat training due to their lethal and vicious nature. There are currently only a handful of men that know these techniques in the United States and United Kingdom.

[22] Personal research notes, 1994 to 2018.

[23] Alexander, *Bubishi: Martial Arts Spirit*, p. 39.

bat techniques that worked — and worked extremely well. These techniques did not utilize a bi-hourly cycle of energy as their basis, but were based on gross motor skills and aggressive closing with an opponent.[24] The strikes were aimed at the anatomically weak structures of the body (from a Western perspective) and brute force was utilized in their execution. The techniques are devastating and extremely lethal in close combat situations, which was proven repeatedly in real-life encounters during the years that the Marines were engaged against the Japanese. The numbers of enemy troops that these techniques killed are staggering. The healing aspects of Traditional Chinese Medicine, in which acupuncture is a cornerstone, are different than the martial aspects of the science. Erle Montaigue stated, "Acupuncture is not Dim-Mak, nor is Dim-Mak acupuncture."[25] Some individuals have only given Traditional Chinese Medicine a cursory examination and pronounced themselves as experts in the field. They then conduct classes and seminars where they expound this concept, law or theory to students that are new to this ancient science. The material is so radical to the Western mind that concepts like Yin/Yang, Five Elements, Main Meridians, Qi, etc., are often accepted without further examination. Often the material is presented in a manner that is best described as skewed. It contains enough factual information that it is often accepted by the student, but upon closer examination is clearly a false representation of the laws of Traditional Chinese Medicine.[26] In those cases it is very unfortunate for the student.

As students of these arts we should not accept anything as factual until we have personally researched it. I include the material in this book in that statement. Anything presented to you, verbal or written, should be considered as suspect until its sources can be verified. I question everything presented and to accept nothing as fact until I conduct my own research to substantiate the material. That has propelled my personal development and was a refreshing counter to the usually "Don't question — Just do" quips that I had grown ac-

---

[24] Montaigue, *Advanced Dim-Mak*, pp. 94-115, Montaigue discusses the Reptilian Brain and the relation that it has with aggressive behavior. Basically, when in a combative encounter you should unleash the natural animal instinct to survive. Animals do not think about technique when they are attacked, they just react with extreme aggression in an effort to survive. The Reptilian Brain, and its involvement with aggressive behavior, is documented in numerous sources that relate to Behavioral Psychology.

[25] Montaigue, *Dim-Mak Death Point Striking*, p. xix — Dim-Mak refers to the Chinese term that is applied to the "death strikes," which are outlined in documents like the *Bubishi*.

[26] There have been numerous occasions when well-known pressure point instructors have made statements that cannot be validated by Traditional Chinese Medicine. Some have appeared in print and video, but many such statements have occurred during seminars. Be careful of what you read and hear — it may not be true and actually hinder your development. I suggest that each student research any statement independently and arrive at their own conclusions.

customed to in the martial arts scene. The results of questioning everything and the product of an overly curious mind are presented in this book, but don't take my word on it. I challenge you to research the material before accepting it as fact. All that I have done is "reverse engineer" the sometimes overwhelming volumes of Traditional Chinese Medicine textbooks, interviewed TCM doctors, and studied with some of the best pressure point practitioners in the west. If you decide to embark on a similar journey then I expect that our paths might cross at some point.

Master Points

According to the teachings of Traditional Chinese Medicine there are a set of eight points that have direct influence of the Extraordinary Vessels in acupuncture treatment. Each of the points is associated with a specific Extraordinary Vessel. The eight Extraordinary Vessels are also arranged in four pairs and the Master points are stimulated in pairs to correct energetic imbalances of the affected vessel(s). The teachings of this method date back to 1439 when Xu Feng wrote *Zhen Jiu Da Quan*. That is the first time that a complete and systematic treatment description of the Extraordinary Vessels is found. It is not known if these treatments where developed at an earlier time and passed on to Xu Feng, or that he developed them himself.[27] Regardless, considering the antiquity of the material it is interesting to examine and attempt to apply to martial science. A list of the Master Points is found in Table 16-6.

Master Points	Associated Vessel
SP-4	Thrusting
PC-6	Yin Linking
SI-3	Governing
BL-62	Yang Heel
GB-41	Girdle
TW-5	Yang Linking
LU-7	Conception
KI-6	Yin Heel

Table 16-6: *Master Points and their associated Vessel. The pairing is illustrated by shading.*

---

[27] Matsumoto & Birch, *Extraordinary Vessels*, pp. 5–6.

Remember that this data has been documented from a healing perspective.[28] The process of "reverse engineering" the healing data has been a common tool of the author, and other Western pressure point practitioners, in gaining an understanding of the "non-healing" implications of Traditional Chinese Medicine. From a healing perspective the stimulation of SP-4 and PC-6 will aid in relieving energetic imbalances in the heart, chest and stomach.[29] The other Master points have effect on other parts of the body, notably the extremities, and will not be covered in this text due to the already established importance of attacking the heart.

I have found it curious that PC-6 was not included in the 36 Vital Points by the author(s) of the *Bubishi*. Out of the two Master points that are being considered, SP-4 and PC-6, the latter is extremely accessible in most combative situations. SP-4 is located near the bottom edge of the inner aspect of the foot and would be difficult to access in a combative situation. PC-6 is located on the inner side of the forearm and numerous techniques can disrupt the energy flow of this point. It is also an intersection point for the Pericardium and Triple Warmer meridians. We have already established the importance of intersection points in attacking the energetic system of the body. Strikes to this point will cause a major energy disruption to the Fire meridian. The only conclusion that can be arrived at concerning the exclusion of PC-6 in the 36 Vital Points is that it drains energy from the Fire meridians. PC-6 is a "drainage" point and that striking it will drain energy in the opponent.[30] That makes PC-6 effective in self-defense situations, but will not accentuate the excessive energetic state of the Heart, which is desired from a combative viewpoint, if it is struck.

For years the *Bubishi* was held as a secret text that was passed down from instructor to serious student. It has been a cherished source of martial technique and virtue for the Okinawans, and now it can be to their Western counterparts. The depth of this document is only touched upon in the presentation of the material in this book. Future efforts in examining the martial applications of the *Bubishi* are planned.

---

[28] Kiiko Matsumoto & Stephen Birch, *Hara Diagnosis; Reflections on the Sea* (Brookline, MA: Paradigm Publications, 1988), pp. 361–362.

[29] Matsumoto & Birch, *Extraordinary Vessels*, pp. 7–8.

[30] Personal research notes, 1994 to 2018.

Pinpoint Strikes?

There have been numerous discussions among martial artists concerning the use of pressure point techniques in an actual combative situation. Those that do not believe the validity of the science are many times the same ones that believe it requires pinpoint striking of the Chinese acupuncture points. This can be understandable due to the manner that some instructors present the art during seminars and on video, but is far from the truth. Pressure point techniques do not require pinpoint accuracy to be effective. Techniques that can be considered as "blunt trauma" strikes can be utilized with great success. The idea that you have to use pinpoint accuracy in fighting violates the principles of Body Alarm Reaction that we learned earlier in this book. Striking with that type of accuracy is not feasible in a real-life situation.

One manner to consider pressure point strikes is that you are not striking individual acupuncture points. Instead, you are striking pressure point clusters. The healing aspects of acupuncture treatment require the insertion of a small needle into a specific point. The combative application of Traditional Chinese Medicine does not have to be that exact. It is like comparing the kinetic energy delivered from a cannon to that of a pinprick. A martial technique strikes the body with a tremendous amount of kinetic energy. The impact delivers that energy in a large area, which is one hundred times greater than the effect of being needled.

Consider the study of Terminal Ballistics for example. Terminal Ballistics is the science of what happens when a bullet enters the flesh of a person. The path that the bullet follows will cause tissue damage, which is due to the actual passing of the foreign object through the tissue. This is referred to as the Primary Wound Channel. Kinetic energy from the round, as it is passing through the body, will cause trauma to tissue that is surrounding the primary wound channel. This is referred to as the Secondary Wound Channel and is dependent upon such factors as the velocity and size of the bullet. Understanding Terminal Ballistics has some relationship to the effects of a strike in the martial arts. See Figures 16-1, 16-2 and 16-3 for reference.

The actual point of impact from a strike, or Primary Impact Point, can be compared to the Primary Wound Channel. The force, or kinetic energy, of that strike will transfer through the tissue that is under the impact point and in surrounding tissue, which is referred to as the Secondary Energy Channel. This can be compared to the Secondary Wound Channel. The greater the force on impact equals to a greater amount of secondary tissue trauma. A forceful strike that is aimed at an acupuncture point will not only disrupts that point, but it

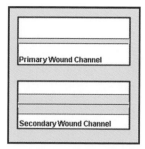

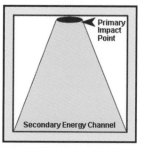

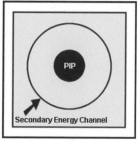

Figure 16-1: Primary Wound Channel is depicted in the top figure and the Secondary Wound Channel is in the bottom. The Primary Wound Channel is much smaller in size than the Secondary.

Figure 16-2: The top of the cone represents the Primary Impact Point. The Secondary Energy Channel is generated in a cone below the PIP. The Secondary Energy Disruption that radiates outward from the PIP is shown in 16-3.

Figure 16-3: Depicts the radiating energy disruption of a strike in relation to the Primary Impact Point (PIP).

will disrupt points that are in close physical proximity. With this in mind is it possible to effectively disrupt the energy of an acupuncture point by just striking close, but not directly on it? Yes and the energetic effects of the strike are not greatly diminished as some would like to make you believe.

Secondly, during the study of the energetic system of the body we tend to focus on one meridian at a time. We often forget that the Main Meridians are bilateral. We often overlook that there are other meridians that run in close physical proximity to the one that we are examining. A strike to the side of the neck, which is aimed at ST-9, will likely disrupt ST-10, LI-17, LI-18, SI-16 and SI-17 in addition to ST-9. You will probably get a couple of points on the jaw line or below the ear as well. This is not to mention the technique of rapid-fire strikes to the same target, which has a dramatic effect of the body. The argument that pressure point techniques require pinpoint accuracy is pure bunk.

The laws that govern realistic unarmed combat do not radically change for a pressure point stylist. They remain the same and the use of pinpoint strikes is not applicable in striking during pressure point fighting. There is a sub-art in numerous Chinese martial art styles called *Qi Na*, which translates to seizing and grasping. It involves various joint attacks and control techniques that allow for easy adaptation for utilizing acupuncture points. It should be noted that some systems specially teach attacking pressure point during *qi na*, which requires greater accuracy. This is in direct contrasts with striking. Remember that strikes are aimed at acupuncture point clusters and not individual points during the initial stages of an encounter. Once you have established a position of dominance, which means that the opponent is stunned or otherwise temporally disabled and in a tactically weak position, you can take that extra split-second to focus on a specific point like GV-15/16 for a finishing blow. That should be the only time that you actually focus on striking a specific point.

CONCLUSION

"All truth passes through three stages: First, it is ridiculed. Second, it is violently opposed. Third, it is accepted as being self-evident."
Arthur Schopenhauer

Hopefully, the information provided in this book will assist you on your quest of understanding the often confusing material pertaining to the Extraordinary Vessels in numerous Traditional Chinese Medicine textbooks. By gaining knowledge of how they function and interact with the twelve Main Meridians you will grow as a student of the martial arts. The majority of the martial arts have their roots in the Far East, as we all know, and by gaining insight into them we are able to see through the eyes of the founders of these disciplines. The combative aspect of the arts is apparent after examining the material presented in this book. The various methods and systems that sprang from China and Okinawa were designed with unarmed combat as the focus.[1] They were not concerned with tournaments, or trophies, or belt rankings. Instead they were focused on extremely efficient methods to kill or disable an opponent.

It is obvious that the author(s) of the *Bubishi* understood the value of attacking the Extraordinary Vessels. They even list the "shut off" points of the Yin and Yang Linking Vessels, which have been proven as critical in the ability to correct energetic imbalances. We can determine some of their intent by understanding the theories and laws that govern Traditional Chinese Medicine and applying them to martial technique. The results prove that the information that was provided by that classic document was intended to kill and/or disable opponents. This transcends the normal self-defense mindset of the majority of martial artist and encompasses the true "warrior arts," which was the actual intent of the founders. The idea that many students practice the "martial" arts is far removed from reality. Unfortunately, the reality is that many students only practice methods that are based upon the martial arts. The material presented in this book is martial. It reflects knowledge that is deemed necessary in a combative situation, not in a tournament ring or for gratification of an ego. The

---

[1] Taika Seiyu Oyata, *Ryu-Te No Michi*, Independence, MO: Oyata Enterprises, Inc., 1998, p. 3–19.

evolution from Western martial artist to a warrior is not for everyone and each person should reflect upon that before starting that journey.

There are numerous individuals that still doubt the effectiveness of pressure point fighting in the west. The idea of striking specific little acupuncture points on the body has been criticized by some respected Western martial artists. This is even reflected by Alexander in his commentary concerning the *Bubishi*.[2] His interpretations are that the points must be struck with pinpoint accuracy and utilize your hands and fingers, which have been conditioned to the point that they can penetrate the body like a spear.[3] Both translations of the *Bubishi*, the McCarthy and Alexander/Penland, contain commentary concerning the Western anatomical features in relation to the Chinese acupuncture points, as does this book. The Alexander/Penland (see Appendix) version even completely ignores the acupuncture point names and associates the vital point locations with Western anatomy.[4] This is understandable considering that we are accustomed to that paradigm, but is of little help in understanding the principles that led to the formation of the Eastern fighting traditions.

We can have all the knowledge that there is to offer, but if we cannot apply that knowledge it is useless. Many Westerners are currently applying Traditional Chinese Medicine to the martial arts. It does not require pinpoint accuracy like many instructors claim. Techniques that could be described as "blunt trauma" strikes, which are aimed at the vital points, can be utilized in pressure point fighting with great effect. Those that think pressure point fighting requires extremely accurate pinpoint strikes should reconsider their viewpoint.

Many Western martial arts instructors doubt the validity of pressure point techniques because they do not understand them or have been exposed to the art by someone that is not properly trained or a fraud. Considering that many of these instructors have spent years perfecting the elementary basics of their specific systems, it is difficult for them to admit that there are advanced areas of understanding that they do not know. One example of an exception is the late Allen Wheeler. Wheeler, like many others, was first exposed to the concept of pressure point fighting from seminars that were becoming common in the 1990s. Wheeler was in his seventies at that time and head of a major martial arts organization; the Okinawan Karate Union. He saw the validity in the techniques and made a continual effort through his last years at gaining a higher understanding. Wheeler passed away in 2005, but through his efforts, the sci-

---

[2] Alexander & Penland, *Bubishi: Martial Art Spirit*, p. xviii.
[3] Ibid., pp. 52–58.
[4] Ibid., pp. 68–79.

ence of Traditional Chinese Medicine, as applied to the martial arts, is being taught and researched by many of his students today. More instructors should follow his example.

One of the things that you might notice in the course of reading this book is that Asian martial arts instructors are rarely mentioned. In fact, the vast majority of the Traditional Chinese Medicine textbooks that were used as references were written by Westerners. This might seem curious to some, but the fact remains that both the martial arts and Traditional Chinese Medicine have been in the west for several decades. There seems to just be something about the martial arts that cause the student to want to pay homage, and substantial money, to Asians for instruction and rank. Unfortunately, those instructors are often lacking in their understanding of the more advanced aspects of the arts or are unwilling to teach it to Westerners. It is time that Westerners decide on the course of the arts that we practice and teach. Western combative arts are alive and well, but may require the student some effort in finding a qualified instructor. There is an emerging number of highly qualified individuals in the Western martial arts scene that are extremely talented and capable of helping students understand the more advanced aspects of the arts. Granted, as far as excellent Asian instructors that are willing to teach these concepts, there are a few available to Western students depending on your geographic location. Do your research and you can find solid instruction.

The idea that the martial arts contain secret techniques is appealing to some, but those "secret techniques" actually are not secret at all. They are techniques that were developed and refined in a different world than the one accepted in the West. They are the result of seeing the world through the eyes of Traditional Chinese Medicine, which on close examination has many parallels with Western science. The knowledge contained in the East is not mystical or secret. It is available to anyone that desires to learn and apply its teaching to the martial arts. The results are undeniable to anyone that has ever experienced a pressure point knockout or the extreme efficiency of techniques that are based on Eastern methods. Unfortunately, the exact reason of how it works cannot yet be explained by Western science, which is somewhat confounding to the Western academic. Regardless, it does work and work very efficiently, but understanding it requires that we view it in the eyes of its founders. Those eyes saw the world from a different point of view - that of Traditional Chinese Medicine and Taoist logic.

Many instructors that focus on the military close combat techniques and other effective non-Eastern fighting disciplines, have a less than favorable opinion concerning martial arts and for good reason. I firmly agree that the Western martial arts have evolved, or maybe "de-evolved," into a gross misrepresentation of the original combative methods. Too much emphasis on character development and feeling good about oneself were added to many styles as the ancient teachings became more mainstream to the public in the later part of the last century. Secondly, the ego gratification of obtaining various belts and ranks has further caused an overall decline. The "old school" of the martial arts did not concern itself with rank, tournaments, and student enrollment. It was more concerned with teaching aggressive and efficient techniques that allowed the practitioner to survive violent encounters. There was no focus on rank, title or the pretty little patch covered uniforms that are common today. In fact, the "old school" martial arts were taught to a very small student base, which is in direct contrast to the commercially oriented schools that are commonplace in our era. The martial arts have become big business and that has led to a great lessening in the overall abilities of those that claim the title of "martial artist." To the close combat oriented practitioner the material presented in this book might seem a little too "Eastern." On a close examination of the empty-handed killing techniques that are outlined the *Bubishi* there is a great deal in common with the proven Western methods. The techniques that were taught to the United States Marine Raiders, OSS Operatives, and British Commandos during the Second World War are some of the most highly effective unarmed killing techniques that are known. The breakdown of the "science" of the *Bubishi*, which until now remained a mystery to Westerners, illustrates techniques that attack the body in an extremely similar manner. The difference is that one is based on the Eastern perspective and the other from the west.[5] Both methods are striving for the same result, which is the quick and efficient ability to "take out" an adversary.

It is my sincere wish that you grow as a martial artist and as a person. The knowledge that is outlined in this book requires that the possessor is a mature, stable, and thoughtful human being. The ability to take the life of an opponent holds the highest degree of responsibility that is known to man. It is not to be treated lightly and dissemination of this material to your students should be after great consideration is given to their maturity and character.

---

[5] William E. Fairbairn, the source of many of the WWII era unarmed killing techniques, studied the traditional martial arts during his early military career while being stationed in the Far East. This influence and his extensive field testing methods both before and during the war, led to the development of some of the most lethal techniques in unarmed combat that are known.

APPENDIX

n addition to the excellent scholarly work of Patrick McCarthy, there have been other translations of the *Bubishi* by Western authors. George Alexander and Ken Penland published a translation of the work, but from a different source as the one utilized by McCarthy. This is in keeping with the fact that there are different versions of the *Bubishi*, which has spread to several branches of Okinawan martial arts through the years. The 36 Vital Points presented in the Alexander/Penland translation are included for historical reference and as a comparison to the McCarthy translation. The major difference is the use of the Chinese name of the various points, some of which are what I have deemed as being the *martial point names*. In my research into the phenomenon of 36 Vital Points in Chinese martial arts systems, I have discovered the use of point names, in Chinese, that do not match the established and accepted point name as it is used in the healing tradition of Traditional Chinese Medicine. After conferring with several individuals that are fluent in Mandarin Chinese, comparing some of the old printed material to both Wades-Giles and pinyin translation methods, and gaining more of an understanding of Chinese culture, I have concluded that some of these point names were used exclusively for martial description of the points. Often, in an effort to determine the exact point, I have found myself spending copious amount of time peering over crude drawings found in some of the early Chinese sources. Some of it was successful, but some of it has remained elusive. Considering the number thirty-six is of importance in the cultural use of numerology in Chinese society, it would be correct to assume that it would be found in different Chinese martial arts systems. This has been validated by the work of David S. Nisan and Liu Kangyi in their book, *The General Tian Wubeizhi: the Bubishi in Chinese Martial Arts History*. This book goes into great detail of the research on the origins of the *Bubishi*, which links it to the Bronze Statue Notebook that was developed in China that first appeared during the 17th century. It should be noted that the Okinawan pronunciation of "*Wubeizhi*" is "*Bubishi*," which I believe conclusively validates Nisan and Liu's theory. As more and more research is done by martial scholars, it is becoming apparent that *Bubishi* is rooted in Chinese martial knowledge. I have also discovered the use of 36 Vital Points in both

Shaolin arts and Yin Style Baguazhang, the latter being the system that I have been practicing since 2003. Unfortunately, both these sources utilize many of the martial point names rather than the more common TCM point names. Several of these martial point names have yet to be determined in association with the healing traditions names, but it is my hope that this will be overcome through more research. It is my intention to eventually publish my research on commonality of 36 Vital Points in association with geographical dispersed martial systems in China, with some that are far removed from the Southern districts that had direct influence on the *Bubishi*.

As stated earlier, the Alexander/Penland translation does not list the points by number, but rather by the Chinese term for that point. Unfortunately, many of the Chinese terms do not correspond with commonly accepted Chinese point names found in Traditional Chinese Medicine textbooks. The associated diagram of the point locations was used to locate the points and that information is included in Table A-1. The names that they attribute to the points are still a mystery and probably reflect a different Chinese dialect.[1]

Alexander/PenlandTranslation								
#	Point Name	Point #	#	Point Name	Point #	#	Point Name	Point #
1	Pai Hui	GV-22	10	Ko Chu	GB-3	19	Chien Ching	ST-12
2	Chi Men	CV-22	11	Wen Ting	ST-6[2]	20	Yao Men	GV-14
3	Tang Men	CV-15	12	Sai Chiao	ST-9[3]	21	Feng Yen	SI-14
4	Shen Chueh	CV-8	13	Suan Chi	CV-17	22	Yoo Tung	BL-43
5	Hui Yin	LI-4	14	Chang Tai	ST-17	23	Feng Wei	LV-14[5]
6	Nao Hu	GV-16	15	Ke Men	SP-21[4]	24	Ching Chu	GB-24[6]
7	Tien Hsi	TW-17	16	Chang Men	LV-13	25	Hsiao Yao	GB-25
8	Pei Liang	GV-10	17	Wei Lung	GV-3	26	Wun Mei	HT-5
9	Ming Men	GV-6	18	Yun Chuan	KI-1	27	Tai Chung	LV-3

---

[1] *Grasping the Wind*, an excellent resource concerning the Chinese terms that are attributed to acupuncture points, was used in an attempt to decipher the terms used in the Alexander/Penland translation to no avail.

[2] This point is unclear in the Alexander/Penland translation, but given the general location is near ST-6.

[3] ST-9 is used for this point, but it remains unclear from the Alexander/Penland translation.

[4] This point is unclear in the Alexander/Penland translation, but given the general location is near SP-21.

[5] This point is unclear in the Alexander/Penland translation, but given the general location is near LV-14.

[6] This point is unclear in the Alexander/Penland translation, but given the general location is near GB-24.

Alexander/PenlandTranslation								
#	**Point Name**	**Point #**	**#**	**Point Name**	**Point #**	**#**	**Point Name**	**Point #**
28	Tsi Ku	TW-15[7]	31	Tsi Chuh	LI-10	34	Wei Chun	BL-40
29	Tien Chu	SI-16	32	Ho Ku	LI-4	35	Chu Ping	BL-56
30	Pi Yu	SI-10[8]	33	Pai High	LV-11	36	Kung Shun	BL-62

Table A-1: *The Thirty-six Vital Points: Alexander/Penland Translation.*[9]

There are some obvious differences between the two published lists of Vital Points. This is attributed to the fact that the original *Bubishi* was copied by hand from instructor to student. That apparently occurred over at least one hundred and fifty years and maybe for a much longer period. Secondly, it is theorized that different instructors might have had a different series of points that they felt were important and changed the original thirty-six points to match their individual experience. Regardless, one of the more striking differences is that the Alexander/Penland translation includes KI-1, which is located on the sole of the foot. This point proves to be extremely difficult to access during a combative encounter. It does have significance from an energetic viewpoint, but given the anatomical location of the point it seems odd that it was listed. Table A-2 shows a comparison of the two translations of the 36 Vital Points listed in the *Bubishi.*

Comparison of McCarthy and Alexander/Penland					
#	**McCarthy**	**Alexander/Penland**	**#**	**McCarthy**	**Alexander/Penland**
1	GV-22	GV-22	6	TW-17	TW-17
2	CV-22	CV-22	7	GV-26	SP-21[10]
3	GB-3	GB-3	8	CV-24	GV-10
4	Eyes	CV-8	9	LU-8	GV-6
5	Ears	LI-4	10	TW-2	LV-14

[7] This point is unclear in the Alexander/Penland translation, but given the general location is near TW-15.

[8] The actual location of this point is unclear. The original drawing, which was used by Alexander, shows it on the top of the deltoid muscle.

[9] This list of the 36 Vital Points is not used in the text for obvious reasons. The fact that the cryptic Chinese names were used for the point locations makes it difficult to determine the exact points that were passed down in the document.

[10] This point is unclear in the Alexander/Penland translation, but given the general location is near SP-21.

		Comparison of McCarthy and Alexander/Penland			
#	McCarthy	Alexander/Penland	#	McCarthy	Alexander/Penland
11	GV-24	ST-6[11]	24	LV-13	LV-13
12	ST-9	ST-9[12]	25	LV-11	GB-25
13	GV-16	GV-16	26	HT-5	HT-5
14	GV-1	ST-17	27	LV-3	LV-3
15	CV-18	CV-17	28	LU-3	TW-15[13]
16	CV-15	CV-15	29	SI-16	SI-16
17	HT-1	GV-3	30	GB-31	SI-10[14]
18	BL-43	BL-43	31	LI-10	LI-10
19	ST-12	ST-12	32	LI-4	LI-4
20	GV-14	GV-14	33	KI- 6	LV-11
21	CV-4	SI-14	34	BL-40	BL-40
22	CV-1	KI-1	35	BL-51	BL-56
23	GB-24	GB-24	36	BL-62	BL-62

Table A-2: *Comparison of McCarthy and Alexander/Penland 36 Vital Points (Shaded points are those that are common to both lists or are in close physical proximity).*

The Alexander/Penland translation has sixteen different points when compared to the McCarthy version. Besides the KI-1 inclusion that is covered above, there are a couple of curious differences. There are ten points that are directly associated with the Extraordinary Vessels in the Alexander/Penland translation. That is in contrast to the fourteen that are found in the McCarthy translation. It is obvious that Alexander and Penland included BL-56 and KI-1, which are both missing from the McCarthy version. Other points may actually be in common between the two translations, but given the manner that Alexander and Penland presented the information it is difficult to determine. The McCarthy translation of the 36 Vital Points, which appears to be both more extensive and informative, are dissected in this book.

---

[11] This point is unclear in the Alexander/Penland translation, but given the general location is near ST-6.

[12] ST-9 is used for this point, but it remains unclear from the Alexander/Penland translation. It is obviously close to ST-9, which is an extremely important point to martial artists.

[13] This point is unclear in the Alexander/Penland translation, but given the general location is near TW-15.

[14] The actual location of this point is unclear. The original drawing, which was used by Alexander, shows it on the top of the deltoid muscle.

BIBLIOGRAPHY

Alexander, George W., and Ken Penland. *Bubishi: Martial Arts Spirit*. Lake Worth, FL: Yamazato, 1993.

Anatomical Atlas of Chinese Acupuncture Points. Jinan, China: Shandong Science and Technology, 1990.

Beinfield, Harriet, and Efrem Korngold. *Between Heaven and Earth: A Guide to Chinese Medicine*. New York: Ballantine, 1991.

Bishop, Mark. *Okinawan Karate: Teachers, Styles and Secret Techniques*. London: A&C Black, 1989.

Chia, Mantak, and Maneewan Chia. *Chi Nei Tsang: Internal Organs of Chi Massage*. Huntington, NY: Healing Tao, 1990.

Chuen, Lam Kam. *The Way of Energy*. New York: Simon & Schuster, 1991.

Clark, Rick. *Pressure Point Fighting*. Boston: Tuttle, 2001.

Coleman, James C., James N. Butcher and Robert C. Carson. *Abnormal Psychology and Modern Life*. Glenview, IL: Scott, Foresman and Co., 1976.

Consterdine, Peter. *Streetwise*. Leeds, UK: Protective Publications, 1997.

Ellis, Andrew, Nigel Wiseman and Ken Boss. *Fundamentals of Chinese Acupuncture*. Brookline, MA: Paradigm, 1991.

————. *Grasping the Wind*, Brookline, MA: Paradigm, 1989.

Fairbairn, W.E. *Get Tough! How to Win in Hand-to-Hand Fighting*, Boulder, CO: Paladin, 1979.

Frantzis, B.K. *The Power of Internal Martial Arts*. Berkeley, CA: North Atlantic, 1998.

Funakoshi, Gichin. *Karate-do Kyumon*. Tokyo: Kodansha, 1988

Gach, Michael Reed. *Acupressure's Potent Points: A Guide to Self-Care for Common Ailments*. New York: Bantam, 1990.

Goldberg, Stephen. *Clinical Anatomy Made Ridiculously Simple*. Miami: MedMaster, 1984.

Gray, Henry, F.R.S. *Gray's Anatomy*. New York: Gramercy, 1977.

Grossman, Dave. *On Killing*. Boston: Back Bay Books, 1995.

Kaptchuk, Ted J. *The Web That Has No Weaver: Understanding Chinese Medicine*. Chicago: Congdon & Weed, 1983.

Kushi, Michio. *How to See Your Health: Book of Oriental Diagnosis*. Tokyo: Japan Publications, 1980.

Larre, Claude, and Elisabeth de la Vallee. *The Eight Extraordinary Meridians*. Cambridge, MA: Monkey, 1997.

Maciocia, Giovanni. *The Foundations of Chinese Medicine*. Edinburgh, UK: Churchill

Livingstone, 1989.

Mann, Felix. *Acupuncture, The Ancient Chinese Art of Healing and How It Works Scientifically*. New York: Vintage, 1962.

Matsumoto, Kiiko, and Stephen Birch. *Extraordinary Vessels*. Brookline, MA: Paradigm, 1986.

————. *Five Elements and Ten Stems*. Brookline, MA: Paradigm, 1983.

————. *Hara Diagnosis: Reflections on the Sea*. Brookline, MA: Paradigm, 1988.

McCarthy, Patrick. *The Bible of Karate: Bubishi*. Boston: Tuttle, 1995.

McConnell, James V. *Understanding Human Behavior*. New York: Holt, Rinehart and Winston, 1974.

Moneymaker, Rick. *Torite-Jutsu Reference Manual*. Chattanooga, TN: Northshore Communications, 1997.

———— and Tom Muncy. *Torite-Jutsu Technique Manual*. Chattanooga, TN: Northshore Communications, 1999.

Montaigue, Erle. *Advanced Dim-Mak*. Boulder, CO: Paladin, 1994.

————. *Dim-Mak: Death-Point Striking*. Boulder, CO: Paladin, 1993.

————. *Dim-Mak's 12 Most Deadly Katas*. Boulder, CO: Paladin, 1995.

————. *Ultimate Dim-Mak*. Boulder, CO: Paladin, 1996.

Nam, Park Bok, and Dan Miller. *The Fundamentals of Pa Kua Chang Volume One*. Burbank, CA: Unique Publications, 1999.

Ni, Maoshing. *The Yellow Emperor's Classic of Medicine*. Boston and London: Shambhala, 1995.

Nisan, David S., and Liu Kangyi. *The General Tian Wubeizhi: the Bubishi in Chinese Martial Arts History*. Taipei; Lionbooks Martial Arts, 2016.

Ohashi. *Reading the Body: Ohashi's Book of Oriental Diagnosis*. New York: Penguin, 1991.

Optimum Time for Acupuncture. Jinan, China: Shandong Science and Technology, 1988.

Oyata, Taika Seiyu. *Ryu-Te No Michi*. Independence, MO: Oyata, 1998.

Reich, Wilhelm. *Character Analysis*. New York: Simon & Schuster, 1933.

Ross, Jeremy. *Acupuncture Point Combinations*. Edinburgh, UK: Churchill Livingstone, 1995.

Selye, Hans. *The Stress of Life*. New York: McGraw-Hill, 1956.

Teeguarden, Iona Marsaa. *A Complete Guide to Acupressure*. Tokyo: Japan Publications, 1996.

Walker, A. Flane, and Richard C. Bauer. *The Ancient Art of Life and Death*. Boulder, CO: Paladin, 2002.

Yang, Jwing-Ming. *Muscle/Tendon Changing & Marrow/Brain Washing Chi Kung*. Jamaica Plains, MA: YMAA Publication Center, 1989.

————. *The Root of Chinese Chi Kung*. Jamaica Plains, MA: YMAA Publication Center, 1989.

POINT INDEX

Page numbers in italics refer to tables and illustrations.

BL-1, *74, 75, 76, 78, 79, 84, 143, 145*
BL-12, 123, *143, 145*
BL-14, *198*
BL-40, *18, 174*, 196, *212, 213*
BL-43, *18, 174*, 187, *212, 213*
BL-51, *18, 174*, 188, *213*
BL-52, *198*
BL-59, *78, 143, 145*
BL-61, *78, 79, 143, 145*
BL-62, 15n9, *18, 78*, 79, 80, *143, 145, 173, 174*, 175, 196, *201, 212, 213*
BL-63, 88, *94*, 95, *143, 145*, 161

CV-1, *18*, 20, 26, 31, 44, 59, 61, *62, 87, 173*, 189, 190, 198, *213*
CV-2, 34, 35, 63, 91, 123, *198*
CV-3, 34
CV-4, *18, 32*, 34, 80, 173, *189*, 213
CV-5, 34, 35
CV-6, 35, *198*
CV-7, 35
CV-8, *32*, 35, *212, 213*
CV-9, 35
CV-10, 35, *36*
CV-11, 36
CV-12, 37
CV-13, *37*
CV-14, 37, 38, 63
CV-15, *18, 37, 173*, 186, *212, 213*
CV-16, 38
CV-17, *32*, 38–40, 149, 186, *212, 213*
CV-18, *18*, 39, 40, *173*, 187, *213*
CV-19, 40

CV-20, 40
CV-21, 40
CV-22, 18, *32*, 40, *42*, 87, 88, *90*, 92, 163, 164, *173*, 182–184, *212, 213*
CV-23, 41, *90*, 93
CV-24, *18*, 31, 41, *174*, 181, *213*

GB-3, *18, 174*, 178, *212, 213*
GB-13, 97, 98, *143, 145*
GB-14, *94*, 97, *143, 145*
GB-15, 97, 98, *143, 145*
GB-16, 98, *143, 145*
GB-17, 98, *143, 145*
GB-18, 98, *143, 145*
GB-19, 98, *143, 145*
GB-20, *78*, 79, 84, 85, 93, *94*, 95, 98, 99, 119, *143, 145*, 161, 162, 193
GB-21, 96, 97, *143, 145*
GB-24, *18, 174*, 190, 198, *212, 213*
GB-25, *212, 213*
GB-26, 70, *143, 145*
GB-27, 70, *71, 143, 145*
GB-28, *68, 70, 143, 145*
GB-29, *78*, 79, 81, *143, 145*
GB-31, *18*, 118, *174*, 195, 196, *213*
GB-35, *94*, 95, *143, 145*
GB-36, 95
GB-41, 15n9, *201*
GV-1, *18*, 44, 46–48, *174*, 188, *213*
GV-2, 48
GV-3, 48–51, *212, 213*
GV-4, *45*, 50
GV-5, 50

217

GV-6, 50, *212, 213*
GV-7, 50
GV-8, *45*, 50
GV-9, 51, 52
GV-10, 51, *212, 213*
GV-11, 51
GV-12, 51
GV-13, 52
GV-14, 18, *45*, 52, 97, *174*, 185, *212, 213*
GV-15, 44, 52, 53, 85, 88, *94*, 99, 161–164, 176, 205
GV-16, *18, 45*, 52, 53, 79, 85, 88, *94*, 99, 161–163, 164, *174*, 176, 184, 203, 205, *212, 213*
GV-17, 53, 54
GV-18, 54, 55
GV-19, 55
GV-20, *45*, 55
GV-21, 55
GV-22, *18*, 55, 56, *173*, 177, 178, *212, 213*
GV-23, 56
GV-24, 18, 56, *173*, 178, *213*
GV-25, 56
GV-26, *18*, 56, 57, 173, 180, *213*
GV-27, 56
GV-28, 44, 57

HT-1, *18, 174*, 186, 187
HT-4, 176
HT-5, *18, 174*, 176, 193–195, 212, 213
HT-6, 176
HT-7, 176
HT-8, *198*

KI-6, 15n9, *18*, 75, *143*, 145, *174*, 175, 196, *201, 213*
KI-8, 75, *143*, 145
KI-9, 88, *90*, 91, *143*, 145, 163
KI-11, 61, 63, 88, 123, *143*, 145
KI-21, *60*, 61, 63, 88, 123, *143*, 145

LI-4, *18*, 195, *212, 213*
LI-10, *18, 174*, 192, 193, 198, *212, 213*
LI-14, *94*, 95, *96, 143, 145*
LI-15, 81, 82, *143, 145*
LI-16, *78*, 81, 97, *143, 145*
LI-17, 204
LI-18, 181, 204
LU-1, *198*
LU-3, *18, 174*, 192, 193, *213*
LU-7, 15n9, 176, *201*
LU-8, *18, 174*, 176, 193, 194, *213*
LV-3, *18, 174*, 197, *212, 213*
LV-11, *18, 174*, 191, *212, 213*
LV-13, *18, 68, 69, 78*, 81, *143, 145, 173, 174*, 191, *212, 213*
LV-14, 87, *90*, 92, *143, 145*, 163, 190, 198, *212, 213*

PC-6, 15n9, *201*, 202

SI-3, 15n9, *201*
SI-10, *78*, 81, *94, 96, 143, 145*, 160, 161, *212, 213*
SI-16, *18, 174*, 181, 182, 204, *212, 213*
SI-17, 214
SP-4, 15n9, *201*, 202
SP-13, *90*, 91, *143*, 145, 163
SP-14, 198
SP-15, *90*, 91, 92, *143, 145*, 163
SP-16, *90*, 92, *143, 145*, 163
ST-3, 15n9, *60*, 61, 63, 82, 123, *143*, 144, *145*
ST-4, *78*, 82, *83, 143*, 144, *145*
ST-8, 97, *143*, 144, *145*
ST-9, *18*, 19, *74*, 75, 76, *143*, 144, *145, 174*, 182, 209, *212, 213*
ST-10, 204
ST-11, 204
ST-12, *18, 74*, 75, *77, 143*, 144, *145, 174*, 183, *184, 212, 213*
ST-17, *212, 213*
ST-25, *198*

ST-30, *60*, 61, 63, 123, *143*, 144, *145*

TW-2, *18*, *174*, 195, *213*
TW-4, 176
TW-5, 15n9, *201*

TW-12, 195
TW-13, 96, *143*, *145*, 147, 160
TW-15, *94*, *143*, *145*, 160, *212*, *213*
TW-17, *18*, *174*, 180, *212*, *213*

GENERAL INDEX

Page numbers in italics refer to tables and illustrations.

Acupuncture Points, 14–17, 19, 20, 31, 41, 61, 87, 93, 175, 176, 181, 182, 184, 201, 203–205, 208

Adam's apple, 41, 76, 93, 182

air *qi*, 146,

alarm point, 20, 34, 37, 38, 69, 92, 149n6, 189–191

Alexander, George, 16n15, 173n1, 211

Alexander/Penland translation (*Bubishi*). See *Bubishi*

anterior cutaneous nerve, 34

anterior jugular vein, 41, 76, 93, 182

aortic arch, 40, 92

arrhythmia, 38, 162

biomechanical attack, 69

Birch, Stephen, 112

Bladder, *19*, 26, 27, 34, 46, 53, 56, 67, 75, 76, 84, 88, *89*, 93, 98, *105*, *112*, *113*, 114, 120, 124–126, 140, 142, 144, 145, 147, 151, 154, 175, 178, 185, 187, 188, 190, 196, *197*

Body Alarm Reaction (BAR), 12, 14, 129–141, 150, 153–157, 159, 162, 203, 122, 123, 124, 126, 128, 157; and fight-or-flight, 133; and General Adaptation Syndrome, 129, 130, 131n6

Branch Meridians, 13

Bubishi, 7, 9, 12, 13, 15n11, 16, 17, 19–21, 25n2, 33, 34, 39, 40, 41, 46, 52, 55, 56, 61, 69, 75, 76, 79, 85, 92, 99, 142, 157, 164, 173–176, 179, 181, 184–187, 191, 195–200, 202, 207, 208, 210–213; Alexander/Penland translation, 19, 173, 208, 210–214; McCarthy translation, 12, 16, 17, *18*, 19, 142n1, 173, 175, 198, 208, 211, *213*, 214

center core, 26, 27, 98

Chia, Mantak, 67

China, 16, 18, 91, 69, 173n1, 175, 207, 211, 212

Chinese classics: *Ling Shu*, 14, 16; *Nei Jing*, 14–16, 26, 31, 109; *Su Wen*, 14, 16, 25n1, 149; *Zhen Jiu Da Cheng*, 15, 16; *Zhen Jiu Da Quan*, 15, 16, 201

chong mai. *See* Extraordinary Vessels

coccygeal nerve, 47, 48

coccyx bone, 44, 46, 47, 188

Conception Vessel. *See* Extraordinary Vessels

Consterdine, Peter, 132n7, 140n17, 159

cutaneous cervical nerve, 41, 76, 93, 181, 182

Cycle of Control, 110, 111, 114, 144, 151–153, 159, 193, 196, 197

Cycle of Creation, 109–111, 114, 151–153

Cycle of Destruction, 109

Dim Ching, 17

Dim Hsueh, 17

Dim Mak, 9, 17, 150, 200

Diurnal Cycle, 9, 15n11, 46, 107n6, 197–199

Dragon Society International, 127n1, 130n5, 131n6

ears, *18*, 179, 180, *213*
earth body type, 119, 121, 122, 140, 143, 146, 150–157, 174
earth (element), 109–114, 118, 142, 144, 145, 147, 148
eighth intercostal nerve, 36
Elemental Body Types, 117–122, 150, 151, 153–157. *See also* earth body type; fire body type; metal body type; water body type; wood body type
eleventh intercostal artery, 50
eleventh intercostal nerve, 34, 35
eleventh thoracic nerve, 50
eleventh vertebra, 50
energetic core, 27, 36, 63, 64, 123
Energy Belts, 67
energy center, 26, 36, 47, 188, 189
Extraordinary Vessels, 12–15, 20–21, 25–30, 59, 69n4, 79, 87, 109, 115, 123, 125, 127, 140–149, 159–163, 173–175, 178–181, 183, 184, 186–201, 207, 214; *chong mai*, 25, 61; Conception Vessel, 15n9, 25n1, 26, 28, 31–41, 44, 57, 63, 82, 87, 88, 92, 93, 123, 124, *149*, 163, *173*, 183, 186, 189; Girdle Vessel, 15n9, 67–72, 124, 125, *173*, 191; Governing Vessel, 15n9, 25n1, 26, 29–31, 44–57, 59, 73, 85, 88, 97, 99, 123, 124, 149n6, 161, *173*, *174*, 178, 180, 184, 185, 188, 189; *Ren Mai*, 25, 31; Thrusting Vessel, 15n9, 25n1, 26, 33, 59–65, 67, 73, 87, 88, 123, *124*, 189; Yang Heel Vessel, 15n9, 41, 73, 75, 76, *78*, 79–85, 96, 99, 125, *173*, 175, *201*; Yang Linking Vessel, 15n9, 29, 44, 46, 52, 81, 84, 85, 88, 93, *94*, 95–99, 126, 160, 161, *174*, 184, 190, 207; Yin Heel Vessel, 15n9, 73, *74*, 75–77, 79, 84, 125, *174*, 175, 182, 183, 196; Yin Linking

Vessels, 15n9, 40, 41, 87, 89, *90*, 91–93, 126, 163, *173*, 183
Eyes, *18*, 73, 179, *213*

facial nerves, 42, 82, 97
Fairbairn, William E., 210n8
Fight-or-flight. *See* Body Alarm Reaction (BAR)
fire body type, 119, 121, 122, 140, 150–156, 193
fire (element), 109–114, 142, 143, 145–148, 160, 163, 174, 181
first intercostal nerve, 40
first lumbar vertebra, 50, 188
Five Element Theory, 9, 12, 19, 73, 79, 88, 109–115, 117, 141, 150, 193, 195, 197; Cycle of Control, 110, 111, 114, 144, 151–153, 159, 193, 196, 197. *See also* Cycle of Control; Cycle of Creation; Cycle of Destruction; earth body type; earth (element); earth body type; Earth (element); fire body type; fire (element); metal body type; metal (element); Ten Stem theory; water body type; water (element); wood body type; wood (element); wood Meridians
fourth intercostal nerve, 38

Gall Bladder, 67, 69, 70, 76, 81, 84, 88, *89*, 93, 96–99, *105*, *112*, *113*, 114, 118, 119, 121, 125, 126, 140, 142–145, 147, 151, 152, 154, 159, 161, 176, 178, 180, 182, 185, 188, 190, 191, *197*
General Adaptation Syndrome. *See* Body Alarm Reaction (BAR)
Girdle Vessel. *See* Extraordinary Vessels
glossopharyngeal nerve, 41, 93
Goju-ryu Karate, 16
Governing Vessel. *See* Extraordinary Vessels

Heart, *19*, 26, 37–40, *89*, 91, *105*, *112*, *113*, 114, 126, 127, 139, 140, 142, 143, 146, 147, 149, 150, 152, 154, 157, 159–163, 186, 187, 193, 194, *197*, 202
hemorrhoid nerve, 47
Human Battery, 25–31, 44, 46, 59, 67, 87–89, 93, 123, 124, 140, 144, 154, 161, 163, 177
hypoglossal nerve, 41, 93

iliohypogastric nerve, 34, 63, 70
inferior epigastric arteries/veins, 34–36, 63
inferior hemorrhoid artery, 47
inferior labial artery, 41
infraorbital ridge, 41, 82
innominate vein, 40, 92
internal mammary artery, 38–40

Jiaohu Points, 15n9
Jwing-Ming, Yang, 150

Kata, 17, 176, 194; Nepai, 17n17; Niseishi, 17n17; Peichurrin, 17n17; Sanseiru, 17n17; Seipai, 17n17; Seisan, 17n17; Useishi, 17n17
Kidney, *19*, 26, 34, 46, 59, 61, 63, 67, 75, 88, *89*, 91, *105*, *112*, *113*, 114, 120, 124–126, 133, 135, 140, 142, 145–147, 149, 151, 154, 163, 175, 188, 189, 196, *197*

Large Intestine, *20*, 41, 56, 81, 82, 89, 95, 97, *105*, *112*, *113*, 114, 124–126, 140, 142, 144, 146, 154, 180, 181, 185, 192, 195, *197*
Ling Shu. See Chinese classics
Liver, *19*, 27, 34, 67, 69, 87, 88, *89*, 91, 92, *105*, 109, *112*, *113*, 114, 118, 119, 122, 124–126, 133, 135, 140, 142, 144–147, 149, 151, 152, 154, 161, 163, 177, 187, 189–191, 196, 197

lumbar artery, 49, 50, 188
lumbar nerve, 49, 50
Lung, *20*, 37, *89*, 91, *105*, *112*, *113*, 114, 126, 127, 140, 142, 146, 149, 154, 157, 163, 183, 186, 192, *197*

Main Meridians, 12–15, 25–27, 29, 31, 44, 46, 59, 69, 73, 79, 85, 87–89, 99, 105, 106, 109, 112, 113, 115, 123–127, 141–143, 146–150, 162, 175, 197, 198, 200, 204, 207. *See also* Bladder; Gall Bladder; Heart; Kidney; Large Intestine; Liver; Lung; Pericardium; Small Intestine; Spleen; Stomach; Triple Warmer
Marine Raiders, 199, 210
Master Points, 15, 175, 201
Matsumoto, Kiiko, 112
McCarthy, Patrick, 7, 16–19, 142n1, 173, 175, 211, 214
McConnell, James V., 134n14
medial supraclavicular nerve, 40
median sacral artery, 48
metal body type, 120–122, 140, 152–154, 156
metal (element), 109–114, 142–148, 150, 151, 155, 159, 163, 174, 193
Miyagi, Chojun, 16
Montaigue, Erle, 135n14, 150, 200

Nei Jing. See Chinese classics
Nepai. *See* kata
ninth intercostal artery, 51
ninth thoracic vertebra, 51
Niseishi. *See* kata

obturator artery, 34
obturator nerve, 191
Okinawa, 12, 16, 18, 173n1, 175, 177, 202, 207, 211
Okinawan Karate Union, 208
ophthalmic arteries, 41, 82
OSS, *199*, 210

Pareto's 80–20 law, 176
Peichurrin. *See* kata
Penland, Ken, 16n15, 173n1, 211
Pericardium, *19*, 26, 38, 89, *105*, *112*, *113*, 126, 142, 143, 146, 147, 149, 150, 152, 159–161, 175, *197*, 202
perineal artery, 33, 62
perineal nerve, 33, 62
Primary Energetic Targeta, 12, 141, 159

Qi, 13, 19, 25–27, 46, 55, 67n3, 73, 140, 150, 154, 183, 184, 200
Qi Jing Ba Mai, 13
Qi na, 204, 205
Qigong, 13, 29, 55
Qing dynasty, 18
Quadrant Theory, 12

Reich, Dr. Wilhelm, 67
reptilian brain, 135n14, 200n24,
Root Vessels, 13

sacral hiatus, 48
Sanseiru. *See* kata
second intercostal nerve, 40
Segmental Theory, 69
Seipai. *See* kata
Seisan. *See* kata
Selye, Hans, 129, 130, 131n6, 139, 140, 154
Shichen points, 12, 198, 199
sixth intercostal nerve, 38
Small Intestine, *19*, 26, 34, 37, 38, 76, 81, 82, 84, *89*, 96, *105*, *112*, *113*, 114, 124–126, 140, 142, 144, 147, 152, 154, 159–161, 181, 185, 189, 193, 194, *197*
Spleen, 19, 26, 34, 35, 38, 67, 69, *89*, 91, 92, 105, *112*, 113, 114, 124, 126, 140, 142, 144–147, 149, 154, 163, 175, 189, 191, *197*
sternum, 40, 92

Stomach, 19, 26, 27, 37, 41, 49, 56, 57, 63, 67, 75, 76, 82, 84, *89*, 95, 97, *105*, *112*, 113, 114, 124–126, 140, 142, 144, 145, 147, 154, 178, 179, 181–183, 185, 187, *197*, 202
Su Wen. See Chinese classics
subcostal nerve, 34, 70
superficial epigastric, 34-35, 63
suprasternal notch, 40, 92-93, 183

Ten Stem theory, 114
tenth intercostal artery, 50, 92
tenth intercostal nerve, 35
tenth thoracic nerve, 50
terminal ballistics, 203
third intercostal nerve, 39
Thrusting Vessel. *See* Extraordinary Vessels
Traditional Chinese Medicine (TCM), 9, 11–17, 19, 20, 25–27, 29, 31, 33, 41, 44, 59, 61, 67, 69, 73n3, 91, 93, 95, 103–107, 109, 110n1, 117, 122, 126, 130, 131n6, 139, 140n17, 141, 143, 145, 146, 149, 150, 159, 164, 173, 175, 180, 181, 183, 186, 187, 190, 191, 193, 197–203, 207–209, 211, 212; reverse engineering of, 11, 14, 201, 202
Triple Warmer, *19*, 26, 34, 37, 38, 84, 89, 96, 97, 99, *105*, *112*, *113*, 124, 126, 142, 147, 152, 159, 160, 161, 179, 180, 185, 195, *197*, 202

Useishi. *See* kata

Viet Cong, 38
Vietnam War, 38
Vital Points, 9, 12, 16-21, 25n2, 173, 176, 179, 180, 182, 184, 185, 187, 131, 133, 134, 151, 153, 156, 157, 169, 170, 171, 173–179, 185, 186, 188, 190, 194–198, 202, 208, 211–214

water body type, 120, 121, 140, 150, 153, 154, 156

water (element), 88, 109–114, 124, 142, 143, 145–148, 151–155, 174

Wheeler, Allen, 208

Wood body type, 118, 121, 140, 150–157,

Wood (element), 88, 109–114, 142–148, 161

Wood Meridians, 67, 118, 119, 151–154, 156, 159

World War II, 179, 199

Yang, 31, 44, 46, 49, 52, 55, 59, 73, 87–89, 93, 104–107, *108*, 113, 114, 122, 124–127, 142–148, 159, 161, 163, 184, 185, 195

Yang Heel Vessel. *See* Extraordinary Vessels

Yang Linking Vessel. *See* Extraordinary Vessels

Yiming, Jin, 175

Yin, 31, 44, 46, *49*, 59, 73, 87–89, 91, 104–107, *108*, 113, 114, 124–126, 142–149, 152, 160–163, 183, 189, 197

Yin Heel Vessel. *See* Extraordinary Vessels

Yin Linking Vessel. *See* Extraordinary Vessels

Yin/Yang, 9, 12, 19, 46, 103–107, 109, 127, 144, *145*, 200

Zhen Jiu Da Cheng. *See* Chinese classics

Zhen Jiu Da Quan. *See* Chinese classics